ADVENTURERS AND VISIONARIES
SAN FRANCISCO

BY RICHARD H. DILLON

SAN FRANCISCO
Adventurers and Visionaries

A pictorial and entertaining commentary on the growth and development of San Francisco, California.

By Richard H. Dillon

Publisher
Douglas S. Drown

Editor
Sharon R. Mason

Historical Photography Editor
Gary F. Kurutz

Current Photographer
Mark Snyder

Art Director
Rusty Johnson

Assistant Art Director
J. Michael Martin

Project Directors
Joyce Moffett
Faith Ver Mehren

Production Manager
Mickey Thompson

Editorial Coordinator
BJ Mallinger

Copyright 1983 by Continental Heritage Press, Inc.
P.O. Box 1620, Tulsa, Oklahoma, 74101.
All rights reserved.

Library of Congress Catalog Card Number: 83-070414

ISBN: 0-932786-35-3

San Francisco: Adventurers and Visionaries is one of the American Portrait Series published by Continental Heritage Press. Others include:

The rescue crew of the U.S. Lifeboat Station on Ocean Beach posed in their special "whaleboat" readied for action on its launching wagon.

3

San Francisco at night—in the 19th century, as
painted by Ferdinand Richardt from some point
on Telegraph Hill (above); and heading toward
the 21st century (below).

The coaling wharf of the Pacific Mail Steamship Company was captured by C.E. Watkins on film around 1871. Note the photo-wagon at center.

SPONSORS AND BENEFACTORS

The following San Francisco area firms, organizations and individuals have invested toward the quality production of this historic book and have thereby expressed their commitment to the future of this great city and to the support of the book's principal sponsor, the Society of California Pioneers.

Ace Pharmacy
*American Building Maintenance Industries
Armor Elevator Co., Inc.
*Arthur Andersen & Co.
*Bank of America
Beatrice Foods Company
Mrs. Philip Kendall Bekeart
Boyd Lighting Co.
Calvin Bullock, Ltd.
*Children's Hospital of San Francisco
*Del Monte Corporation
*Emporium-Capwell
*The Fairmont Hotel & Tower
*Fireman's Fund
*Forderer Cornice Works
*Franklin Hospital/Ralph K. Davies Medical Center
*French Hospital Medical Center
*Guittard Chocolate Company
*Heald Colleges of California
Randall W. Hill
*John Howell - Books
*Johnson & Higgins
*Just Desserts
Lazzari Fuel Co. Inc.
*The Mark Hopkins
*McCutchen, Doyle, Brown and Enersen
*McKesson Corporation
*Gabriel Moulin Studios
*Pacific Medical Center
Packaging Graphics Service
*John Parrott
*The Port of San Francisco
Ross Electronic Dist. Co. Inc.
*St. Mary's Hospital and Medical Center
*San Francisco Ballet
*San Francisco Opera
*San Francisco State University
*The San Francisco Symphony
*Schroeder's Cafe
Kurt E. and Martha Schulze
Schulze Manufacturing
Scotch House - Scottish Imports Ltd.
*See's Candy Shops, Inc.
Shade Foods, Incorporated
*Southern Pacific
Spencer Stuart and Associates
*Standard Oil Company of California
*Stone, Marraccini & Patterson, Architects and Planners
Sunnyvale Valve & Fitting Co.
*Sutro & Co. Incorporated
*Tadich Grill
James Howard Tayler
Tayler Products Corporation
*Transamerica Corporation
*University of San Francisco
VWR Scientific Inc.
W & B/Collins Contractors
Walker Engraving Company
Walker/Graphics
*Wells Fargo Bank, N.A.
*West Coast Life Insurance Company
Willard Marine Decking
Williams & Burrows, Inc.
*Williams, Dimond & Co.

*Denotes Corporate Sponsors. The histories of these organizations and individuals appear in a special section beginning on page 171.

The geometry of San Francisco's sunset skyline, as seen from Treasure Island.

San Francisco is perched at the north end of a great peninsula, its west side a long, sandy beach sometimes visited by cetaceans (dead or alive) as well as by citizens.

FOREWORD by Albert Shumate, M.D.

Richard H. Dillon's *San Francisco: Adventurers and Visionaries* is a fascinating, lively account of the City by the Golden Gate. Historian Dillon has drawn upon his broad knowledge of Western America and the perspective gained as author of many books on many aspects of the city's development.

Dillon's history is unique in that it deals at length with the city's first inhabitants, the Indians, and also its latest, covering the whole

span from the sixteenth century to the present. It thus differs from the principal histories previously published.

The earliest, *The Annals of San Francisco*, devotes only a few pages to the aborigines, and since it was published in 1854 recounts only the beginning of the city. John S. Hittell's *History of the City of San Francisco*, dedicated as was the *Annals* to The Society of California Pioneers, carried the account forward to its

date of publication, 1878. Most of its pages relate the history of the city's 28 years since California had become a state. Zoeth Skinner Eldredge's *The Beginnings of San Francisco,* published in 1912, is mainly concerned with the early explorations and the years of Spanish and Mexican domain.

Two more recent histories, Oscar Lewis' *San Francisco: Mission to Metropolis,* and John J. McGloin's *The Story of a City,* also differ from Dillon's account. The former ends with the 1960s and the latter begins with the European period.

Now *San Francisco: Adventurers and Visionaries* adds many previously unpublished facts and gives us the whole span of the history of the city. Its spirited style reflects San Francisco's sparkling, eventful story. Richard Dillon is to be complimented for adding greatly to our knowledge and understanding of San Francisco.

San Francisco's urban style seems predicated on pizzazz. A precipitous descent down Lombard Street (left); Vaillancourt Fountain in Justin Herman Plaza at Embarcadero Center (top left); Embarcadero Center stairs (top right); Murals in the Mission District (above left); Chinatown Lion Dance during Chinese New Year celebration (above right).

Seal Rocks are visited more often by sea lions than by seals, and very rarely by humans.

CONTENTS

CHAPTER 1.

LAY OF THE LAND

SAN FRANCISCO

Popular usage restricts the term "the Peninsula" to the San Mateo County suburbs south of town, but there is no mistaking the fact that San Francisco is a peninsular city. Occupying the northern end of a massive, 30-mile-long peninsula, the city is almost surrounded by water. Only on the south does the exciting metropolis abut on dry land. Even in the Financial District's "Wall Street of the West," deep-shadowed by skyscrapers, one senses a salty tang in the air, usually accompanied by a sea breeze and patches of fog.

On the north, the peninsula is separated from Marin County by the deep moat of the tide-ripped Golden Gate—*Yalupa* to the Indians, something like Sunset Strait to these poetic people. It was matter-of-fact *La Boca del Puerto de San Francisco*, the Mouth of the Port of San Francisco, to the no-nonsense Spaniards. To the romantic Hellenophile, John C. Fremont, it was *Chrysopylae*, Golden Gate in Greek.

On the east side of the city lies the broad expanse of San Francisco Bay, an inland sea, one of the world's great landlocked harbors. Forty miles of frontage is urban peninsula, the remainder tidal flats and marshlands which contrast greatly with the sandy beaches and steep cliffs of San Francisco's oceanside.

The seaport of San Francisco extends its borders across the Gate to grasp at the very tips of Marin County and Points Bonita, Cavallo and Blunt (on Angel Island). Most San Franciscans do not realize—and most Marinites refuse to believe—that San Francisco claims not only the Needles, the pointed rocks leeward of Lime Point, but even Fort Baker's Horseshoe Cove. To the westward, San Francisco is expansionist indeed. It reaches far into the setting sun to collect, as city property, the scattered rocks of the Farallon Islands, 32 miles out to sea from the city.

For years, San Francisco was likened to Rome as a city built upon seven hills. This is because a baker's half-dozen are of great historical importance—Telegraph, Nob, Russian and Rincon hills, Twin Peaks and Mt. Davidson. (Once-prominent Rincon Hill has all but vanished, decapitated in the 1930s to provide a massive anchorage for the city's end of the San Francisco-Oakland Bay Bridge.)

Although technically a Mediterranean climate of only two seasons, wet winters and dry summers, San Francisco—with its boasted natural air conditioning—is usually a bit on the cool side. Temperatures are moderate, seldom reaching the 80s in the warmest weather. There is no snow, and frost rarely troubles city gardeners.

The city's reputation as a fogbound sister of London is quite undeserved. Tule fogs, the dense, dank and gloomy "pea soupers" of winter, are rare. The prevailing westerlies push these condensation fogs, which rise up out of the marshes of tules or bulrushes, away from the peninsula. The common ocean fogs of summer—snowy white cascades toppling over the Sausalito hills—are sucked inland by the high temperatures and low pressures of the Central Valley. The synergistic combination of the fogs and almost ceaseless wind makes for a chilling experience. The sometimes year-round combination is responsible for the absence of both convertibles and swimming pools in San Francisco.

The City by the Golden Gate enjoys adequate rainfall for its temperature and latitude, averaging about 22 inches a year; but because of rapid runoff from steep terrain and the porosity of its sand dunes, the city has always been short of water. There is no river within the city limits and most of the small streams are arroyos, or intermittent creeks. Even these, like Hayes and Mission creeks and most of Islais Creek, have gone underground, buried beneath tons of cobbles, concrete and asphalt. Lobos Creek is an exception. After emerging from under Mountain Lake's Park-Presidio Boulevard, it wends its way through the relative wilderness of the Presidio to die at Baker's Beach.

While running streams have always been in short supply, still-water lakes were common in primeval San Francisco. Rainwater and perennial springs still feed one large natural lake and several smaller ones. Lake Merced, now cut in two by a causeway, is by far the largest body of water within the city's borders. Separated from the ocean only by a narrow strip of land holding Fleishhacker Zoo and old Fort Funston, Lake Merced probably emptied into the Pacific until it was landlocked by an earthquake.

Second in historical importance to Lake Merced is Mountain or Presidio Lake. This much smaller body of water was reduced to half its original size in the 1930s by the dumping of rock and soil in the construction of the adjacent Park-Presidio Boulevard approach to the Golden Gate Bridge.

Just west of Stern Grove is boggish little Laguna Puerca—Pig Lake or, colloquially, Dirty Lake. Euphemists have taken to calling it Pine Lake and even Crest Lake in order to upgrade its image. Laguna Honda is a curiosity—half lake, half reservoir. Once fed by a creek, it was long ago paved over into a reservoir.

Except for the Chain of Lakes in Golden Gate Park, San Francisco's other primeval lakes have been obliterated by "progress." Laguna Seca once lay in the lee of Twin Peaks. Lake Geneva is now buried deep beneath Geneva Avenue. The most historic of the vanished lakes is shallow Laguna de los Dolores, which once ran to the bay from Mission San Francisco de Asís. It gave its name to Mission Dolores and, with Mission Creek, was responsible for the siting of the Franciscan establishment in 1776. The most interesting of the lost lakes is Washerwoman's Lagoon in North Beach, entombed beneath Franklin, Octavia, Filbert and Lombard streets. There, laundresses labored to cope with mountains of soiled linen generated by filthy 49ers.

The Financial District had twin lakelets. Pear-shaped, brackish Laguna Salina was at Jackson and Montgomery streets; Laguna Dulce lay at Sacramento and Montgomery.

San Francisco is not perfect; it is, however, faultless, although sandwiched nervously between two great seismic seams, much too close to both of them for comfort. The Hayward Fault runs along the Berkeley Hills to the east; the more famous, and dangerous, San Andreas lies sulking offshore, submerged in the sea until it rears up to rip the Olema Valley trench across Marin County from Bolinas Lagoon to fjord-like Tomales Bay.

A HIDDEN PARADISE

Early Spaniards found the western side of the great peninsula to be a desolate, sand-blasted sahara of dunes, but in the lee of the hills and huddled in gullies, the bayside was lightly wooded with live oaks, willows, bay (laurels) and buckeyes. More of the vegetation was in chaparral, the so-called "elfin forest" of brush which clothes so much of the Coast Range. San Francisco's site was a natural garden of amazing variety.

The chaparral was home for a variety of small rep-

tiles and mammals; larger critters were coyotes, deer, wildcats, raccoons, mountain lions, black bears and the greatly feared grizzlies, well-named *Ursus horribilis*. Lazing about the strands were sea lions, while sporting in the water were inquisitive harbor seals and playful sea otters.

The San Francisco peninsula was one great aviary. High above the timid quail and mourning doves swung flights of migrating swans, ducks and geese. Year-round residents were the soaring birds of prey—eagles and hawks. Kingfishers and ospreys searched the waters from aloft, and at dusk came the nocturnal hunters, the owls. Turkey vultures cleaned up carrion, sometimes joined by their giant cousins, California condors, as well as by rowdy jays, magpies, crows and ravens.

Almost surrounded by water, the site of San Francisco was a haven for myriad shorebirds, even the phalaropes, awks and stormy petrels of story and legend. Farther ashore darted swifts and swallows, larks, blackbirds, hummingbirds, wrens, bush tits, chickadees, nuthatches, thrushes, mockingbirds, thrashers, vireos, cedar waxwings, Baltimore orioles, sparrows, finches, towhees, juncos and Western tanagers.

The natives of San Francisco's peninsula put up with a sand-blasted life, hiding in rude brush and

tule huts. Why? Becuse of their taste for shellfish. San Francisco Bay teemed with fish, clams and shrimps, and the opposite shore provided additional abalones, mussels, seaweed and more clams. Small wonder that the major Indian monuments to survive were shell mounds or kitchen middens ringing the bay shore.

The earliest people represented simple hunting and gathering folk who flourished by 2500 B.C. By the Middle Horizon time, they were producing bone, stone and shell artifacts—bowls, fishhooks, arrow points, pipes and charms. As their tools improved, they evolved into the Late Horizon period. These Penutians, replacing an earlier Hokan language stock, were efficient acorn hunters and meal grinders. Their bone and shell work became more sophisticated and, in a curious dead-end of advancing technology, they briefly supplanted their efficient bows and arrows with spear-throwers.

The Spanish dubbed the earliest San Franciscans simply *Los Costeños*, the Coastal People, later Anglicized to Costanoans by the Americans. (In recent years

attempts have been made to substitute the tribal name Ohlones for the Hispanic-gringo term.)

The *Costeños'* few handicrafts were baskets and excellent reed canoes or *balsas*. They also made nets, not only for fishing and hunting, but for carrying loads. The earliest San Franciscans also excelled in weaponry. They were not a warlike race and much preferred athletics, gaming, dancing or singing to fighting, but they were great hunters. The men fashioned strong bows and arrows, spears and harpoons, tipping the points with sharp obsidian— volcanic glass—traded from the North Bay.

The aboriginal San Franciscans were adept anglers, using hooks and lines, nets, spears and harpoons. Skilled hunters of deer and elk as well as birds and smaller animals, they used their bows and arrows, nets, clubs, spears and braided snares effecively. Excellent boatmen, their reed canoes enabled them to take not only fish, but also harbor seals, sea otters, sea lions, porpoises and even an occasional whale to vary their diet. Other dietary staples included all kinds of seeds, nuts, bulbs, roots, tubers and grasses and insects. Hence the demeaning Yankee term for

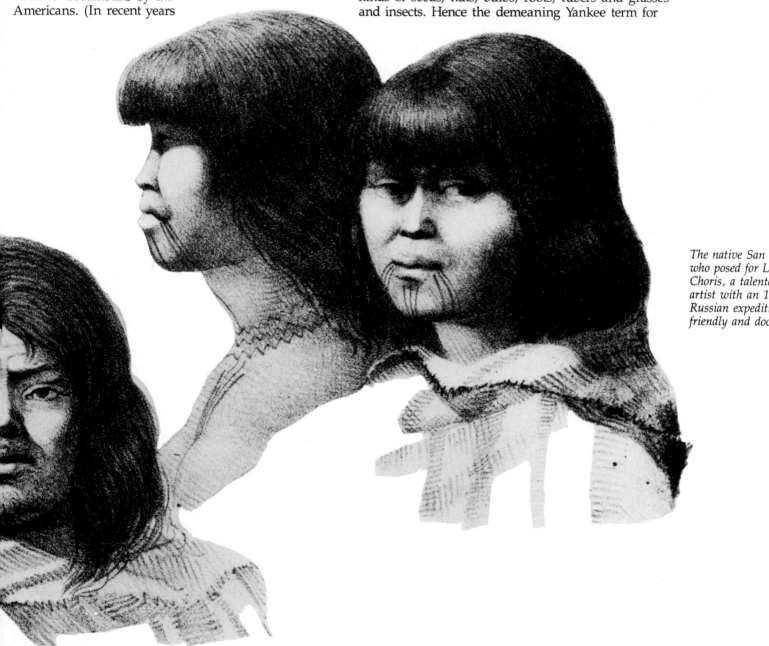

The native San Franciscans who posed for Louis Choris, a talented German artist with an 1816 Russian expedition, were friendly and docile people.

19

the Indians, Diggers. Actually, the Costanoans did not have to learn to plow or plant because nature was so kind to them. Their larders were usually filled to bursting at all seasons. The nearest they came to agricultural practices was the selective, controlled burning of the land which encouraged new crops of fresh, sweet grasses.

The *Costeños* were tribal in name only. Never a unified political group, they formed a loose grouping broken into perhaps 40 bands, each headed by a chief who was usually a man, occasionally a woman. Each small village had a sub-chief or headman. Little actual authority was delegated to a chief. The first San Franciscans were a democratic, peaceful people. There was no caste system; no princes and no untouchables.

Their religion was negligible in European eyes, probably because of their lack of funereal ceremonies. They were extremely reticent about the dead, whom they sometimes buried, sometimes cremated. It was the strongest of all taboos even to refer to the deceased. There were shamans who practiced the primordial psychology of witchcraft; also herbalism; the assigning and relieving of taboos; and fetishism, making offerings of feather wands or sprinklings of acorn meal to such gods as Eagle, wily Coyote and Hummingbird.

Happy with their lot on earth, the *Costeños* raised no temples. Just as they carried on no wars of conquest because they ate better than most other Native Americans, and with a lot less effort, they lived for the day. They saw snow only across the water on Mt. Tamalpais or Mt. Diablo and rarely shivered in a local frost. The men's only clothing was usually a mantle or cloak of rabbit skins and perhaps rude sandals. If they were still cold, they covered themselves with mud. Women, for decency's sake, wore a tule or bark apron and, for sex appeal, a facial tattoo.

These original San Franciscans were sedentary and docile, never straying very far or for very long from their beloved clam beds and mussel colonies. They did make periodic migrations to the adjacent hills, mostly for acorn gleaning, but also for deer and tule elk hunting. They visited nearby marshes for wildfowl and strolled the wild ocean shore to scout for stranded whales, dead birds and sick sea lions.

The *Costeños* numbered somewhere between 7,000 and 10,000 at their peak population, when the first Spaniards arrived. Although their lands extended from the deep moat of the Golden Gate—cutting them off from the Coast Miwok of Marin only a few miles away—to the mountainous Big Sur coast to the south, only a few thousand souls lived on the end of the peninsula itself. They were rugged environmentalists, respecting and enjoying a land of plenty with which they were in complete harmony.

Not until 1769 were the *Costeños* seen by European eyes, thanks to the rocky and often fog-shrouded Golden Gate. Incredibly, the most gifted explorers in the service of the king of Spain and the queen of England were unable to find the Golden Gate and thus unlock the harbor of harbors.

The first navigator to cruise along the outside coast of San Francisco was Juan Rodríguez Cabrillo, in November 1542. Cabrillo reconnoitered the California coastline as far north as the site of later Fort Ross. He discovered the Farralon Islands but failed to discern

Juan Rodríguez Cabrillo.

the Golden Gate before foul weather drove him back south. The narrow strait was hidden between great bluffs and invisible from the deck of a vessel at sea, obscured by the bay islands and hills behind it. Cabrillo died early in 1543 of complications from an injury incurred on San Miguel Island off Southern California, but his pilot, Bartolomé Ferrelo (Ferrer), explored the coast all the way to Oregon. Again, the Spaniards failed to spy out the narrow Golden Gate marking the end of the San Francisco peninsula.

The first European to land in today's San Francisco County (on the Farallon Islands) was Francis Drake, later Sir Francis, famous patriot of the English—and infamous pirate to the Spanish. After raiding ships and seaports in the Pacific Ocean off Latin America, Drake hustled his *Golden Hinde* north to "a convenient and fit harborough" to careen her in June 1579 before completing his circumnavigation of the world.

It is unlikely that even this talented Devonian sea dog found the Golden Gate or San Francisco Bay. Most historians believe that he beached his ship in Drake's Bay in Marin County, well to the north of the Golden Gate. There he took possession of the coast for Queen Elizabeth, calling it Nova Albion, and set up a brass plate on a post to verify his claim.

Sir Francis Drake.

Sebastián Rodríguez Cermeño, a Hispanized Portuguese, brought the Manila galleon *San Augustín* into San Francisco waters in November 1595 in search, ironically, of a safe port for treasure-laden galleons wishing to break the long passage home to Acapulco from the Philippines. Like Drake, he anchored in the shallow and exposed Drake's Bay which, confusingly, he called San Francisco Bay. A storm came up and wrecked the galleon on November 30. Although he must have hugged the coast in his retreat to Mexico in the crowded ship's launch, even Cermeño failed to see the Golden Gate although he, like Drake, landed on the Farallones.

Nor was the doughty Basque sailor, Sebastián Vizcaíno, any more fortunate in his search of 1603, although he found and named prominent Punta de los Reyes to the north of the Gate.

Probably all of the early navigators were so awed by the rocky coast and wild waves of the ill-named Pacific that they gave the San Francisco-Marin headlands of the Golden Gate a very wide berth. It would take a landlubber, a soldier, to find the sailors' harbor of harbors.

THE SACRED EXPEDITION

An over-extended and decadent Spain dillied and dallied for decades about establishing a presence in far-off California. Finally, New Spain acted. In 1769, the *visitador general* in Mexico City, Don José de Gálvez, acting on behalf of King Carlos III of Spain, dispatched Don Gaspar de Portolá to settle the northern coast of California. Ac-

As San Francisco Bay opened out before them, members of Don Gaspar de Portolá's 1769 expedition called a halt to marvel at its vastness. Painting by Walter Francis.

companied by Father Junípero Serra, most prominent of the Franciscans, Portolá set out by land on May 15 on what was grandly titled the Sacred Expedition, reaching San Diego Bay on June 29, 1769. He was preceded by another overland party under Captain Francisco de Rivera y Moncada, which had set out on March 24. The *San Carlos* and *San Antonio* sailed from Mexico to rendezvous with the two land detachments.

Leaving Father Serra to build his first California mission at San Diego, Portolá took some of his best men and strongest horses northward. The little party marched up the coast on July 14, to find it growing more and more rugged. Portolá pushed on to Montara Mountain, from which he could see the Farallones and Point Reyes, both known to him from reports and charts of Spanish navigators. On November 1, Portolá sent out a reconnoitering party led by the founder of one of San Francisco's proudest clans, Sergeant José Ortega.

Ortega worked up the peninsula, plowed his way across the dunes to hard, wet sand on Ocean Beach and turned the corner of the Golden Gate at Seal Rocks. From the hills behind today's South Tower of the Golden Gate Bridge, the noncommissioned officer gazed upon the immensity of San Francisco Bay, spreading for miles before his eyes. It was November 2, 1769. Only a footsoldier, Ortega cursed the bay and the frustrating strait that connected it with the ocean. His orders were to find a route to Point Reyes, and now he was blocked from reaching that prominent headland. Further exploration of the coast was impractical, if not impossible, so Ortega retreated next day to Portolá's camp.

The commander, with his men weary and sick, was as disgusted with his ill luck as was his sergeant. He failed as completely as his subordinate to appreciate the importance of the discovery and established his provincial capital at Monterey Bay.

It would take a far-sighted priest, Pedro Font, to sense the great value of the harbor of harbors, "where all the navies of the world might fit." As Font stared in awe at the bay, seven years later, he predicted that if the peninsula were settled, European-style, "there would not be anything more beautiful in the world." He called the great haven "a miracle of nature."

San Francisco Bay, long unseen by sea explorers, waited until 1769 to be discovered by landlubbers from Mexico, as depicted by Walter Francis in 1909.

CHAPTER 2.

COLONISTS

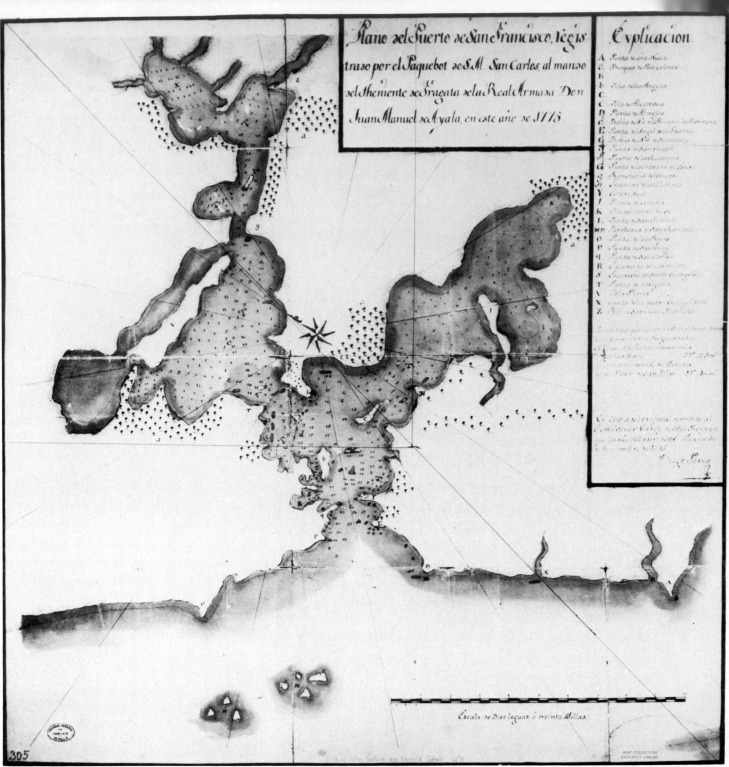

Captain Juan Manuel de Ayala's skilled Basque pilot, Jose de Cañizares, drew the first charts of the San Francisco area (above) in 1775. Ayala was the first navigator to enter the Golden Gate when he brought the packet San Carlos (right) "inside" late in 1775.

SAN FRANCISCO

Such a superb port as San Francisco was impossible to neglect entirely, even by wasted, exhausted Spain. To do so would be to forfeit it to Russia, France or England. So in 1775 the decision was made by a new viceroy of New Spain, Antonio Bucareli, to establish an outpost on San Francisco Bay.

On September 19, 1775, Captain Juan Bautista de Anza set forth from the Presidio of Tubac just south of Tucson in Arizona, then Sonora. De Anza made a remarkable march of 1,500 miles in six months, much of it across furnace-hot deserts, and led his party of soldiers, priests and colonists into newly founded Mission San Gabriel in January 1776 with the loss of only a single person by death, and probably a few deserters. His party had actually grown from several births on the arduous march, and he arrived in California with 244 people.

From San Gabriel, De Anza took his followers up the coast to Monterey, then returned to Sonora for another batch of colonists. By the end of his second expedition, men, women and children were poised at Monterey to begin the settlement of San Francisco.

Meanwhile, the supply ship *San Carlos* had been sent by Bucareli to explore San Francisco Bay. She was the first known vessel to pass through the Golden Gate and enter the bay—on August 5, 1775. Between then and September 17, Captain Juan Manuel de Ayala and his chief pilot, Jose de Cañizares, explored and mapped the great body of water, including its satellite bays and even such tidal streams as Petaluma Creek. When they returned to San Blas, their report was a favorable one, and their map and its place names were of great use to the settlers.

De Anza took Father Font, Lieutenant José Moraga and eleven of his strongest men to the very tip of the San Francisco peninsula on March 28, 1776. There, at a whitish bluff on the inside of the point, he erected a cross to mark the site of his future fort which would protect the missionaries and their Indian charges. (The site, on Cantíl Blanco, the White Cliff, has now disappeared, a victim of excavations from 1853-61 for Fort Point.)

After Font blessed the presidial cross, De Anza led his men southeast three miles to a well-watered site for the mission. He chose the sunny, sheltered bank of a lagoon that discharged into San Francisco Bay via a small stream. A second cross was set up there to claim the mission site.

De Anza was San Francisco's first hero. A splendid soldier, many of his colonists wept openly when he left them to return to Sonora. De Anza recalled, "I was deeply moved by their gratitude and affection, which I reciprocate." He praised his California colonists as people of fidelity who never deserted him.

Rivera y Moncada, military *commandante* of Upper California, was almost a disaster for nascent San Francisco. He opposed the settlement, wanting the newcomers to reinforce the scanty population of the

capital at Monterey. He quarreled with De Anza and forbade the latter's trusted lieutenant, José Moraga, from carrying out his original instructions.

Finally, word came from Mexico City overruling Rivera y Moncada. Even so, the obstructionist officer gave Moraga orders to establish only a presidio, not a mission. Wisely, the stalwart soldier and the clergyman ignored him.

Accompanying Moraga's first company of colonists was Father Francisco Palóu who, on the morning of June 29, said Mass on the shore of Laguna de Nuestra Señora de Los Dolores, the Lake of Our Lady of Sorrows. This small lagoon gave Mission San Francisco de Asís its popular name, Mission Dolores. While camped there to await the return of the *San Carlos* with supplies to build the military post, the wife of one of the enlisted men gave birth to a daughter, the first non-Indian native San Franciscan of history.

Colonizer of San Francisco, Don Juan Bautista de Anza, painting by Walter Francis.

The missionaries converted their Indian wards to Roman Catholicism, but allowed them to continue with many of their old customs. Louis Choris pictured dancers on the Mission plaza in 1816 (above) and playing the classic "stick game" (below).

With food, tools, supplies and men from the *San Carlos*, Moraga celebrated the completion of the first primitive Presidio building on September 17, 1776 with a Mass and civil ceremonies. (Some local historians prefer this date to June 29 as the foundation date for the city of San Francisco.)

The heart of the military base was first a fortification some 275 feet square built in the form of a palisade. Redwood logs were upended and sunk into the ground to form a solid wooden wall around a compound. The stockade boasted at first just one cannon borrowed from the *San Carlos*, intended to command the strategic strait of the Golden Gate.

On October 9, 1776, Palóu formally dedicated a small wooden Mission Dolores. The church was soon replaced by another temporary wooden structure, then by a more substantial adobe on a new site in order to allow the lagoon-side area to be tilled as a garden.

CONVERTING THE INFIDELS

Relations between the colonists and the Indians were excellent at first. The relationship deteriorated somewhat when the Franciscans tried to transform the "savages" into good Christians. In their zeal to convert these infidels, the padres often were insensitive, sometimes even devoid of good sense. They were accused by their critics of breaking up families by their practice of separating the young women into a dormitory to protect them from the advances of soldiers as well as young Indian men, and to have mixed the tribes together willy-nilly, as the Mission became the home of non-*Costeños* as well as locals. Certainly the Fathers drilled their charges in a work ethic—gardening, truck farming, grain harvesting, herding, brickmaking and weaving—that was as alien to these gentle, unenterprising people as phrenology or higher mathematics.

The padres were not deliberately cruel to their wards, but they were strict disciplinarians. Sometimes even the kindness of the padres boomeranged. They gave their Christian neophytes a two-week vacation from their labors each year. The Indians were allowed to return home on an honor system. Most of them returned to Mission Dolores, but others defected. Some joined renegades, or rebel leaders, who carried on a guerrilla war with the whites.

The fortnights of leave were the Indians' happiest times. The German explorer for the Russians, Otto von Kotzebue, who visited the settlement in 1816, recorded, "I, myself, have seen them going home in crowds, with loud rejoicing."

Kotzebue exaggerated wildly when he claimed that 300 out of the total Indian population of San Francisco died each year. The turnover was large, but many of the losses were due to desertion, not death, or were simply absences-with-leave. Crammed together physically, the Indians exchanged diseases, although it is not at all certain that they died like flies, as critics of the mission enterprise insist. But the cutting, foggy sea winds did not help the sick, either, especially those with respiratory disorders. For that reason, a sub-mission or *asistencia* was founded in sunny Marin County in 1817. It shortly became the full-fledged Mission San Rafael. There the sickliest Indians were sent to recuperate. Even earlier, neophytes were transferred to warmer missions—to Santa Clara when it was founded in 1777, and later (1823) to the last of the missions, San Francisco de Solano, in Sonoma.

Mission Dolores was not a whopping success. It did not reach the size or prosperity of most of the other Alta California missions. The sandy soil and often-overcast skies permitted only meager grain harvests, and the hilly terrain kept the peninsula's herds of horses and cattle small compared to those running on richer pasture lands. The Mission settlement, however, was huge by *Costeño* standards. The massive Mission church (the same one we view today) was built of four-foot-thick walls of adobe bricks supporting a red tile roof on hand-hewn redwood logs tied together with rawhide thongs and pinned with wooden pegs. Alongside the church lay the *campo santo*, the holy ground of the cemetery.

The priests' quarters and Indians' barracks that circled the church were, in turn, surrounded by cultivated fields. Crops of corn, wheat, beans, peas and potatoes were harvested to support the communal kitchen. A representative of each family came at meal time to receive its rations. Each family was assigned its own garden plot separate from the community's fields. The Indians passed much of their free time there, tending their watermelons and cantaloupes, pumpkins, onions and garlic. They even planted fruit trees, berries and grapevines.

The most productive shop in the Mission complex was the woolen mill where weavers, mostly women, manned twenty large looms. There were two mule-powered grist mills which ground flour for the Mission and supplied the Presidio—when it could come up with the cash. When it could not, the padres found themselves with a surplus of flour, which they traded to the occasional vessel that came to anchor in the bay. This modest, informal and very illegal trade was the only business carried on in the settlement except for out-and-out smuggling. Presidio officers winked at the smuggling and more open trading, both illegal, but the governors at Monterey kept their taboo on San Francisco Bay. Monterey remained the only port of entry; magnificent San Francisco Bay was off limits (at least officially) to ships as a port of call.

GARRISON DUTY

By around 1778, a building of solid adobe bricks was completed within the paling of the Presidio. Around 1791, the commandant's quarters was finished. The original Cantíl Blanco battery was steadily improved, and in 1794 a strong point, the Castillo de San Joaquín, was added to San Francisco's feeble defenses. Its garrison was only a corporal's guard of six men, but its battery was composed of eight bronze twelve-pounders cast in Peru.

The Presidio was always under-armed and under-manned by a rag-tag company of slovenly, unpaid and bootless *soldados*. Their only break in the boring routine of garrison duty—which consisted largely of

herding a few head of cattle and carrying on sub-
sistence gardening—was drinking, wenching and perhaps a little music. From time to time there was a
dance or a fiesta. A real treat was a bull and bear
fight held on feast days at the Mission Dolores.

Occasionally there was the excitement of a punitive
expedition to round up runaway neophytes,
renegades and wild Indians, with exploration and
mapping a useful bonus. The favorite Indian hideout
was the watery maze of rivers, sloughs and great tule
beds of the swampy Sacramento-San Joaquin River
Delta, then called simply the *Tulares*. From the jungle
of a marshland, the still-savage tribes raided Mission
herds and drove the captured stock into the swamps.

Several Spanish officers and enlisted men of the

Presidio made names for themselves in these campaigns into the interior. Begun by Fages and De Anza in 1772 and 1776, Presidio commandant Captain José Moraga continued them in 1776. In 1806, Moraga's son, Gabriel, destined to become the greatest Spanish explorer of California, entered the Delta in command of a punitive force. He was followed that same year by his second cousin, Luís Argüello. The younger Moraga led further expeditions in 1808 and 1818, and Argüello again in 1817. Promoted from sergeant to ensign, José Antonio Sánchez led a party into the interior in 1826, but the last great campaign was Moraga's of 1821. He explored all the way to the northern end of the Sacramento Valley. An epidemic of malaria brought to the Delta by Hudson's Bay Company beaver trappers in 1833 virtually wiped out

A lithograph, after a drawing by Louis Choris, faithfully recorded life at San Francisco's Presidio in Spanish times.

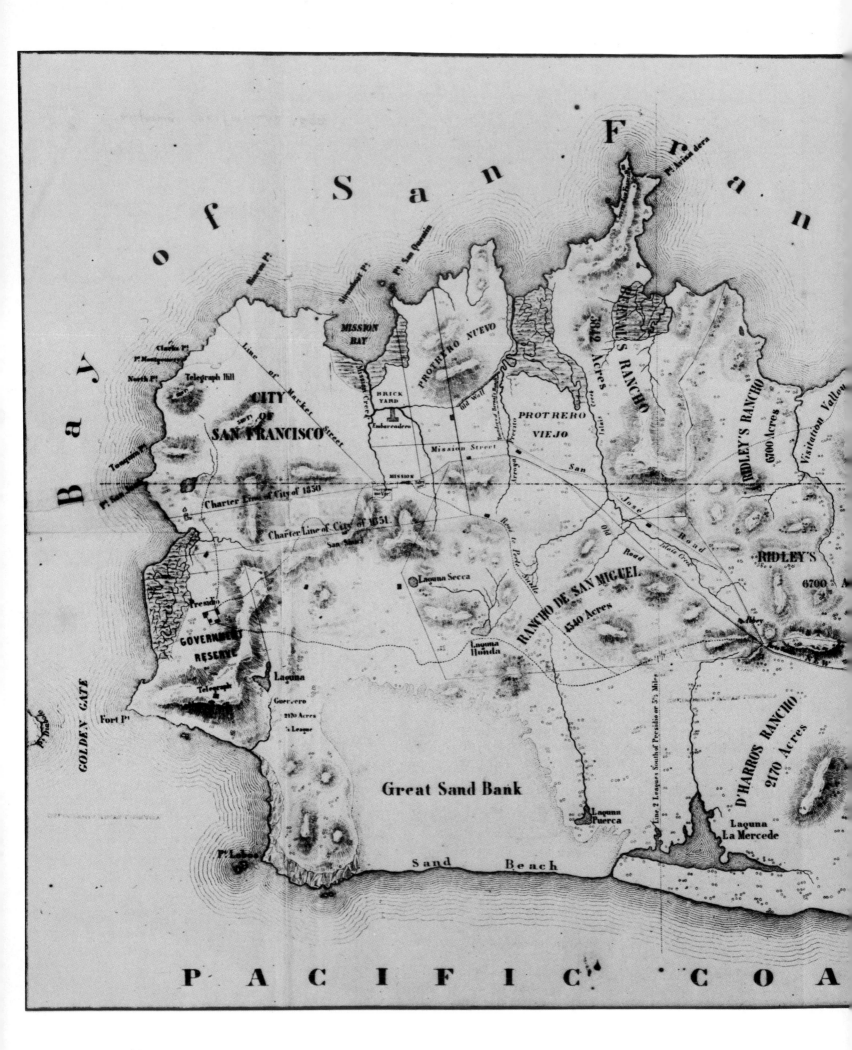

Bay of San Fran

MISSION BAY

Clarks Pt
Pt Montgomery
North Pt
Telegraph Hill

CITY OF SAN FRANCISCO

Telegraph

Pt Se

Charter Line of City of 1850

Charter Line of City of 1851
San

BRICK YARD

Embarcadero

MISSION

PROTRERO NUEVO

Old Wall

Mission Street

PROTRERO VIEJO

Pt San Quentin

BERNES RANCHO

RIDLEY'S RANCHO
6700 Acres

Visitation Valley

RIDLEY'S
6700 A

Laguna Secca

RANCHO DE SAN MIGUEL
4540 Acres

Laguna Honda

Presidio

GOVERNMENT RESERVE

Laguna
Guerrero
2170 Acres
's League

GOLDEN GATE

Fort Pt

Pt Lobos

Great Sand Bank

Laguna Puerca

Line 2 Leagues South of Presidio or 5½ Mile

D'HARROS RANCHO
2170 Acres

Laguna La Mercede

Sand Beach

P A C I F I C   C O A

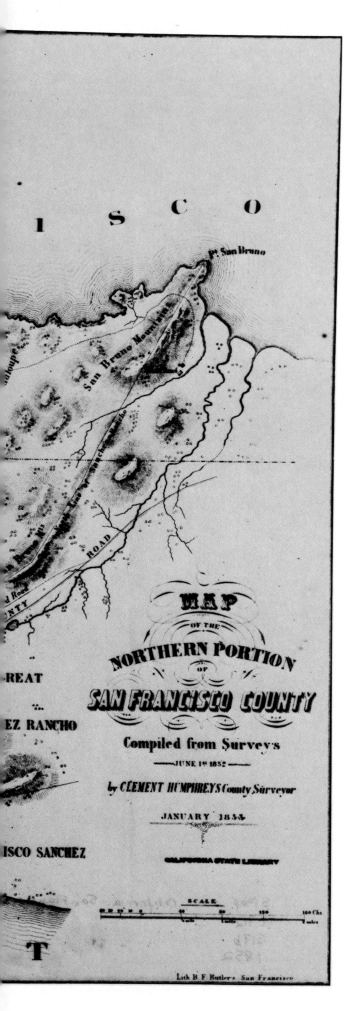

the Indians and made further expeditions from the Presidio unnecessary.

It was not until November 14, 1792, seventeen years after the *San Carlos*, that a foreign skipper entered San Francisco Bay. Lieutenant George Vancouver brought his ship *Discovery* around to anchor in Yerba Buena Cove (an inner harbor extending from Clark's Point on the north to Rincon Point), named for a local wild mint, *la yerba buena*, the good herb, without noticing the supposedly frowning fort on the Golden Gate's south bluff.

Commandant Luís Argüello gave the English officer permission to stake up a tent on the beach while his men secured wood, water and food to provision the ship. This modest canvas shelter was the first structure to be erected on the site of the future city's downtown, halfway between the Presidio and the Mission.

When Vancouver toured the Presidio, he saw the result of neglect by Mexico City and Madrid. Its 35 uniformed inhabitants, their families and a few Indian servants lived in thatch-roofed huts with earthen floors and drafty windows innocent of glazing. Vancouver noted only a single rusty old cannon in a defensive position, crudely lashed with rawhide to a rotten gun carriage.

Several positive things that Vancouver noticed about impoverished San Francisco were the kindness, generosity and graceful hospitality of its people, all traits that would distinguish the eventual city there. The meat and other foods kindly provided him by the Spanish rescued Vancouver's crew from malnutrition and scurvy.

A survey of 1855 recorded the old San Francisco cattle ranchos of the Mexican period (left).

STARVED FOR VISITORS

Neglected by Spain, San Francisco was all but abandoned by Mexico when independence came in 1821. Captain Frederick William Beechey, of H.M.S. *Blossom*, described the Presidio of 1825 as dilapidated, and "little better than a heap of rubbish and bones on which jackals [coyotes], dogs, and vultures were constantly preying."

Foreigners and their vessels were still prohibited from visiting San Francisco when Mexico took over. Naturally, most shipmasters and many Californians ignored the taboo since the Presidio was powerless to enforce the edict even if the commandant agreed with it, which was unlikely. San Franciscans were starved for trade, goods, news, visitors.

So it was that a parade of ships followed Vancouver's *Discovery* into San Francisco Bay. Nikolai Rezanov of Alaska's Russian American Company arrived in a Yankee ship, the *Juno*, in 1806. The Russian was well-received, especially by Concepción Argüello, the 15-year-old daughter of the commandant, José D. Argüello. She fell head over heels in love with him, and Rezanov got Argüello's consent to marriage. Unfortunately, the Russian died on his way to Moscow to get permission from the Orthodox Church to marry a Roman Catholic. "Concha" waited for him for years, then entered a convent as the first California-born nun of the Dominican order.

The Russians sent other ships to trade and hunt,

31

illegally, for sea otters from camps on the Farallon Islands. In 1812, the Russians disregraded Spanish territoriality entirely and planted their Fort Ross colony on the Redwood Coast north of San Francisco. The feeble Presidio could not oust the Slavs, nor did it try to do so.

Traders followed explorers in the wake of the *Juno*. Already word was being spread of San Francisco's great advantages over Monterey Bay. Its harbor was a hundred times safer; it had the finest drinking water on the coast just across the Gate in Sausalito; there was no customs house and there were no duties to pay, assuming that one could bully or bluff one's way into trade with the locals.

When California became part of an independent Mexico in 1822, its small population hardly noticed the change, at first. But in 1834, San Francisco and all of California were jarred out of complacency by a proclamation of Governor José Figueroa secularizing the missions. The friars of the Franciscan order would be replaced by secular priests, and the missions would become parish churches. The Indian neophytes would be released from the jurisdiction of the missionaries, whose property would be converted into Indian pueblos, with each family given land and livestock. Like so many well-meaning reforms, it did not work. Taking effect in stages during 1834, 1835 and 1836, it destroyed the mission system, but took the Indians along with it. Although only half the property was to be held by civil administrators and half given to the Indians, all of the Mission lands ended up in private (white) hands. The rising class of California *rancheros* prospered; the Indians scattered, often drifting aimlessly.

By 1841, Mission Dolores was a shambles. The herders' stock had long since dispersed. The fields were yielding bumper crops of weeds. The 1,500 Indians of 1816 had declined to 400 by 1834; in 1841 only 50 demoralized individuals clung to the ruins. The friars were gone and no curate replaced them. The faithful had to wait for an occasional priest to ride in to hold services.

The only silvery streak in an otherwise cloudy sky was the rise of cattle *ranchos* in California, even in constricted San Francisco. Only two dozen grazing permits or land grants had been made in Spanish times. After the Mexican Republic began to run California, its governors handed out, by 1846, over 600 grants involving eight million acres of pasture lands. A surplus of cattle on these new ranches brought New England skippers to San Francisco to engage in the hide and tallow trade. Belatedly and accidentally, prosperity came to Mexico's weakest province.

Young Don José C. Bernal, seen with Doña Carmen Cebrián, was a member of a prominent San Francisco ranchero *clan of Mexican days.*

CHAPTER 3

YANQUI SEAPORT

Just as secularization seemed ready to destroy what was left of San Francisco, the port without a town was saved. A small commerce began on the flimsy foundations of petty smuggling. Russian vessels came from Sitka for wheat and beef to ease starvation in Alaska. Whaling ships began to call for wood and water. Trading vessels wandered in from New England and Hawaii. Commerce grew as Mexico liberalized Spain's old restrictions on fraternization with foreigners. The trend increased with sentiment for separatism, even independence, in California. Finally, cattle ranching began to play a dominant role as both cause and effect of the new trade. Virtually all business was in tallow and hides, the latter for New England's shoe factories. It brought a modest prosperity.

Hide brigs began to anchor between Yerba Buena Island and the mainland cove in the 1830s. They sent small boats ashore to pick up hide bags of tallow and stiff cowhides on the gravelly beach between Clark's Point and Rincon Point, toward Mission Bay.

Trade attracted foreign settlers, men of varying backgrounds, tastes and nationalities who resembled one another only in business aptitude and acumen. Even in the 1830s, the tiny port was distinct from its fellow California settlements. From the first year of its existence, San Francisco was a cosmopolitan society of Mexicans, Americans, Britons, Hawaiians, South Americans, French, Russians, Germans, Danes, Dutch and other Europeans—even a West Indian pioneer.

At first, Americans tended to look down on San Franciscans. They contrasted their own industry and education with the lax values of untutored, simple and seemingly slothful Spaniards. Author Richard Henry Dana, although liberal in comparison to most of his New England peers, typed *Californios* as "an idle, thriftless people," whose women displayed an excessive fondness for dress.

The city of San Francisco had its beginning circa December 7, 1834 when the first *ayuntamiento* or town council was organized. Francisco de Haro was chosen to be the first *alcalde* of the still-to-be-developed pueblo. The office was the Mexican equivalent of mayor, with the added duties of municipal magistrate or justice of the peace. Beneath him was a second *alcalde*, or vice mayor, and a syndic; above him was a sub-prefect for the district; then, in Monterey, a prefect, virtually a lieutenant governor, and finally the governor.

The appointment was duly confirmed by Governor José Figueroa; De Haro's instructions were to develop the port by reserving land extending 600 yards from the beach for governmental purposes and to measure off the land above that line for a townsite. Because the Presidio was in such an advanced state of decay, there was no help from that quarter. San Francisco would grow without a taproot in either the military or the mission settlement, which lay almost equidistant from the townsite. De Haro would, however,

Francisco de Haro, the first Mexican alcalde of the port-village of Yerba Buena.

have the assistance of a talented ex-seaman, William Richardson, who found himself "on the beach" in San Francisco.

CAPTAIN WILLIAM RICHARDSON

The true founder of the future city of San Francisco was not its first *alcalde* but the Englishman, Richardson. He sailed through the Golden Gate on August 2, 1822 as first mate of the British whaler *L'Orient*. Richardson fell for San Francisco like the proverbial ton of adobes. On October 7 he petitioned the governor for the privilege of permanent residence. Pablo Vicente de Solá, like so many pragmatic California politicians, was ready to bend the law that forbade settlement by foreigners. On October 12 he granted Richardson's request, appreciating the Londoner's expertise in both navigation and carpentry—two skills in short supply around San Francisco. Richardson soon melted into the mainstream, converting to Catholicism, marrying María Antonia Martínez, the daughter of Presidio commander Ignacio Martínez, and becoming a naturalized Mexican citizen in 1830.

The ex-whaler built a launch and also a surf boat, thereby beginning San Francisco's shipbuilding industry. He ran the launch on the bay, ferrying passengers and carrying grain and local produce, as well as hides and tallow. He trained six or eight Indians as crewmen, carpenters and boatwrights, and with his *Costeño* crew, Richardson explored every slough, inlet and mudflat of San Francisco Bay.

Richardson dreamed of greatness for the port and wished to play a role in its development. In 1825 he applied to the governor for the grant of a lot above Yerba Buena Cove, and again in 1828 and 1834. All of these applications were rejected, but the persistent Londoner tried again in 1835. This time, Governor Figueroa asked him the extent of the property that he desired. Richardson gave him a *diseño*, or sketch map, of a clearing of the brushy slope about 750 yards southwest of the anchorage of Yerba Buena Cove.

In anticipation of the formal grant, he pitched a tent on the site as of June 25, the effective date of San Francisco's 1835 founding. The village, town and city which grew up there was called Yerba Buena. Richardson fenced off his property and replaced his temporary canvas home with an American-style house built of lumber. In 1836, when the land grant was actually signed by San Francisco's new *alcalde*, José Joaquín Estudillo, Richardson built a proper home for his family, a large one-and-a-half-story dwelling of adobe bricks. As the village of Yerba Buena drew inhabitants, they came to call it *La Casa Grande*, the Big House. (It occupied much of the area of present-day 827-845 Grant Avenue.) The building served as a combination trading post and family residence. The first town council met there; the first court convened

Captain William Richardson.

in it; the first Protestant services were held in this home of a Catholic convert. It was also, later, the site of the first capital trial of the Vigilance Committee.

The governor appointed Richardson port captain in 1835, although he did not receive his official commission until 1837. From then until 1844, Richardson was the only harbor, bay, bar and ocean pilot at San Francisco. Commodore Robert F. Stockton named him collector of the port during the early American period as a reward for his piloting services on the Navy's flagship *Congress*.

Captain Richardson, who died in 1856, was one of the most respected men in all California. Historian Hubert H. Bancroft pronounced Richardson "a skilful sailor and an energetic man of business." The Englishman's own son described him as "clipper-built, well designed for speed and strength." Captain William Heath Davis, who knew him best, wrote that all became firmly attached to him because of his goodness of heart. The handsome, good-natured sailor with the musical voice could never say no to anyone. "He had not a single enemy, because his heart and nature were so noble."

THE PIONEERS

Captain Richardson's first neighbor was Jacob Primer Leese, a fine-looking Yankee from Ohio. Only 29, he had already had an adventurous career as a trapper and Santa Fe trader before moving to Los Angeles in 1833 and to San Francisco in 1836. Leese was determined to become San Francisco's resident hide and tallow trader. He procured a 300-yard lot adjoining Richardson's place on the south (later the site of the first St. Francis Hotel, at Montgomery and Clay streets).

The indefatigable Leese hurried work on his fine 60-by-25-foot wooden building, a combined trading post and dwelling. It was completed just in time for a combination house-warming and Independence Day party on July 4, 1836. The event was a real humdinger, and as a result of the Ohioan's example, Independence Day parties for both the United States (July 4) and Mexico (September 16) were celebrated in later years, usually at Leese's place.

Jacob Leese married Rosalía, sister of the rising

young officer Mariano Guadalupe Vallejo, in 1837. That same year, the Buckeye became a "whitewashed" (naturalized) Mexican citizen. Leese's daughter Rosalía, born in 1838, was the first white child born in civil San Francisco, then Yerba Buena.

Nathan Spear and William S. Hinckley soon joined their partner Leese in San Francisco. Hinckley was an open, talkative and sometimes-tipsy Bostonian, but an educated man of pleasant address. A widower, he married Susana Martínez and became Richardson's brother-in-law. Hinckley became San Francisco's first Anglo-Saxon *alcalde* in 1844. He was well-fitted for the post and discharged his duties creditably, then succeeded Francisco Sánchez as port captain in 1845. He was the most pro-Mexican of the *extranjeros*, or foreigners.

Spear had pioneered trading in Hawaii and the South Pacific. He came to California in 1831 but, unlike Richardson and Hinckley, was ineligible for a grant of land because he would not become a Mexican citizen. Starting in the deck house of the British bark *Kent*, Spear became a prosperous merchant. He built a store alongside the ship's cabin, and soon owned a six-mule-powered flour mill and two schooners Yerba Buena Island came to be called Goat Island after Spear pastured his animals on it. By 1841, his business building and residence was the most impressive in the little colony of about 30 families. Spear moved away in 1846, but when his Hawaiian wife died he returned and lived in San Francisco until his death a few years later at age 46.

Spear's nephew was Captain William Heath (Kanaka Bill) Davis, a half-Hawaiian born in Honolulu in 1822. He came to California three times as a youth on Hawaiian trading vessels. On his third trip in 1838 he stayed on as his uncle's store clerk. Davis married the ex-*alcalde's* daughter, María de Jesús Estudillo, in 1847 when he was already a prominent merchant and ship owner. He found that liquor was the best article of commerce in hard-swigging San Francisco. Buying New England rum in Honolulu for $1 a gallon, plus 30 cents duty, he sold it for $3 to $4 and could hardly land it fast enough to supply the demand.

Davis later built the first brick building of more than one story and rented it to the U.S. government for $36,000 a year. At the urging of W.D.M. Howard, he allowed himself to be elected to the *ayuntamiento* in 1848-49, but bungling by a business partner, combined with uninsured losses in the great fire of 1851, almost ruined Kanaka Bill. He is best remembered for his gossipy book of remembrances, *Seventy-Five Years in California*, which remains a minor regional classic.

In 1837, Leese, Spear and Hinckley obtained from Alcalde Ignacio Martínez a grant of 300 yards on the west side of what was becoming Montgomery Street. The partners built a trading post on the lot, easily the village's largest structure—a two-story frame building with dormer windows, an architectural rarity for Spanish California.

Leese was given three 300-yard lots on Dupont and Sacramento streets and three more beyond the town's limits. Governor Alvarado made him and Salvador Vallejo a unique grant, right on the water. In fact, it was on the deepest water of the cove at La Punta de la Loma Alta (High Hill Point), later Clark's Point.

Leese was the first Anglo in San Francisco to be given a land grant ranch.

The Leese/Spear/Hinckley partnership dominated West Coast business until it broke up in 1838 when Spear took a violent dislike to Leese. Leese dissolved the business and moved to Sonoma. Spear and Hinckley remained at Clay and Montgomery for a few more years.

In 1841, Dr. John McLoughlin bought the partners' old store for the Hudson's Bay Company, and chose his own son-in-law, William Glen Rae, to be the company's factor in San Francisco. The HBC ("Here Before Christ," its rivals joked, sourly) opened for business in September, stocking a miscellaneous assortment of English goods.

Manager Rae was tall, handsome and vain, but also hospitable and generous, a gentleman with a wife and children. He made a successful operation of the store, sending launches darting across the bay to pick up hides and tallow for barter. He was highly respected, even though he had some business reverses and backed the wrong side in one of the territory's frequent power struggles.

In January 1845, the public learned that Rae had been unfaithful to his wife, "having succumbed to the fascinations of a California lady." The sensitive Scot was so overcome with disgrace and mortification that he shot himself, becoming the first of a long line of San Francisco suicides. After Rae's death, British Vice Consul James Alexander Forbes closed the store. The company never reopened it, but sold it to Henry Mellus and W.D.M. Howard.

The next pioneer San Franciscan to arrive on the scene was William Alexander Leidesdorff, an enterprising mulatto gentleman born in the Danish West Indies. He arrived in command of his own ship, already well-to-do from his profits as a New Orleans cotton broker. He dispensed dry goods, groceries and hardware in exchange for rawhides, first from a building owned by John Fuller, then from his own residence and store. He built a two-story adobe at the intersection of Clay and Kearny streets (now Portsmouth Square), adding a bar and billiard room in 1846 and finishing the upper floor in 1847. The building became Brown's Hotel, then the City Hotel, popular until it burned in the 1850s.

Yerba Buena by 1837 was a bona fide port for hide droghers and whaleships. George H. Baker's lithograph is from an original drawing by Captain Jean Jacques Vioget.

William Leidesdorff, a leading citizen of Yerba Buena.

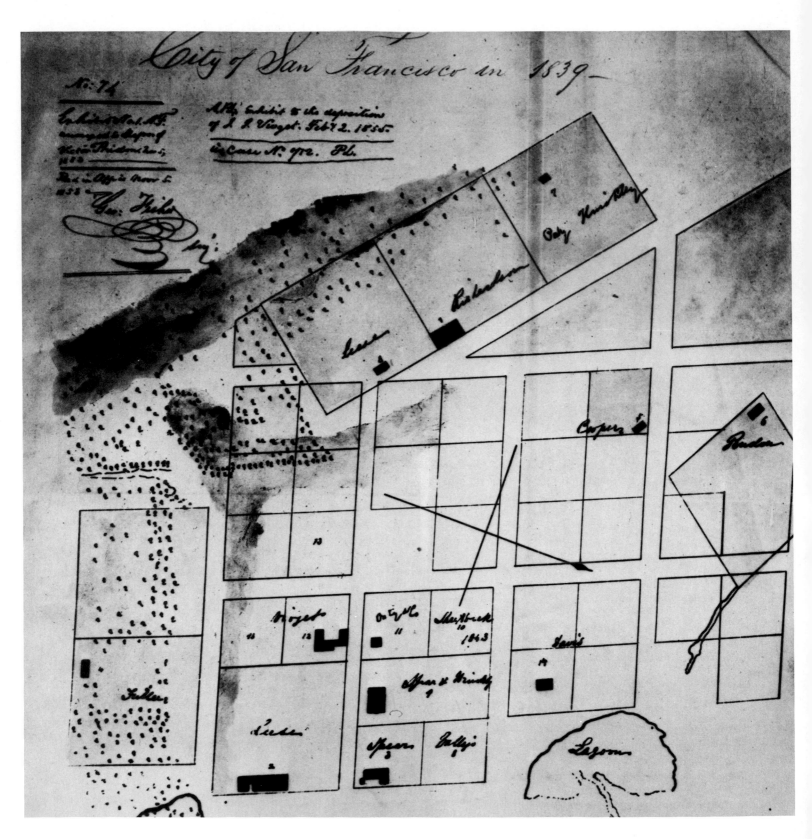

City of San Francisco in 1839

Jean Jacques Vioget made the first plat of Yerba Buena in 1839.

Leidesdorff was chosen to be a member of the first school board, a councilman on the first two American *ayuntamientos*, city treasurer and vice consul of the United States in San Francisco. The Danish West Indian was vain, very proud of his consular uniform with brass buttons and gold lace. He hobbled about with the assistance of a cane and a dozen half-dressed Indians. He built a warehouse near the water and added a stubby wharf where Captain Stephen Smith of Bodega brought the first redwood lumber for San Francisco's growth.

Bachelor Leidesdorff died in 1848 at the age of 38. He owned more of San Francisco than anyone else and left a large and valuable estate, although crippled with $60,000 in debts.

There were few Mexican families in Yerba Buena/ San Francisco proper, and some spent only the winter months there. A prominent native was Second Alcalde José de Jesús Noé, described by sailor-writer Joseph Downey as the town's majordomo—"the big gun of the village."

Near the shambles of Mission Dolores lived Fran-

38

The Presidio was probably a good deal more decrepit when the Stars and Stripes finally flew over it in 1846 than in the picture (left) offered by an unknown woodcut artist.

cisco Guerrero, both *alcalde* and sub-prefect. He encouraged immigration by "progressive" foreigners and freely predicted that California would soon pass into American hands. Guerrero was one of the early victims of the license that turned to violence in Americanized San Francisco. Due to testify in litigation over Mission Dolores property, he was murdered in broad daylight in 1851.

Francisco de Haro, ex-*alcalde* and syndic, also lived out by the mission, as did Francisco Sánchez. The latter had to put down a mutiny in the harbor and did so a bit too drastically by running his sword clean through a mutineer, killing him and pinning him to the bloody deck. Sánchez was shaken by the incident and resigned his post as port captain in favor of Hinckley.

Travelers to Yerba Buena from Monterey often broke their journeys at the *ranchos* outside of town, knowing they would be warmly welcomed. Dr. Marius Duvall, who visited José de la Cruz Sánchez's rancho in 1846, found the one-story adobe anything but neat, and its owner negligent in personal appearance. But what a hospitable fellow he was! He offered the surgeon a stew of chicken with rice, wheat tortillas and coffee, then a bed for the night.

A sailor almost as important as Richardson arrived in Yerba Buena in 1837—Jean Jacques Vioget, a bespectacled 38-year-old civil engineer. Master of his own vessel, Vioget came only to trade, but fell in love with San Francisco. He stayed put and became a naturalized citizen in 1840. An excellent artist, Alcalde de Haro hired him as surveyor and cartographer in 1839 to make a plat of Yerba Buena. Vioget turned out to be a real community asset. A jolly fellow, he kept a grocery store and tavern/billiard parlor that was one of the very first San Francisco saloons.

In 1844 the Mexican government finally recognized that San Francisco was destined to be no mean port and built a mission-style customs house on the corner of the plaza. The customs house did not stop smuggling, although it did stimulate legitimate trade by attracting the attention of more skippers to San Francisco.

By 1845, the town was bursting its cartographic bounds, so Alcalde José Sánchez doubled the size of Yerba Buena, extending it as far as today's Sutter, Stockton and Green streets. Montgomery remained the waterfront avenue.

Although the cadre of pioneering San Franciscans was of a dazzling variety, it was a tightly knit extended family of close friends, from *alcalde* to peon. Since there was, as yet, no city hall, town clerk Ridley kept the *alcalde's* official map of the township—nearly illegible from erasures and the attentions of greasy fingers—in the safest place in town, behind the bar of his saloon.

A PRIZE OF WAR

The year 1841 saw a slight and temporary leveling off of San Francisco's growth and prosperity as Alvarado issued decrees to limit foreign trade. It was a futile gesture—much too little and much, much too late. The presence in the harbor of Lieutenant Charles Wilkes' Exploring Expedition warships and the arrival at Sutter's Fort of the first overland company of emigrants, pointedly reminded the governor of America's continuing interest in the port. Cadwalader Ringgold, one of Wilkes' lieutenants, made the first accurate survey and chart of the bay and Sacramento River. Even the most illiterate peon could now read the handwriting on the wall—and it was in English.

In 1842, Uncle Sam tipped his heavy hand. Commodore Thomas Catesby Jones seized Monterey when he received mistaken intelligence that the United States and Mexico were at war. The red-faced Welshman quickly hauled down the American flag, made his apologies to the dumbfounded Mexican authorities and slunk away to sea.

Just four years later, the 200 Yerba Buenans in 50-odd buildings were hardly surprised when

The major Spanish-style building in early San Francisco was the tiled-roof Customs House, built in 1844 by local Indians.

the *Portsmouth*, to be *alcalde*, possibly because he knew a little Spanish. Bartlett was later confirmed in office by the town's first general election on September 15, 1846. When his sloop left the bay to help recapture Southern California, Bartlett was left behind to continue his *alcalde*ship—to the great joy of the *Portsmouth*'s crew and to "the manifest discomfort of the townspeople, who hated him as cordially as we did," wrote diarist Joseph Downey, Bartlett's clerk.

Rumors of an impending attack on San Francisco by Castro and fear that Britain's Royal Navy might take the side of Mexico led Montgomery to urge American whalers to hole up in San Francisco and Richardson's Bay. There were eight to ten of them at anchor by August 1846. A lookout was placed atop Loma Alta (now Telegraph Hill) to spy out approaching sails, and the gun from the *Portsmouth's* launch was set up in the Plaza where a log blockhouse was going up. Meanwhile, an earthen battery to replace the old Castillo de San Joaquin was being constructed on a hillock 100 yards below Clark's Point. Soon the battery (from which today's Battery Street takes its name) was bristling with armament. But no powder was provided and no garrison, although Howard's amateur soldiers mustered a company of artillerymen. The battery was officially named Fort Montgomery, but it was also called Fort Missroon, Fort Pick-and-be-Damned and, mostly, Missroon's Folly.

Shortly after Commodore Robert F. Stockton was welcomed to town on October 3, 1846, with a parade, buffet and ball at Leidesdorff's, he took away the new gun carriages, leaving the old cannon propped up by sticks. A disgusted Missroon hauled down the flag and abandoned the strong point.

The only real invasion of Yerba Buena occurred on July 31, 1846 and involved no Mexicans, only peaceable Mormons. The 238 passengers, mostly Saints, arrived on the chartered *Brooklyn*. Samuel Brannan had planned to rendezvous with Brigham Young at San Francisco to establish a Mormon colony, but Young halted at Salt Lake.

Brannan was a Down Easter who early traded Maine for Ohio, where he became a journeyman printer. Converted to Mormonism, he was chosen by Young to lead the maritime exodus because of his dynamic personality. He had his hands full on the voyage. Sam had to tongue-lash and excommunicate three men and the object of their affection, the well-named Mrs. Lucy Eager, for "licentious and wicked conduct...of the most disgraceful character."

As if lascivious followers were not enough, Elder Brannan had expected to arrive in a Mexican port. Fresh from persecution in Illinois and Missouri, the Mormons felt their hearts sink as they saw the Stars and Stripes over Portsmouth Plaza. Boats from the *Portsmouth* landed the Mormons, who pitched neat white tents in a lot opposite the customs house. By the onset of the rainy season, they had scattered—to occupy all the vacant buildings in town, at the Mission and at the Presidio.

Yerba Buena did not become a Mormon town, although the *Brooklyn's* passenger list about doubled its population. Defections were numerous and eventually included the leader. Brannan himself was excommunicated for supposedly pocketing some of the church's tithes. As early as September 1847, the Mor-

Manifest Destiny again reared its ugly head in the shape of the Bear Flag Revolt. The ambitious, aggressive and ambivalent explorer, John C. Fremont, figuratively patted the rebel "Grizzlies" on the head. He and Dr. Robert Semple marched on San Francisco on July 1-2, 1846.

Since Alcalde Hinckley was unavailable (he was dead, as of the very day before, on his return from a meeting of Mexican citizens ordered by General José Castro at Santa Clara), Semple arrested Robert Ridley, a naturalized Mexican citizen and the port captain.

The reason for the Bear Flag rebels' "seizure" of San Francisco was apparent enough to recently arrived Edwin Bryant. "This place is doubtless destined to become one of the largest and most opulent commercial cities in the world and, under American authority, it will rise with astonishing rapidity." He was right. Between 1846 and 1848, San Francisco was the most thriving town on the Pacific Coast, at a time when no one had yet dreamed of gold.

The Mexican War broke right on the heels of the Bear Flag "conquest." On July 9, 1846, 70 armed Marines and sailors marched unopposed to the Plaza. There, Lieutenant John S. Missroon, executive officer of the U.S.S. *Portsmouth*, raised the Stars and Stripes over the customs house, and Captain John B. Montgomery read a proclamation of conquest. The proclamation, however, only formalized a *fait accompli*. San Francisco had been a Yankee port in Mexico since Richardson secured his foresail to redwood posts eleven years earlier.

Captain Henry B. Watson was appointed military commandant of Yerba Buena by Montgomery. He stationed a garrison of two dozen of his Marines in the customs house, now converted to a barracks. Twenty or thirty civilians also organized themselves into a militia company captained by W.D.M. Howard. They elected officers and began drilling to be ready to help the Navy defend San Francisco against recapture by the Mexicans.

On August 26, 1946, Captain Montgomery appointed Washington Allon Bartlett, third lieutenant of

mon establishment began to break up with the sale of property held in common. Brannan finally became a real apostate, taking to drink and ending up in a pauper's grave in 1889, although in his prime he was probably San Francisco's first millionaire.

The most important event of Alcalde Bartlett's "reign" was the appointment in 1847 of a surveyor of San Francisco. Vioget's early effort was by now badly dated. Jasper O'Farrell, an Irish civil engineer, had arrived in California from Mazatlan, deserting at Sausalito while cooper of a whaleship. The Mexican government named him surveyor general of Alta California. Now the U.S. military governor appointed him surveyor of San Francisco.

O'Farrell first corrected the street intersections; Vioget had been off on his right angles by two and a half degrees. (This correction is still called O'Farrell's Swing.) To rearrange the grid lines of his streets, the Irishman had to move back some fences and amend property lines. He then created 100-foot-wide Market Street, capable of handling fleets of yet-uninvented streetcars. It ran "on the bias," diagonally from the Embarcadero toward Twin Peaks.

Probably because of O'Farrell's survey, town lots began to increase in price from their base of $12 to $15. Wartime San Francisco became so cramped that the military governor in late 1847 allowed the mudflats of Yerba Buena Cove, euphemized as "water lots," to be sold. This was both to extend the city limits and to bolster the city's coffers. (Since there were no city taxes as yet, Alcalde Bartlett ran his government with fines—usually from $5 to $10—collected largely from drunken whalers or other sailors on liberty who violated the sunset curfew.) The expansion, from Montgomery to Sloat (later Sansome) Street, was expected to be adequate for twenty years of urban growth.

Sam Brannan founded San Franciso's first newspaper, the *California Star*, in January 1847. Brannan proved to be a much better newspaperman than cleric. He came through pretty well on his promise to publish an independent newspaper of quality, fairness and truth. In his editorializing, he praised America's traditional freedom of the press and worried aloud over California's strange status—he concluded that no one really knew by what laws, Mexican or American, the conquered territory was being governed.

Brannan also pioneered a staple of San Francisco journalism, the legal notice. In January 1847 he anounced for the *alcalde* that all hogs in town had to be penned up and that all strays would be seized and their owners fined $5 per porker. In both Spanish and English, he next warned that Jonathan Fuller was no longer responsible for the debts of his wife. The really big news of this nature was his report of Bartlett's proclamation ordering that "San Francisco" be substituted for "Yerba Buena" on all official documents and communications as of January 30, 1847.

ON THE BRINK OF THE GOLD RUSH

P olitics aside, pre-Gold Rush San Francisco was a splendid place. Although it was already working on a world-class reputation as a hard-drinking town, violent it was not. It was a golden age, when captains, supercargoes and pursers were treated like gods, setting the stage for the greatest liberty port of them all. The *extranjeros* had adopted the native lifestyle, an eternal routine of loafing, smoking, dancing and (alas) too much drinking. The islands in the bay were still wooded, the waters were thick with fish and shellfish. Hunting of canvasbacks, mallards, widgeon and teal was easy and bountiful.

At the end of May 1847, the town enjoyed its first grand illumination in which whale oil lamps, tallow

---

candles, bonfires and tar barrels blazed merrily to light up the buildings as guns and firecrackers boomed in salutes to General Zachary Taylor's great victory over Santa Anna at Buena Vista.

That July, the town's sale of lots began and the *alcalde* got himself an interim council to help him govern until the election scheduled for September 13. The most important ordinance fueled land speculation by rescinding the old rule that lots had to be fenced and occupied by a building within a year of purchase. Real estate gambling now began to rival gaming with cards and chips.

The *Star* estimated in 1847 that San Francisco would grow by 300 to 500 houses per year. A June census of the city's 50 square blocks showed a total of 459 persons, four-fifths of them young, 273 of them literate. The figure included 375 whites—247 males and 128 females. Some 228 persons were Americans and 38 *Californios*. The diversity was astounding—27 Germans, 22 English, 14 Irish and an equal number of Scots, 6 Swiss, 5 Canadians and 21 people of miscellaneous national origin. There were surprises— 34 Indians and already 10 blacks. Hawaiians constituted almost ten percent of the population with 40 residents.

A special school census at year's end brought the population count to 850. By the time gold was discovered, there were 1,000 San Franciscans in 200 buildings. A dozen mercantile houses were in competition and two wharves represented rival sections of the city—the Broadway Wharf and Central Wharf, at the foot of Clay Street. Mellus and Howard were the leading businessmen. In 1845 they had bought the Hudson's Bay Company building (which later became the U.S. Hotel). Alongside it they built the first brick building in town and took in Talbot H. Green as a partner.

Like so many 'Frisco pioneers, Henry Mellus was Massachusetts-born. A sailor on the *Pilgrim* in 1835, he worked his way up to clerk and supercargo before becoming a partner with W.D.M. Howard in 1845. Although Downey described his career as one of "varying fortunes," he became wealthy and much later was elected mayor of Los Angeles.

Howard, who came to California to enter the hide trade in 1839 when he was 20, was a bold entrepreneur. He was a prime mover in Central Wharf's construction, so that vessels could offload on a dock in deep water at great savings over the lightering of cargo ashore in small boats. He backed Sam Brannan in gold mining ventures that made them both rich. He helped him organize the Society of California Pioneers and was its first president in 1850-53. He reorganized his old volunteer defense company into a 100-man militia unit called the California Guard. Howard and Mellus bought the city its first fire engine in 1851.

Mellus had an apoplectic seizure in 1850 that ruined his health, and he sold out his interest in the business to Howard and Green. He later claimed he had been tricked. Howard, sore as a boil, saw to it that the city renamed Mellus Street, and it remains today Natoma Street. Howard's health declined quickly in 1854 and he spent his dying days in the Oriental Hotel. As a generous benefactor of his adopted city, Howard was honored by having a street named

Five powerful merchant princes posed for a photographer in the early 1850s. Left to right, seated, were Jacob P. Leese, Thomas O. Larkin and W.D.M. Howard. The man standing left rear next to Sam Brannan is unidentified.

for him South of Market. Unlike Mellus Street, Howard Street stuck.

As for Green, he was a candidate for mayor in 1850 when someone recognized him as a Philadelphia fugitive, Paul Geddes. He denied everything, but took off for the East, ostensibly to clear matters up. He did not return for several years.

Hides and tallow still led San Francisco's exports on the eve of the Gold Rush, followed by wheat, furs, soap, some lumber and a little wine and brandy. San Francisco was California's major port and a close rival of the busiest port of the Pacific, Honolulu. There was a flourishing trade between the two harbors. During the last quarter of 1847, San Francisco imported $53,590 worth of goods and exported about $50,000. For the year ending April 1848, 85 merchant vessels dropped their hooks off San Francisco's Embarcadero.

Education came to San Francisco in April 1847 with J.D. Marston's private school. By December, a community drive had placed a public schoolhouse in the Plaza. Thomas Douglas became the first teacher in April 1848 with an annual stipend from the trustees of $1,000. Pupils paid fees ranging from $5 to $10 a term. The ugly little school building was used as a quasi-church, as a polling place in Thaddeus Leavenworth's election as *alcalde* and as a temporary courthouse during the partisan power plays of Leavenworth's embattled incumbency. It also served as a jail for City Marshal Malachi Fallon before being torn down as a public nuisance.

Schools and churches went hand in hand in the 1840s; there was no concern for separation of church and state—as long as the religion was Protestant. Timothy Dwight Hunt, Presbyterian divine from Hawaii, was appointed the city's official chaplain at a salary of $2,500 a year. He preached in the schoolhouse.

Jasper O'Farrell's ornate membership certificate in the Society of California Pioneers shows the artistic skill of C.C. Nahl.

POLITICS

When Alcalde Bartlett was released after capture by the Mexicans during the Mexican War, he returned to office, ousting the acting *alcalde*, George Hyde. The governor appointed Edwin Bryant to succeed him on February 22, 1847. Bryant served as chief magistrate and mayor only to June, but he saw O'Farrell's survey completed and began the sale of the lucrative beach and water lots. In just three years, 1,200 lots were sold for occupancy or re-sale at minimal prices—$10 to $25. But speculation came to the fore with the choice waterfront properties; these sold readily at prices up to $600 each.

The military governor appointed Hyde to succeed Bryant. The lawyer off the *Brooklyn* was experienced —he had served as *alcalde* of San Jose, as second *alcalde* of San Francisco (Bartlett's assistant) and acting *alcalde* during Bartlett's captivity—but his tenure was wracked by controversy. He was accused of giving away great hunks of land and tampering with the official city map.

Local politics were heating up. The appointed council of July was replaced by an elected one in September 1847. Intended to help Hyde govern, the council instead belabored and embarrassed him. *Alcalde* and council were soon playing a political game of Hyde and seek. During the summer of 1847, there was a great public outcry for Hyde's removal. A grassroots movement for true democracy, perhaps the origin of San Francisco's trademark philosophy—Always Question Authority—was afoot. The people were demanding free elections in place of imposed appointments by a military oligarchy. Thaddeus M. Leavenworth, preacher, physician and druggist, was elected *alcalde* on August 29, 1848, with 99 votes to his opponent's 76. The election was declared invalid when it was pointed out that there had been insufficient prior public notice of the election and that citizens of Mexican descent had been discouraged from voting. Levenworth ran again on October 3 and was elected, fair and square, by a huge margin. Only 158 people bothered to vote, however, and Leavenworth was soon the target of more criticism than Bartlett and Hyde combined.

There was a second murder in 1848 near Clark's Point. Soon there were disgraceful disorders in the streets, even bloody fights. The *alcalde's* authority was defied, and Leavenworth's personal safety was threatened. There were two rival town councils; at one point, briefly, three! An illegal legislative assembly was formed to seize power and did so, capturing the city archives. Its partisans, brandishing a hangman's noose, actually drove the *alcalde* into hiding.

The bitter political partisanship destabilized infant San Francisco and kicked the door to power wide open for entry by opportunistic and ruthless men. The stage was set for violence and criminality, and the legalized violence that was its sad antidote—vigilantism.

CHAPTER 4

Splendid Isolation

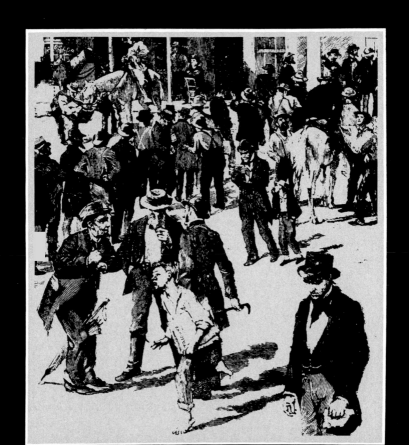

Gold was discovered at Coloma on January 24, 1848, but San Francisco was not ignited by the California Gold Rush until May. It was not that word of riches traveled all that slowly; the delayed reaction was caused by San Francisco's skepticism of the news.

Captain John Sutter hurried gold samples to Dr. Victor Forgeaud for tests, but the San Francisco physician at first thought them to be only fool's gold, worthless iron pyrites. When finally convinced that it was the real stuff, he told publisher Sam Brannan. The latter hurried out an April 1 special edition of his newspaper. Brannan's "extra" failed to excite San Francisco's doubting Thomases because of Forgeaud's initial blunder, compounded by the *Star* editor Edward Kemble's journalistic blooper. He pronounced California's gold placers "a sham...got up to guzzle the gullible."

Brannan now took drastic action to shock the townspeople out of their lethargy. Sam tramped up and down Montgomery Street brandishing a quinine bottle full of gold dust and bellowing, "Gold! Gold from the American River!"

That did the trick. A mad rush for the mines was delayed only momentarily by San Francisco's first major funeral. William Leidesdorff died just a few

The last issue of the Californian, suspended when the majority of its subscribers and advertisers lit out for the diggings.

ANDRÉ CASTAIGNE. 1891.

The post office in San Francisco, 1849-50, featured a long general-delivery line of 49ers.

Yerba Buena Cove became a beehive of activity during the "Rush for the Gold Regions." Well-heeled homeward-bound miners (inset) had a choice of clippers or Panama steamers of the Pacific Mail Steamship Company.

days after Brannan's dramatic promotion of the mines. Once the obsequies were out of the way, San Franciscans stampeded to the placers and spread word southward to ignite a rush from the rest of California.

The rush turned the city into a ghost town by late summer. The *Star* groused, "Everything wears a desolate and somber look, everything is dull, monotonous, dead." In June, both papers suspended publication for want of customers as well as pressmen. By that fall, all but seven of San Francisco's able-bodied adult males had lit out for the diggings.

LIFE IN EL DORADO

During the winter of 1848, miners began to return from the raw mining camps, either content with their existing pokes of gold dust and nuggets, disillusioned by failure to find riches, or inoculated against gold fever and the miserable life of manual labor that mining entailed. Enough families were back home by December for school to reopen and for a public meeting of concerned citizens to urge the creation of a provisional state government to end the benign anarchy prevailing in California.

The returnees brought the population of the city back to 2,000 by January and 5,000 by July 1849. They saw $850,000 worth of nuggets and "dust" strip merchants' shelves bare in the first sixteen weeks of the rush for riches and realized that they had an El Dorado right in their own backyard.

Between New Year's Day and July 1849, 10,000 Forty-niners hit the beach at Yerba Buena Cove. During the second half of the year, each and every month saw 4,000 more gold hunters land at the Embarcadero. In 1850, 36,000 more Argonauts came, the arrival of their ships now announced by a semaphore atop Telegraph Hill. Immigration dropped in 1851 to about 33,000, then peaked in 1852 with 66,988 arrivals.

All of the arrivals, even transients camping in Portsmouth Square, dropped their quota of gold on San Francisco. Most moved on to the mines but, even so, the city's population doubled every ten days.

The Pacific Mail Steamship Company's sidewheeler China was typical of the fast steamers tying San Francisco to "the States."

Long Wharf in the days when the city's population doubled every ten days.

Even before San Francisco was a metropolis, it was a cosmopolis—with Turks, Yankees, Chinese and Mexican Californios mixing on the streets.

Carleton E. Watkins photographed Washerwoman's Lagoon and the sand dunes of North Beach in 1858.

By 1851, San Francisco was a major American City. Its first official map, by William Eddy, included "imaginary" streets (submerged) and so-called water lots to be reclaimed by filling.

The pedestrian was an endangered species in early San Francisco. The streets swarmed with wharf rats the size of lunch boxes, but a greater danger were the packs of wild dogs that ran the streets at night.

Bayard Taylor could only estimate that the port grew by 3,000 to 30,000 people in the last quarter of 1849 alone. A census was impossible; everyone was too busy hustling about making money to count or be counted.

Abandoned vessels soon formed a ghost fleet lying at anchor off the Embarcadero—a rotten row of 774 ships by 1851. Some were dismantled for lumber; others, like the *Apollo*, were hauled ashore for warehouses or to serve as stores. The old *Panama* was converted into a church, the *Euphemia* made over into a jail.

Wharves resumed their march eastward over the mudflats in search of deep water as the few stores built out over the polluted shallows on pilings proved inadequate for unloading lighters. The shallows were first filled by pick-and-shovel-wielding Pats or Paddies, but these Irishmen were soon superseded by steam "paddies." Mixed with the earthen fill and the rock ballast dropped by vessels was a great dump of unwanted goods, a kitchen midden indicating to future archaeologists the bad investments and busted monopolies of the 49ers. One observer described layers of junk—strata of cookstoves, boxes and bales of leaf tobacco, once-precious rolls of sheet lead for roofing, fancy gold-washing machines and bundles of filthy clothes.

Dirty linen had to be shipped to Honolulu, even Canton, as the gold-hungry hordes quickly overtaxed the laundresses of Washerwoman's Lagoon, out by North Beach. The first real laundry there—Chinese—reduced the price of washing shirts from $8 to only $5 a dozen. The second establishment, Ansel Easton's, not only got rich on the contract to launder the Pacific Mail Steamship Company's endless bundles of soiled linen, it guaranteed success for the city's first soapmaker, Thomas Bergin and Sons.

At dusk, the streets swarmed with gargantuan rats, not just the Norwegian or wharf rats that jumped ship like the 49ers, but all varieties and mongrel combinations—gray, black and white—until the tough grays drove out the rest. There was a veritable plague of the rodents during 1850-53. Damage by the huge

By 1854, the intersection of Pine and Kearny had been "tamed" by the addition of board sidewalks and planked streets (above). The view up Montgomery Street from California Street in June 1854 revealed a solid Downtown of stone and brick business buildings (left).

53

The quick and the dead were always at odds in crowded San Francisco. The deceased made their last stand at Lone Mountain Cemetery, but eventually were exiled even from that remote hill to Colma, down the Peninsula.

INTERNATIONAL HOTEL,

JACKSON STREET, BETWEEN MONTGOMERY AND KEARNY.

SAN FRANCISCO, CAL.

D. N. HUNT, - - - - PROPRIETOR.

Rooms, by the Day, Week or Month, with or without Board, at Reasonable Prices.

FAMILIES

Furnished with Suits of Rooms. The Rooms are commodious and well ventilated, and Persons visiting San Francisco may rest assured that all the comforts and quiet found in a Private House, will be met with at this Hotel.

THE "INTERNATIONAL COACH,"

Is always in attendance to convey Passengers to and from the Boats,

AT ONE DOLLAR FOR EACH PERSON.

Town Talk Print, 149 Washington Street.

The 200-room International was among the first truly elegant hotels in the Far West. The Annals of San Francisco *described it as "admirably adapted in all respects to the purposes for which it has been constructed."*

vermin was second only to the losses from fire.

The streets were being graded, and seemingly bottomless quagmires at intersections were filled with junk before they could swallow pedestrians and carriages whole in the torrential season of 1849-50 that brought 50 inches of rain. As late as 1855, a pedestrian drowned by falling into a hole on the waterfront's Davis Street. Plank sidewalks, spiked in place against the winter rains, helped subdue the stinging dust storms of windblown sand and replaced rickety and makeshift "pitfall sidewalks" on such populous streets as Kearny.

Piles of redwood lumber from Mendocino City failed to keep pace with the demand for housing. Briefly, the business of lodging and boarding newcomers threatened to rival the gambling, boozing and commercialized wenching that passed for local industries. The hulk *Niantic*, originally dragged high and dry for a storehouse, was re-converted to a hotel. Flea-infested boarding houses were carelessly thrown together all over town, some with lines of bunks in three tiers, occupied in shifts. The grasping proprietors of a few merely chalked off areas on the floor. In these squares, a tired traveler could at least throw down his bedroll and his tired body, grateful for a roof over his head.

The need for housing drove property prices sky-high. Shanties commanded $800 a month in rent. A lot worth a barrel of bad whiskey in 1847 went for $18,000 in 1849. A vacant lot with no takers at $5,000 suddenly sold for $10,000 when adjacent Broadway Wharf replaced many Whitehall boats and lighters running between anchorage and beach.

Wags were not strangers to San Francisco, even when its thoroughfares were dirt streets. In the early 1850s some gents sighted through "telescopic" whiskey bottles and modeled ladies' hoops for an anonymous photographer.

French Consul Jacques Moerenhout described land speculation as so extravagant as to be "approaching madness," with values up by 1,000 percent. Land was so scarce that graveyards grasshopped all over town from North Beach, Russian Hill and Happy Valley to Yerba Buena Cemetery (today's Civic Center), then to Lone Mountain. Finally, to make way for the living, all of San Francisco's dead, except the Presidio military and one clergyman on Franklin Street, were exiled down the peninsula to Colma.

The need for housing and board not only bred fleabags, it produced the first hotels and restaurants of any quality in the Far West. The St. Francis, International and Oriental Hotels, the Parker House and Rassette House were shortly succeeded by truly luxurious hotels—the Lick House, James Donahue's Occidental, the Baldwin Hotel and, greatest of them all, the Palace Hotel of William Ralston and William Sharon in 1875.

English pubs, or ale houses, were popular for a spell. McClaren's Hotel near Woodward's Gardens was famous for its long-necked bottles of Allsop's Ale, its Stilton and Cheshire cheeses and its crisp bread and fresh ranch butter. Barry and Patten's was the first gentleman's saloon, with no gambling, only billiards, and its oil paintings chaste in character. It immediately became famous for its free lunch.

San Francisco at first made do with so-so French restaurants like Lafayette, and Raphael's in the Tehama House, but soon had a chic Delmonico's and a Poulet d'Or, quickly bastardized into the Poodle

Dog. The Wigwam was the ancestor of such esteemed seafood houses of today as Tadich's and Sam's Grill, but Charles Elleard's place in 1850 was the first bona fide oyster bar.

The Parker House of Robert Parker and John Henry Brown was posh for its day. No expense was spared to make it a comfortable place. When the Parker House partners found that the panes were too small for the window sashes, they simply rushed a clipper to Honolulu for glass of the correct size. Everybody was invited to a housewarming, grand ball and supper; class distinctions did not arrive until the 1850s.

One of the city's first devastating fires, in 1851, shortly destroyed the hotel along with the El Dorado gambling saloon and Dennison's Exchange. Were it not for the inch-thick mud coating the streets, the whole downtown might have gone up in smoke. David Broderick and Andrew Kohler saved the east side of Washington Street, including the pioneering Miner's Exchange Bank, by shoveling viscous mud against the walls of the threatened building to make it fire resistant. The Miner's Exchange Bank made necessary loans on the best security for only ten percent a month. This rate was not usurious in 1849; gamblers were sometimes eager to pay ten percent *an hour* for a transfusion of dinero when they anticipated a hot streak of luck.

Since 24,000 men arrived during the last half of 1849 but only 500 women—many of them members of the world's hoariest profession—a pattern of living was set up early for all times. With practically no

Coffee houses, ale houses and saloons served as men's social clubs in San Francisco during the 1850s. The stovepipe-hatted gents were just twenty years too early for the Bohemian Club.

homes or families, restaurants and places of entertainment became absolute necessities. But the male loners who crowded around the doughtnuts-and-coffee bar on the *Apollo* were eager for something besides shelter, grub and the diversions of drink and female company. They had earlier been infected with gold fever; now they came down with 'Frisco's virulent disease, gambling fever.

By 1853, the *Christian Herald* was twitting San Francisco for its 46 gambling dens as well as its 48 bawdy houses and 537 saloons. Cynic Hinton Helper opined that the best bad things obtainable were to be found in the city: "...purer liquors, better seegars, finer tobacco, truer guns and pistols, larger dirks and bowie knives, and prettier courtesans."

Even the *Annals of San Francisco*, compiled in 1855 by two local newspapermen and a doctor who were perversely proud of rough-and-tumble San Francisco, had to admit that its population ran to "hot-headed young men, flush of money and half-frantic with excitement, and lewd girls freed from the necessity of all moral restraint."

It was commonly said that San Franciscans would bet on anything—from a friendly game of pool to handicapping a cockroach race. The best-known building in town was not City Hall but the El Dorado gambling palace. At all hours in such temples of chance as the Tontine, La Sociedad, Empire, El Dorado, Parker House and Veranda, there was music, the tinkle of dealers' bells calling for drinks or cigars, the rattle of chuck-a-luck games, the clink of Mexican

dollars and the quieter click of ivory checks or counters.

The *Annals*, less than a decade later, looked back on the flush times as if on ancient history. The compilers described gambling saloons as: "...glittering like fairy palaces....In the larger saloons beautiful women dealt out the cards or turned the roulette wheel, while lascivious pictures hung on the walls....All was mad, feverish mirth, where fortunes were lost or won upon the green cloth in the twinkling of an eye."

Gambling, although illegal, was widespread in old San Francisco and was even the theme of advertisers.

GRIZZLY TAMER

Market hunters were common in beef-short San Francisco during the 1850s, providing venison, wild ducks and geese to establishments like the New World Market, but Grizzly Adams (1812-1860) was a super-hunter. The eccentric mountain man was John Adams of Massachussetts. For some reason, he disguised his identity by taking his brother's name, James Capen Adams, during his years on the Coast. He was the West's greatest animal tamer, indeed the only man who ever domesticated Ursus horribilis—the grizzly. Adams made pets of grizzly bears. They not only carried his packs, they would fight their wild kin in his defense.

Grizzly Adams exhibited his animals—bears, wolves, mountain lions, elk and deer—in a Clay Street menagerie not far from the New World Market. He called it the Mountaineer Museum. Along with the Woodward's Gardens Zoo, it can be considered the ancestor of today's Fleishhacker Zoo.

P.T. Barnum got wind of San Francisco's mountain man and enticed him to New York in 1860 with the offer of a partnership in his museum, but Adams's health was failing from head wounds received in a hand-to-paw fight with a wild grizzly, and he died in New York that same year.

Grizzly Adams took his bears by wagon to his Mountaineer Museum on Clay Street, not far from the New World Market.

FROM DUCKS TO HOUNDS

Already the cosmopolitan instant-city was questioning authority, extolling self-reliance and the determined readiness to grapple with adversity. It tolerated diversity and rugged individualism, even eccentricity, with a ready smile.

San Francisco's flight from authority soon began to exact a heavy price. The greed of a rootless population created an unhealthy civic ethic—a combination of get-rich-quick and every-man-for-himself philosophy. Self-indulgence and hedonism bred a contempt for law and order and the common weal at a time when they were already subservient to profit and loss. Opportunism, gambling and business speculation distracted and bemused an apolitical public. Control of the city, its government enfeebled by lack of taxes, began to slip into the receptive hands of venal politicans and ruthess criminals, even though they made up but a small percentage of the adventurous and visionary young men constituting San Francisco's citizenry.

Mayor Leavenworth had to convert the little log fort into a calaboose for criminals, at first only petty lawbreakers like the Oregonian lunatic known only as Pete. He was incarcerated for cutting the tails off five horses (and shaving their stumps) in order to send fly whisks to London for Queen Victoria's dining table. Pete and Dancing Billy, who clogged away the hours on the porch of Brown's Hotel, were the first of San Francisco's long historical queue of street crazies.

But lunatics were the least of Leavenworth's worries, certainly not the reason the city acquired the old hulk *Euphemia* as a prison brig to replace the tiny log house. Politically, the city was in a confused state as the legislature meddled in its affairs, proffering a series of city charters to be voted on. The overtaxed, hybrid Hispano-American government of *alcaldes* buckled under the weight of thousands of arrivals.

With rival city councils wrangling, gangs of ruffians moved in to take advantage of the moral and fiscal weakness of a derelict city government. Australian ex-convicts, often Irish, banded together in their rough quarter, Sydney Town. These Sydney Coves or Sydney Ducks occupied the area between Clark's Point and Telegraph Hill that would soon become famous as the Barbary Coast of saloon-keepers and shanghaiers.

The late spring of 1849, the ex-felons from Down Under were eclipsed by a band of American rogues, many of them Irish-Americans. Most were discharged Mexican War Volunteers from Colonel Jonathan D. Stevenson's New York Regiment. These desperadoes at first called themselves the Hounds because their organization grew out of ten bounty hunters hired to hound to earth runaway sailors. The bounty hunters got out of hand. They formed a paramilitary unit and were soon specialists in the "protection" or extortion racket.

On Sundays, the Hounds brazenly paraded the streets in quasi-military display, carrying revolvers, dirks and bludgeons openly, with banners flying and fife and drum playing. The Hounds normally raided by night and chose the helpless as their victims, especially the Chileans and their Peruvian and Mexican friends who clustered on Washington Street between Kearny and Montgomery at the base of Telegraph Hill. As their power grew, they became more arrogant and began to invade saloons, to demand free food and drink and perhaps to break up the furniture before leaving.

The leaders were ex-New York Volunteers Captain Sam Roberts, Jack Powers and Tom Edwards. Roberts and company used military discipline and the power of numbers to intimidate ordinary citizens and to terrorize the Latin Americans. There were no street lights and no police force. Law-abiding people got off the streets at dark and bolted their doors.

The Chileans complained to the mayor, but Leavenworth was helpless. When he told the Hounds to desist, they laughed at him. As late as August 1849, Mayor Leavenworth was complaining to the citizens, "We are without a dollar in the public treasury....You are without a single police officer or watchman, and have not the means of confining a prisoner for an hour..."

During a Hounds raid on Chile Town, a man (not a member of the Hounds) was accidentally killed by the *Chilenos*. The toughs used his death to gear up their organization's terrorism. The hoodlums now styled themselves the Regulators. They had the audacity to inform the city that they were now regulating "Spanish foreigners," protecting the community from the Chileans. Perhaps they felt safe in their bullying because of the public's ambivalence. Even the press and later the *Annals* were prejudiced against the poor, "immoral" Latins.

The breaking point for the beleaguered city came

Teacher Mary Myrick posed with her Girls High
School graduating class, boys and all, in 1855.

The Merchants Exchange
on Battery Street, begun in
1849, boasted one of the
West's first libraries, or
reading rooms.
Subscriptions brought the
major newspapers of the
United States and Europe
to local businessmen.

Militant Samuel Brannan was not always as fraternal as in the pose he struck for an unknown artist.

when two of the Regulators shot and badly wounded two *Chilenos.* John McDougal, later governor of California, was an eyewitness. He had had a bellyful of violence. He called to another passerby for assistance and they made citizens' arrests of the culprits. Word of their action spread, and the next day Sam Brannan addressed a mass meeting of irate citizens. Another paramilitary group was formed, this one to help the mayor against the Regulators. Sheriff Hiram H. Ellis swore in somewhere between 150 and 230 special constables, at least 60 of whom were armed with muskets.

The leaders of the militia-like organization were the fiery Brannan, the magnetic and cordial Howard, Dr. Forgeaud and Captain Bezar Simmons. They acted quickly and had soon incarcerated about twenty of the ringleaders of the Regulators. Eight Hounds, including Roberts, were sentenced by a jury trial with counsel (although there were as yet no official courts) to prison terms of up to ten years. Others were fined or forced to post bonds to guarantee their good conduct. But since there was no place to properly incarcerate the prisoners, they finally were released. Most of them either vamoosed for distant parts or went underground.

To prevent a recurrence of the Hounds, San Francisco's last *alcalde,* John Geary, attempted to fill the city's treasury by selling more town lots, requiring liquor licenses and levying fees and lucrative gambling taxes. He and the common council used the funds to set up a court and a police department. But party politics descended to the level of fistfights, and the city experienced its first financial panic. The recession was a mild one, but there were bankruptcies and a run on the few banks.

San Francisco shrugged off the depression and continued to enjoy itself in 1850. Colonel Charles L. Wilson's new plank toll road to Mission Dolores brought the milk punches of roadhouses like the Grizzly and the Mansion House much closer, also the racetracks and bullfights of the Mission area. More good news was the lightness of a cholera epidemic. Best of all, the *Oregon* brought news in October of California's admission to the Union. All business was suspended to celebrate statehood with cannon salutes, bonfires and whooshing rockets. But these were upstaged by a remarkable sound described in the *Annals* as "the universal shout [that] arose from 10,000 voices on the wharves, in the streets, upon the hills, housetops, and the world of shipping in the bay." A second and official celebration followed, with oratory, more fireworks and a big parade that included a colorful contingent of Chinese.

At this time, San Francisco's Chinese were still curiosities, not yet victims of prejudice. There were now about 800 "Celestials" on Tong Yan Gai or China Street, Sacramento Street between Kearny and Dupont (the nucleus of today's Chinatown—the biggest Asian settlement outside the Orient). They also had shrimp fishing camps on various points jutting out into the bay. By now, the Cantonese had a laundry, five restaurants, 33 stores, even two newspapers and several joss houses, or temples.

The Chinese made no trouble for the community, but the same could not be said for the remnants of the Hounds who emerged, once the heat was off, as efficient arsonists. Some of the Irish toughs also

John W. Geary became San Francisco's first mayor in 1850.

turned up among the squatters who now plagued San Francisco. They seized land by force. For Theodore Shillaber to recover his leased Rincon property from squatters, he required the assistance of Captain Erasmus D. Keyes and twenty soldiers from the Presidio to demolish the tents and shanties on the Point. Mayor Geary sent two companies of militia to help Sacramento during its bloody squatter riots. Forgeaud and Woodworth lost property to the squatters because of the new legal interpretation holding that *alcaldes* had no right to grant lots. Joe Folsom fought back simply but effectively; he hired toughs to clear the squatters off his land. Selim and Fred Woodworth, with Stephen Teschemacher, captured a contested sand hill at Market and Second as late as 1853 by arming themselves with pistols and shotguns, plus sandwiches and "stimulants," and routed the squatters. Finally, Squatterism in San Francisco was licked in 1854 by a vigilante-like People's Organization For the Protection of the Rights of Property and Maintenance of Order.

FIRETRAP

San Francisco got its first hand pumper in 1849 —just in time for the first of six major fires that ravaged the city between Christmas Eve of that year and June 22, 1851. Assault, robbery and arson went hand in hand. Some 3,000 buildings worth $30 million were destroyed in the conflagrations, most set by arsonists. Lives were lost as well.

The Christmas Eve blaze took the Parker House but brought about the formation of the first volunteer fire fighters—the Empire, San Francisco and Protection companies. The May 4, 1850 fire broke out, suspiciously, on exactly the same spot. Police prevented pillage by street idlers, and the mayor's reward of $5,000 for suspected incendiaries resulted in several arrests, although all suspects were released for want of evidence. Shortly afterwards, a 12,000-gallon cistern was built in Portsmouth Plaza to aid the understrength, unpaid fire companies. There were now three engines and 90 men, plus a hook-and-ladder company of 45 men. The city encouraged construction downtown of stone and brick buidings with iron doors and window shutters. Buildings with sailcloth walls or roofs were prohibited, and property owners were required to keep six buckets full of water at all times. Heavy fines would henceforth be imposed on anyone who refused to fight fires.

A June fire that burned the base of Central Wharf and spread to residential areas was unusual—it was probably "legitimate," caused by a defective bakery chimney. Mayor Geary signed an ordinance creating a paid city fire department by July 1, but one fatalist, J.L. Riddle, rebuilt his place of business with Chinese matting.

The worst blaze of all, the Great Fire of May 3-4, 1851, was blamed on incendiaries. The fire wiped out sixteen blocks and parts of seven more—about 1,500 to 2,000 buildings. The fire finally swept to the very edges of town before burning itself out. Never before, and not again until the earthquake and fire of 1906, did San Francisco suffer such a disaster. The plank

The Great Fire of May 3-4, 1851 (above) caused the greatest devastation to San Francisco prior to the 1906 earthquake and fire. The "bhoys" of a volunteer fire brigade posed, circa 1855, on Meiggs Wharf for an ambrotype photographer (left).

61

Nonchalant confidence was written all over the features of M.G. Searing, ex-foreman of the Tiger Engine Company of firefighters, as he posed for an unknown photographer.

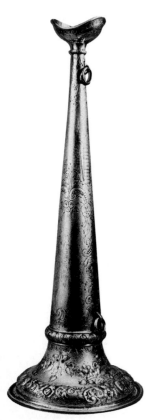

The foreman of a company of firemen carried his speaking trumpet as a symbol of office.

using them to further their own ends with the help of block voting.

San Francisco's six fires, which wiped out Tom Maguire's theater a half-dozen times and destroyed all downtown landmarks, were terrifying. There were hardly any high-rises, so the fire hugged the ground like a great bed of red-hot lava beneath black smoke rolling silently into the bay.

JUDGE LYNCH

After the 1849 eradication of the Hounds, citizens left execution of criminal laws to the constituted authorities. By 1851, however, assaults were increasing. Merchants organized a night patrol to protect themselves against burglaries and arson, but the force was inadequate to cope with crime apparently backed by political corruption.

The press now began to urge creation of another "volunteer police" to replace the inefficient executive department and judicature of the city. Soon the people were ready to take the law back into their own hands again, to issue it in a new form. The *Daily Alta California* wrote, "We deprecate lynch law...[But] how many murders have been committed in this city within a year? And who has been hung or punished for it? Nobody."

In June a Committee of Vigilance was formed by 40 concerned and alarmed citizens, including Brannan, William T. Coleman, Isaac Bluxome, Selim Woodworth and Colonel J.D. Stevenson. It was intended to promote stability and community in a city of increasing anarchy and seemingly endemic chaos. The Vigilantes organized in response to an inflamatory letter to the editor of the *Alta* which demanded the formation of a committee of public safety and the waging of a war of extermination against local criminals. The letter writer concluded, "If there is not spirit enough among us to do it then, in God's name, let the city be burned and our streets flow with the blood of murdered men!"

Until now, San Francisco had been a classless frontier society, leveled by the egalitarian forces of prospecting and placer mining. All men were rendered equal in the search for riches. From now on, an Establishment dominated the Vigilance movement, and vice versa. Middle-class Whig or Republican businessmen squared off against the lower classes—workingmen who were often Irish, Roman Catholics in religion and Democrats by political persuasion.

The true desperadoes among the rowdy street loafers did not march to fife and drum as had the Regulators, but they seemed just as well-organized and villainous. They used fires and false alarms to cause confusion and to screen their depredations. The small jail-brig was full and the police too few and poorly paid. Perjured court testimony was getting guilty criminals off scot-free. More and more talk of lynch law as an antidote was picked up by the press. Soon handbills circulated in a crowd ringing City Hall calling for the code of Judge Lynch. "Let each man be his own executioner," one of the broadsides read. "Fie upon your laws!" They have no force."

The Vigilante organization quickly grew from 200 to 700 and more. A sort of armed chamber of com-

sidewalks kindled the fire, the air spaces beneath them acting like bellows to fan the flames. Firemen fought well, using gunpowder as well as water, but the flames ran along the wooden sidewalks as if they were trails of powder and jumped the firebreaks created by the explosives.

Only five new brick buildings survived on Montgomery Street and perhaps ten or a dozen similar structures elsewhere. The blackened swath ran for three-quarters of a mile north and south and a third of a mile east and west. A few local people wondered if San Francisco would ever recover.

The city was making a brave comeback when, on June 22, it was swept by the last of the great fires. This one took City Hall, the Jenny Lind Theater and the old adobe Customs House. The fire destroyed the old storeships *Apollo*, *Niantic* and *General Harrison* and threatened the city's precious piers, as well as shipping in the harbor, until firebreaks were made by destroying the landward portions of the wharves.

In 1853, San Francisco had 38 cisterns spotted at strategic points. (Their locations are still marked by rings of bricks imbedded in the blacktop pavement of streets.) Efficient volunteer fire companies were locked in generally friendly rivalry. The Empire Company No. 1 was composed of ex-New Yorkers; the Social No. 3 of Bostonians; Knickerbocker No. 5 of staunch Unionists; and Monumental No. 6 of Baltimoreans and other Southerners. By 1855, there were twenty-odd companies backing up the paid fire department. Some of the volunteer companies lasted until 1866 when they were disbanded because politicians were

merce, it was far more tightly organized than its 1849 predecessor and it gave itself a formal name—the Committee of Vigilance—and a constitution. The Vigilante leaders were the ubiquitous rabble-rouser Brannan and the steadier Coleman and Selim Woodworth.

The Vigilantes made 91 arrests, whipped one man, drove many others into exile and hanged four men. Surprisingly, they dismissed charges in 41 cases and handed fifteen men over to the regular authorities for trial. The committee may have seen itself as an auxiliary force to aid the regular system of policing and justice, but of the four men it lynched, none was a murderer, all were merely thieves.

Between 1851 and 1856 the committee's philosophy hardened into one that overreached its initial role and strayed dangerously close to social revolution. Luckily for San Francisco, the vigilance movement leaders (other than Brannan) were sustained by a faith in popular government. With comparative peace and order restored by September 1851, the Vigilantes made good on their pledge and voluntarily handed control of the city back to the constituted authorities, then disbanded.

The movement, however, was anything but dead. Committee members were shortly in action again, this time supporting the very authorities with whom they had been at odds. Waterfront mobs gathered to lynch Captain Robert (Bully) Waterman for his shipboard cruelty on the clipper *Challenge*. Again, it was class strife, and ex-Vigilantes supported the city and Waterman against the angry sailors and wharf loafers who threatened the peace.

Less than five years after breaking up, the Vigilantes were back at their old stand. U.S. Marshal William Richardson made the mistake of insulting Arabella Ryan, the mistress of professional gambler Charles Cora. The marshal's uncalled-for remarks led Cora to accost him in the street, apparently after the belligerent peace officer twice tried to pick a fight with him. Cora's pistol ball killed his opponent on November 17, 1855, but the trial ended in a hung jury because of Richardson's provocation of the incident and the supposition that, since the dead man was also armed, Cora had fired in self-defense.

Meanwhile, a failed and embittered banker-speculator, James King of William, was whipping up enthusiasm for a return to Vigilantism by means of his sensationalist, muckraking paper, the *Evening Bulletin*. The egocentric editor took his strange moniker by adding his father's given name to his own, so as to distinguish himself from "common men" named James King.

King of William's ruthless crusades included vicious attacks on the innocent as well as the presumed guilty. Careless of the truth, he went for the throats of police and judges for their failure to arrest and convict lawbreakers. King of William singled out James P. Casey for special vilification, reminding his readers of Casey's stretch in Sing Sing Prison in New York and accusing him of ballot box stuffing while he was a polls inspector, to get himself elected to the Board of Supervisors. Casey considered these statements slanderous and challenged his tormentor to a duel. When the editor spurned his challenge, Casey stopped him as he crossed Montgomery Street on May

William T. Coleman, the "Lion of the Vigilantes."

Selim E. Woodworth, a prominent Vigilante in 1851.

The Committees of Vigilance were paramilitary organizations, as demonstrated by the daguerreotype of officers of a sharpshooters' company.

James King of William, crusading editor of the Bulletin, *ignited the Second Vigilance Committee with his reckless muckraking —and his death.*

The symbol of the 1856 Vigilantes was the wide-open—vigilant—eye (above). The last violent act of the Great Committee was the 1856 hanging of Joseph Hetherington and Philander Brace, accused murderers, on a gallows erected on Davis Street, between Commercial and Sacramento streets (right).

14, 1856, and said, "James King of William, are you armed?" Casey did not wait for an answer when he saw his foe reach under his cloak, perhaps for a derringer. He fired.

Luckily Coleman, not Brannan, became president of the second vigilance committee, called the Great Committee. In just three days, Coleman built a combined militia and secret society to cure the city's lawlessness, with 2,500 citizens organized into military companies. They protected their headquarters, Fort Vigilance or Fort Gunnybags at 41 Sacramento Street, with sandbags and cannon. The Vigilantes ignored the protests of Mayor James Van Ness in their crusade against the city's rough elements. At the county jail, the Vigilantes demanded the surrender of Casey and Cora. Sheriff David Scannell tried to resist, but it was hopeless, and he surrendered the men.

When James King of William died (possibly from a surgeon's bungling—a sponge was left in his wound), the fate of Casey, and Cora as well, was sealed. Shortly after the martyr-editor's funeral procession wound its way to Lone Mountain Cemetery, Casey and Cora were tried for murder, not manslaughter. Cora's jury split on a verdict, but only a majority, not unanimity, was required by Justice Lynch, so he was convicted and hanged along with Casey. Two other men accused of murder were also lynched.

At least the Great Committee reserved hanging for

accused murderers, not petty thieves. Other targets of Vigilante vengeance, like Judge Edward (Ned) McGowan, suspected of "complicity" in the street shooting of King of William, fled and went into hiding. In all, 30 others, including the jailer Billy Mulligan, found themselves banished, deported as "wharf rats" and disturbers of the peace, destroyers of election purity and "perfect pests to society."

Supposedly to restore order, the Vigilantes now resorted to censorship of the press, kidnapping and unlawful detention, secret trials prejudiced by popular outrage, illegal search and seizure and abolition of due process, legal counsel and writs of habeas corpus.

Few people dared oppose the Vigilance Committee. The press went along, for the most part, even though the Vigilantes executed editor Casey of the *Sunday Times,* and mobs sacked the opposition *Herald,* the paper with the largest circulation. The Vigilantes also ruined the *Daily California Chronicle,* forcing it into bankruptcy in 1858.

An opposition Law and Order Party appeared, but it was dominated by Tammany Democrat pals of those being persecuted by the Vigilantes. Vigilance Committee chairman Coleman kept his head, allowing a neutral body of law-abiding citizens to intercede with the governor, who was outraged at the Vigilantes' impertinence in taking over the city. Governor J. Neely Johnson, an anti-Irish Know Nothing, was so arrogant and rebuffed the non-aligned emissaries so rudely that they gave up in disgust in their efforts to restrain the overreacting committee. The neutral public found little to choose between bullying Vigilantes or shifty Law and Order Democrats backed by a Know Nothing governor and fiery Judge David Terry, who termed the Vigilantes "damned pork merchants."

The Vigilantes won. The crisis ended with an enormous victory parade on July 18, 1856. The committee voluntarily terminated itself and returned control of San Francisco to City Hall. But it spawned a reforming People's Party that held onto city government with a hammerlock after the Civil War forced a realignment of forces.

The declining Whigs were replaced by the American party's bigoted Know Nothings, so-called because of their secrecy about their program, whose main plank was anti-Catholicism. As storm clouds of sectionalism and secession scudded along before the Civil War's outbreak, California's old plotter John C. Fremont emerged as the first presidential candidate of the new Republican party. The Democrats were in disarray, split right down the middle by secession and slavery. U.S. Senator David Broderick was a Tammany politico from New York, but he gave the Northern or Unionist wing of the party genuine leadership. It was composed largely of urban, working-class Irish and Germans. Broderick's rivals were vociferous Southern Democrats led by Senator William Gwin and the hotheaded David Terry. In a speech, Terry called Broderick a traitor. The Irishman retaliated by publicly retracting his early opinion that Terry was that rare bird, an honest judge. Terry demanded satisfaction. Broderick, a man of honor, had to accept the challenge, although he knew little of firearms, while Terry was an expert.

The two politicians met near Lake Merced on

September 13, 1859 for San Francisco's last duel. Broderick, unfamiliar with hair triggers, accidentally discharged his weapon harmlessly into the air. Terry took deliberate aim and shot Broderick in the chest, killing him. At Portsmouth Plaza, 30,000 people turned out to hear the funeral eulogy by Oregon's Senator Edward D. Baker, earlier San Francisco's outstanding orator.

Broderick's death predictably widened the breach in the Democratic ranks, and hastened the shift of allegiances that came with the Civil War. Only a handful of Southern Democrats like Terry, Asbury Harpending, General Albert Sidney Johnston and Reverend William Scott were outspoken defenders of secession and slavery. Scott was driven from his pulpit; Johnston resigned his commission and headed for the Confederate army; Harpending fitted out a Rebel commerce raider on the Embarcadero, but his plot was discovered before he could sail. A few newspapers, like Frederick Marriott's *San Francisco News-Letter*, were shut down or wrecked by mobs. The wartime Governor John G. Downey sent Colonel Patrick Connor with the California Volunteers to hold the Overland Trail against hostile Indians when the Regulars pulled out to fight in the East. He then sent Colonel James Carleton and the California Column to recapture Arizona and New Mexico and to invade Confederate Texas.

Generally, however, the Civil War touched San Francisco but little, except to cut off manufacture from the East and thereby boost local industry. Shipments of "treasure" from San Francisco bolstered the Union, of course, and the city and state strongly supported the Sanitary Fund, ancestor of the Red Cross. The California drive, in fact, supplied it with a million dollars, half of the national total.

FRONTIER COSMOPOLIS

Vigilantism had ruled the 1850s; the War Between the States dominated the '60s, but not to the exclusion of business-as-usual, plus much economic and cultural progress. James and Peter Donahue had brought the Industrial Revolution to town—at least its metallurgical implications—in the 1850s when they converted their smithy into a foundry, the Union Iron Works. In 1854 the Donahue brothers teamed up to light the city's streets with gas lamps. By 1859, the Union Iron Works was facing competition from rival foundries—Vulcan, Risdon, Miners and others.

During the 1860s, Union Iron Works continued to turn out quartz stamp mills and boilers, added heavy industry—railroad locomotives—and assembled the monitor *Camanche*, the first ironclad in Western waters. In 1863, Peter Donahue joined Henry Newhall and others to build San Francisco's first railway, the San Francisco and San Jose Railroad.

Good drinking water was necessary even in a whiskey-slugging port like 'Frisco. Wells and water barged from Sausalito were inadequate. Mountain Lake Water Company tapped a lakelet on the edge of the Presidio until Billy Ralston's Spring Valley Water Company took over.

San Francisco became a hybrid—a strange mixture

Senator David Broderick, leader of California's Northern or Union Democrats, just before the Civil War.

Broderick was the loser in an 1859 duel near Lake Merced with his Southern Democrat rival David Terry.

So barren was "The Rock," Fort Alcatraz, that soil for a garden for officers' wives had to be imported.

During the Civil War and later, San Francisco belatedly attended to its military defenses. An officer's family enjoys an outing at a battery on Angel Island.

Fort Point on the Golden Gate was backed up in the 1860s by an artillery battery on Black Point (Fort Mason), now a part of the Golden Gate Recreation Area.

Reverend and Mrs. Thomas Starr King. Reverend King was the city's conscience during the Civil War. The eloquent Unitarian preacher and graceful writer is, today, one of California's two representatives in Washington's Statuary Hall.

of frontier port and sophisticated cosmopolis. Alongside venison, grizzly steaks, abalone and Dungeness crab would be chilled champagne, either imported from France or shipped down from Agoston Haraszthy's Buena Vista cellars in nearby Sonoma. Rich bon-bons were supplied by Domenico Ghirardelli, the West's "Chocolate King." Richard Henry Dana noted that Continental fashions prevailed in San Francisco by the 1860s, including "French cooking, lunch at noon and dinner at the end of the day, with *cafe noir* after meals..."

Civic pride came early. In 1849, 60 businessmen protested to the city council against the ugly buildings that destroyed the effect of the city's only "ornament," Portsmouth Square. Urban architecture of distinction varied from the $117,000 Parrott Building and great Montgomery Block to delicate and quaint octagonal houses (two of which survive today on Green and Gough streets). The Montgomery Block, or Monkey Block, called "Halleck's Folly," was paid for entirely by legal fees from land litigation cases. There were grand homes on Rincon Hill and in South Park. Churches were going Gothic, but civic architecture remained staunchly Neoclassical in style.

Not even Vigilantism could "Americanize" the small cosmopolis. As early as 1849, Bayard Taylor had found the streets thronged with an international crowd. Samuel C. Upham may have passed Taylor on the polyglot street. He recalled, "Such a meeting of languages and jargons and of tongues the world has seldom seen. It is a modern Babel."

The French were few in number but prominent. They ran the most fashionable department stores— Felix Verdier's Ville de Paris, later the City of Paris; Raphael Weill's The White House. (Weill became one of the Bohemian Club's great amateur chefs and is remembered on menus today by Chicken Ralphael Weill.)

The Italians were not quite ready to assert themselves in North Beach and on Fisherman's Wharf, but the Germans were numerous—around 6,000 of them as early as 1854. These were jolly Teutons, not Prussians. They loved Sunday school picnics and especially their *Mai Fest* (May Day festival) at Russ's Gardens. Many were members of singing societies and the *Turnverein* or gymnasts' union.

There were a few Negroes, all of them free, although like Asians and American Indians they were routinely denied their civil rights—unable to vote, hold office, serve on juries, testify in court or attend public schools. Blacks were mostly laborers, porters, waiters, barbers and cooks, but some were educated— there were Negro newspapers by the 1860s.

As early as the 1850s, the two distinctive Jewish communities were established. The Polish and some English Jews were Conservative or Orthodox members of Sherith Israel synagogue. The more politically liberal German Jews were of Reform Judaism and members of Temple Emanu-el. There were a few Sephardic Jews from Spain and Portugal.

The pioneer of San Francisco's now-large Filipino population was Pedro, last name unknown, a porter at Cross, Hobson and Company. He fell to his death from the open door of a loft. Barry and Patten lamented the tragic accident: "A pleasant, faithful servant, who had the regard of all who knew him."

IRON MAN

*T*he pioneers of industry in the Far West were three adventurous immigrant-Irish brothers, Peter, James and Michael Donahue. They met in San Francisco in 1849 after wandering over North and South America. A machinist, boilermaker and molder, they converted a humble smithy into the Coast's first foundry, iron and brass works and machine shop in 1851.

The Donahues' Union Iron Works turned out stamp mills for California and Nevada mines, the state's first printing press and the West's first heavy locomotives. James died young and Michael moved to Iowa, but Peter Donahue (1822-1885) remained an industrial giant of the city. He constructed the boilers, engines and all other metal work for the Navy's first West Coast-built warship, the U.S.S. Saginaw, later shipwrecked in the South Pacific. He then put together the first ironclad on the Coast, the monitor Comanche, sent to San Francisco in pieces in a sailing ship to defend the port from Confederate raiders during the Civil War.

The Union Iron Works became very important in American shipbuilding. Both the Oregon and Olympia of Spanish American War fame were built there. But Donahue left the foundry and shipyard to go into steamboating and

The birthplace of West Coast industry was Peter Donahue's Union Iron Works, which he sold to Prescott and Scott.

railroading. Already, with James, he had established the San Francisco Gas Company, the first such utility in the West. Peter, like his brothers, was the antithesis of the "stage Irishman" caricatured as a jolly, hard-drinking dimwit. He was shrewd, hard-working, visionary; just the man to make San Francisco industrially independent of the East.

On Independence Day, 1862, crowds gathered on Greenwich Street in the North Beach Area.

In 1865, broad Market Street was already the main drag of a bustling seaport.

HIGH STAKES

Gambling with cards and chips was replaced as early as the 1860s by all manner of business speculation. Risk-taking came naturally to San Franciscans. The city's good fortune was proverbial. The gold boom was immediately succeeded by Nevada's silver bonanza. Even the Civil War brought only prosperity, force-feeding local industry as Eastern competition dried up. The sole disappointment was in the city's high hopes for the transcontinental railroad. It attracted settlers, but instead of an economic boom it triggered a regional recession as a flood of cheap goods smothered the market for local production.

San Francisco seemed indifferent to hard luck and hard times, positive that a fortnight's frenetic activity would mean a "stake" that would lead to new riches. Quick transitions were the norm. It was as if the loony Dr. Elbert Jones was a role model. Everything that the medic touched, at least between alcoholic sprees at Peter Sherreback's Our House bar, turned to gold.

Eccentricity did not hamper "The Generous Miser," James Lick, from becoming a millionaire. The skin-flint philanthropist in hand-me-down clothing built the Lick House hotel, and was a benefactor of the Society of California Pioneers and Lick Observatory on Mt. Hamilton. Demagoguery and drink did not stop Sam Brannan from amassing a million, although the latter habit eventually sent him skidding into poverty and oblivion. J.C. Flood and William S. O'Brien, proprietors of the Auction Lunch, became millionaires by eavesdropping on the conversations of their businessmen-customers. Butcher Henry Miller became California's greatest cattle baron of all time. John Studebaker manufactured carriages to rival Henry Casebolt's before following Henry Ford to automotive fame.

Gold, the heaviest of metals, naturally obeyed the laws of gravity and slid down the Sierra into San Francisco vaults. It was followed in the 1860s by the silver bullion of Nevada. Wealth transformed the Montgomery-Sansome district into the Wall Street of the West, crowded with frantic money-lenders, bankers, brokers, gamblers—and bankrupts.

Capitalists were as common in San Francisco as draymen. Because they were financing industry in San Francisco, they were aware of new technology that was beginning to revolutionize mining and agriculture. The improved equipment allowed a shift to deep quartz (hardrock) mining that gave California mines a new lease on life and transformed Nevada and Arizona, and later Montana, Idaho and Alaska into tribute-paying duchies of imperial San Francisco. The lumbering and fisheries of the Pacific Northwest would also shortly fall in line. This activity stimulated shipping and general commerce, all headquartered in the "capital" of the economic region, San Francisco.

Banking was big business by the 1860s. In 1861, the visionary William C. Ralston, called "The Man Who Built San Francisco," joined Joseph Donohoe to form Donohoe, Kelly and Company. Ralston ran up a personal fortune with the Virginia and Truckee Railroad, the Kimball Carriage Company, a sugar refinery, the Pacific and Mission Woolen Mills, the California Theater and the Grand and the Palace hotels. In 1864, with Darius Ogden Mills as president and himself as cashier, Ralston founded the Bank of California. It dominated West Coast finance after Ralston's shrewd Nevada field agent, William Sharon, virtually took over the Comstock mines by foreclosing on defaulted loans. Soon the West saw a new and powerful cabal, "Ralston's Ring."

By 1870, San Francisco was a fast-paced metropolis, although on a much smaller scale than New York. The city had grown from 1,000 people in 1848 to 50,000 in the 1860s, a population reached by New York, Philadelphia and Boston only after 200 years of growth. It was connected with Virginia City by three stage-and-steamer runs a day that brought $40 million of silver in 1864 alone to 2,000 mining companies (some of them legitimate) that offered handsomely engraved stock certificates on the exchanges.

When even San Francisco industry's powerful new pumps were no longer strong enough to pull up the water that flooded the Comstock's deepest shafts, another visionary San Franciscan came to the rescue. Tobacconist and amateur engineer Adolph Sutro promoted his Sutro Tunnel, a low-level bore seven miles long, to be driven into the base of the mountain to drain the mines. Ralston and Sharon were unwilling to cut a slice of the rich Comstock cake for an outsider, and they tried to squeeze Sutro out. But the Yellow Jacket Mine fire disaster of 1869 won Sutro the support of the miners' union. It pledged him $50,000 which broke the ice. Soon British banks took the plunge, and Sutro Tunnel extended the life of the Nevada mines.

Also in 1869, the Big Four—Sacramento merchants Stanford, Hopkins, Crocker and Huntington—completed their Central Pacific Railroad to connect with the Union Pacific at Promontory, Utah. They had gobbled up Peter Donahue's San Francisco and San

Mark Hopkins (top) was the modest "elder" of the Big Four of the Southern Pacific railroad monopoly. Charles Crocker (above), another member of the powerful quartet.

The Gold Rush attracted many Germans, who formed gymnastic associations like the Turnverein.

71

By the time Carleton Watkins pointed his camera from Rincon Hill, the flat below was packed solid with houses climbing up and over Telegraph Hill.

Jose Railroad, which the city had expected to be the last link of the transcontinental railroad. Instead, the Big Four made Sacramento their terminal and later the Oakland Mole in San Francisco Bay. But the Central Pacific, later the Southern Pacific "Octopus," now walled off the city from any rail competition and had a virtual monopoly on the fleet of ferryboats connecting it to the rest of the world.

Overland Mail coaches and the short-lived Pony Express had done little to tie San Francisco to "the States," and ship passages took weeks. But the transcontinental telegraph (1861) and the Pacific Railroad (1869) ended San Francisco's splended isolation. In general, it was a good thing, but the connection terminated—in its infancy—a remarkably vital and independent regional culture.

In far-off San Francisco, music and theater was at first mostly "borrowed"—performers were on tour from the East—but the city produced its own phenomenal flourishing of journalism and even literature. From the start, San Francisco had been a strange frontier outpost—full of well-educated, well-to-do people with leisure and a hunger for any kind of reading matter. By 1853 there were a dozen local newspapers. The best of the lot was the *Alta California*. Journalism continued strong in the 1870s, but declined in quality and uniqueness in the face of Eastern publishing's easy access to the Coast.

The West's second literary journal, the *Golden Era* (1852), preceded by the *Pacific*, proved to be a seedbed for San Francisco's cultural growth. It was tilled by Bret Harte and Mark Twain, Ina Coolbrith and Joaquin Miller, and led the way for the literary harvests of the *Overland Monthly* days. The West's first extra-illustrated journal was *Hutching's Illustrated California Magazine* of 1856. Only a few years later, Anton Roman pioneered San Francisco's great book trade.

Theater began as early as the summer of 1849 with the songs, skits and recitations of Stephen Masset, also known as Jeems Pipes of Pipesville. The red-faced, dreamy-eyed runt of a bohemian humorist was San Francisco's wandering minstrel.

In the tracks of Masset came Joseph Rowe and his Olympic Circus, which also introduced the Far West to blackface minstrels. His Ethiopian Serenaders were succeeded by the Christy and San Francisco Minstrels. Will Shakespeare was not far behind the elephants, bringing along Junius Brutus Booth and his sons, Edwin and John Wilkes. Edwin Forrest was another local favorite tragedian.

Leland Stanford, president of both the Central Pacific and Southern Pacific, was the best known of San Francisco's railway moguls.

A photographer on Telegraph Hill caught the square-riggers headed for the Golden Gate and the open sea in the 1860s.

Press powerhouses Edward C. Kemble, seated,
and Edward Gilbert were founders of the Daily
Alta, San Francisco's greatest paper.

Petite, much-married (and "mistressed") Lola Montez, who sometimes cleared $16,000 a week, titillated audiences with 1850s cheesecake in *The Spider Dance*. Lola, really half-Irish Eliza Gilbert, married the editor of the local weekly *Town Talk*, Patrick Purdy Hull. The great Lotta Crabtree was her protege. Lola was succeeded as a stage phenomenon by Adah Isaacs Menken—"The Menken"—who cavorted in a flesh-colored leotard in a play called *Mazeppa*. A real beauty who popularized spit curls, Adah also married locally, capturing world champion boxer John C. Heenan, "The Benicia Boy."

Impresarios arrived to guarantee San Francisco a theatrical future. Dr. D.F. (Yankee) Robinson was first, but Tom Maguire was the greatest. He founded a series of Jenny Lind theaters and Maguire's Opera House. Maguire built up two fine stock companies, one for variety and the other for drama.

Doc Robinson brought the first professional singer to the Coast—Boston-born coloratura soprano Elisa Biscaccianti, "The American Thrush." Her delicate voice was said to rival Jenny Lind's. She introduced Italian music to the city and was a tremendous success. Biscaccianti opened an era of fine music that is still going on in the city. She lived in San Francisco for almost a year before resuming her tours.

Biscaccianti was followed in 1853 by Kate Irwin, "The Swan of Erin," who left town $250,000 richer than when she came. She was followed in turn by another Irishwoman, an "unknown." Catherine Hayes introduced opera to San Francisco, singing arias in costume and acting whole operatic scenes. Kate was adopted by the city's firemen as a mascot, anticipating Lillie H. Coit, and did very well, thanks to

San Francisco's first press agent, W.A. Bushnell, whom she later married. Her grace and dignity, as well as her voice, won over the whole town.

Theatrical papers appeared, like *Figaro* and the *Daily Dramatic Chronicle* (and later the *Footlight*), covering everything from Italian opera to the off-color burlesques of the melodeons. Andrew Kohler established a music store, Kohler and Chase.

Rudolph Herald became the city's first musical conductor of both orchestras and choruses. He produced oratorios, but it was Tom Maguire who introduced complete operas and a grand, seventeen-piece orchestra with the Bianchi Opera Company.

In education, San Francisco eventually lost the West's first normal school to San Jose, but got the West's first kindergarten in 1867. St. Ignatius College (now the University of San Francisco) was founded in 1855. The Mercantile and Mechanics Institute became strong subscription libraries preceding the establishment of a public library. Mechanics fairs, starting in 1857, were forerunners of San Francisco's international expositions and influenced California's state fairs to a broader scope. Robert B. Woodward added an art gallery to his zoo and Woodward's Gardens. There Virgil Williams made copies of 100 works of the great masters.

Out of commerce and banking, industry and technology, came an economic, sociopolitical and even cultural imperialism in which San Francisco held sway over an enormous area of the West. This giddy, affluent heyday of Imperial San Francisco lasted from the 1870s until the devastating trauma of the 1906 earthquake and fire.

"Cute as a button" was actress Lotta Crabtree (1847-1924), protege of Lola Montez. She became a national star, the highest-paid theatrical performer in America of her day. Her fortune, estimated at $4 million, she gave to charity. She never forgot the city where she got her start, and in 1875 she gave a great cast-iron fountain and column to the city. It rivals the Donahue (Mechanics) Monument as an object of attention by Market Street strollers.

"Lotta's Pump", as irreverent San Franciscans dubbed it, is also strongly identified with old San Francisco's favorite prima donna, Luisa Tetrazzini. Her local debut at the Tivoli Opera House in 1905 was the beginning of a brilliant career. As a "thank you" to her adopted city, Tetrazzini thrilled 10,000 people crowded into Market Street with a Christmas Eve 1910 vocal concert from a stand erected at Lotta's Fountain.

Lotta's Fountain in pre-earthquake and fire days (right).

Theater in pioneer San Francisco ranged from Shakesperian drama and Italian grand opera to the low-brow melodeons.

Early warnings of the 1906 quake and fire disaster came in 1865 and 1868 when tremors caused buildings to sag and buckle.

'FRISCO'S EARLY WATERHOLES

Bartenders have been legion in San Francisco's history, from pioneer John Henry Brown to Prohibition's Izzy Gomez and on to Shanty Malone. The two greatest mixologists of all were Professor Jerry Thomas of the Occidental Hotel, who invented the once-famous Blue Blazer, and Duncan Nicol, whose specialty was Pisco Punch, made with a secret recipe known only to Nicol (and now lost) from Peruvian Pisco. The Professor is assured of immortality, for he invented the martini, naming it either for Martinez, the Carquinez Strait town, or for the vermouth that he used, Martini and Rossi.

When Professor Thomas left town, Duncan Nicol dominated the local barkeeping scene. Dignified of mien, white of hair and mustache, he started out with the politicians' hangout, the Snug Cafe, next to City Hall. He sold it to one of his barkeeps, Chris Buckley (later the so-called "Blind Boss" of San Francisco), and became a partner in the old Montgomery Block bar, the Bank Exchange. It was from this saloon that James Casey walked into the street to shoot James King of William and bring the Second Vigilance Committee into existence in 1856.

The "Monkey Block" was a hive of bohemians who descended on the Bank Exchange to quench their raging thirsts. Painters William Keith and Jules Tavernier had studios in the building and many writers kept office-studies

Duncan Nicol chatted across the Bank Exchange bar with Johnny Perazzo in 1918.

there, like Mark Twain, Bret Harte, Mary Austin and George Sterling. Gentry mixed with them at the bar, too, since bibliophile Adolph Sutro stored his books in the Montgomery Block and winemaker Arpad Harazthy kept barrels of wine in the building.

A towering presence in early-day San Francisco was the Chinese Giant, a star attraction at Woodward's Gardens.

San Franciscans have always taken their recreation seriously and the city, over the years, has provided not only midwinter fairs, Portolá festivals and international expositions, but also simple resorts for local weekenders, from Russ Gardens, Crystal Palace Garden, the Willows and the Tivoli Gardens (alias Vienna Gardens) to the Cliff House, Sutro Baths and Playland at the Beach.

The early Germans preferred their own Russ Gardens way out at Sixth and Harrison streets—but most other citizens favored Woodward's Gardens, the sunny Mission District property of hotelier Robert B. Woodward. His What Cheer House (1852) on Sacramento Street at Leidesdorff, between Montgomery and Sansome, was a temperance hotel for men that, curiously, prospered in hard-drinking San Francisco.

In 1866, Woodward converted his San Francisco house and grounds at Mission and Thirteenth streets into a pleasure resort. He offered the public botanical gardens, pavilions, a playground, skating area, bandstand, concert stage and a round lake whose circumference was filled with a curved "boat" (like a rim on a wheel) which could be moved by sails and oars. There were taxidermist's tigers, deer and bunnies, also a real, live, eight-foot, three-inch Chinese giant. Events ranged from acrobatics to modern jousting tournaments and on to balloon ascensions. There was an aquarium and a zoo. In his art gallery, Woodward had copies of 100 old masters painted by a local talent, Virgil Williams.

San Francisco's Victorian mini-Disneyland closed in 1883.

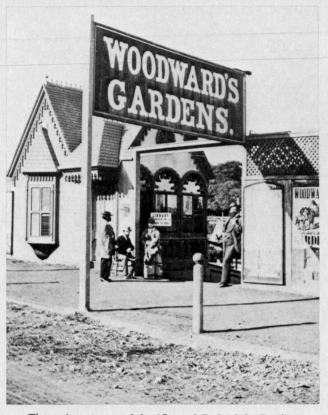

The main entrance of the "Central Park of the Pacific."

A run of horse smelt brought crowds of fishermen in the 1860s to Long Bridge, Vallejo and Front streets, for Eadweard Muybridge to capture with his lens.

CHAPTER 5

IMPERIAL CITY

Employees at the San Francisco Branch of the U.S. Mint posed stiffly for the camera in 1894.

EMPLOYEES
NOT ALLOWED IN THIS RE...

SAN FRANCISCO

The railroad brought more migraines than millions to San Francisco. Yet in the last three decades of the nineteenth century, the gathered momentum of gold and silver wealth—$500 million from the Comstock alone—propelled it into the position of an opulent, powerful, imperial city reigning over the entire West. It was the only place in the Far West that could command capital—lots of it—at will.

ALL THAT GLITTERS

Speculation raged through the post-Civil War decades, especially in Nevada mining stocks. There were three exchanges in the 1870s—the aristocratic San Francisco Stock Exchange, or Big Board; the California Stock Exchange, the Little Board; and the New Board, the Pacific Stock Exchange.

The spectacular rise of shares entranced San Franciscans even more than the spin of roulette wheels. In 1871 the manipulated stock of the Comstock lode's Crown Point Mine shot from $3 to $6,000, reflecting a new "strike"—a fresh and rich vein of ore. In early 1872, the market value of stocks traded on the exchanges increased fivefold to $81 million.

Even with the ligature of the transcontinental railroad, San Francisco was a little "out of sync" economically with the rest of the country. Its crash was a year ahead of the general U.S. panic of 1873. A few insiders grew enormously rich, but most small-timers were wiped out. Yet the public's faith in the market was unshaken. The buyers came right back, figuratively flinging their last coppers to the brokers, and they soon enjoyed a new wave of good times in 1874.

The Crown Point and Belcher Mines were, in historian John S. Hittell's words, at "the flood tide of their prosperity." Even the Crown Point, however, paled beside the fantastic riches of the Consolidated Virginia discovery, which was soon paying $300,000 a month in dividends. It created a new array of mining

magnates to rival the railroad's Big Four. First came Alvinza Hayward and John P. Jones, then the real Silver Kings—James Flood, William S. O'Brien, James Fair and John Mackay, who shoved Ralston and Sharon aside.

But the mines enriched only a small number of adventurers. Only a modest percentage of all the money invested by the general public was ever returned in the form of dividends. Ironically, rich San Francisco now found money in too short supply for adequate investment in local industry; it was all being siphoned off to desert holes in Nevada. The *Call* claimed in 1871 that just 121 men controlled $146 million—tycoons like the Big Four, Ralston, Mills, stagecoach king Ben Holladay and James Phelan, whose fortune was in real estate and liquor.

The reckoning came in 1875. Word leaked out that the ore veins and ledges of the richest Comstock property, the Con-Virginia, and the California mines were nearing exhaustion. The market value of the stocks collapsed, plummeting by $140 million. This fall of the Comstock shares triggered a run on the banks. William Ralston was forced to close the doors of the most powerful financial institution in the West, the Bank of California. It was Black Friday, August 26, 1875. The very next day, Ralston took his usual swim at North Beach—and drowned. Since he was personally more than $5 million in debt, his death was a powerful coincidence, though never proved a suicide. The *Alta* bade the amiable financier a last farewell: "With him has passed something that mere money cannot replace. His was the vast vision of the builders, and his like shall never pass this way again."

Ironically, San Francisco's old staying power reasserted itself and Mills, Ralston, et al, got Ralston's bank back in business in October. There were more deposits than withdrawals on opening day.

By 1880 the city's population had jumped to 233,939, or one-fourth of the state's total. Prosperity had returned; a new stock exchange was built and the Crocker Bank founded in 1883. Reflecting the town's prosperity was the web of street railway lines

Darius Ogden Mills (top) joined with William Ralston to establish the powerful Bank of California in 1864. William Sharon (above), another of Ralston's associates, picked up the pieces after the bank's failure in 1875. One of the shards was the greatest hotel in the West, the Palace Hotel.

A cameraman named Holler invaded the Stock Exchange by night to take one of the city's first instantaneous "flashlight photographs."

Traffic jams at Market, Post and Montgomery streets were still a problem of the future in the late 1860s.

Two-thirds of the entire fleet of the Telegraph Hill Railroad performed for I.W. Taber's camera on Greenwich Street in the 1880s (right). Cars of the Sutter Street Railroad halted at Sutter and Stockton streets in front of Vienna Gardens and Temple Emanu-el (below).

82

The workhorses of the Pacific Coast were the lumber schooners and hay scows herded into berths on the Embarcadero (above).

In 1886 the Majestic *was heeled way over at her wharf for repairs to her bottom (facing page). The Pacific Mail Steamship Company's largest iron steamer, the* City of Peking, *posed for Eadweard Muybridge in the Hunters Point drydock (facing page, inset).*

covering the parts of the city not too hilly for horse cars. Because of O'Farrell's grid, steep streets were unavoidable, and at times horses injured themselves in falls on the slippery rails or even foggy cobbles of the hills.

An eyewitness to one such street accident was Andrew Hallidie, operator of a wire rope (cable) factory supplying the mines. He came up with a solution to the problem. Hallidie placed the world's first cable car on his "endless ropeway" on steep Clay Street in October 1873. The "cables" soon spread to Sutter, California and other hilly streets. However, horse cars were not put out to pasture by the cables. In 1875 there were eight competing railway companies, and only one of them was cable-powered. As late as the 1880s, horse car lines still covered more distance than cable routes. Gertrude Stein's brother Michael consolidated the Market Street Railway Company in 1893, and Mayor Phelan later tried to unify the system further. The nags, unlike the beloved cable cars, were retired after the 1906 quake in favor of electric trolley lines.

By the centennial year of 1876, the Imperial City was booming as never before. The value of assessed taxable property was $269 million. Of some 27,000 buildings, about 4,500 were of brick or stone construction, the rest wooden. That year 1,019 vessels flying the American flag entered the Golden Gate and about 612 foreign ships arrived in port. Wheat was king, covering the Central Valley and other open country, and grains and flour were the leading exports. California was briefly the world's supplier of wheat. Great sailing ships waited patiently in San Francisco and Richardson's bays for the wheat harvest, to haul cargoes of the precious foodstuff to England. Other industries were prospering as well. The Pioneer, Pacific and Mission woolen mills were beginning to be rivaled by tanneries, a dozen of them in the 1870s. Zellerbach Paper Company began to pioneer an important business.

Food, besides wheat and flour, became important in San Francisco. Joseph Brandenstein started the modern coffee business with MJB in 1881, followed by Hills Brothers and J.A. Folger. A. Schilling and Company dealt in coffee, tea and spices. Sugar refining and sales, begun by George Gordon, the builder

The axes of the Chinatown Squad busted up many a warring tong during Chinatown's dark days (right). Chinatown's opium dens were depressing and squalid, but use of the drug declined rapidly after 1911, as the Chinese began to integrate into the mainstream.

of South Park, continued with Coleman and Ralston and boomed with Hawaii's Claus Spreckels. Fisheries, mostly Italian, Dalmatian and Chinese, also began to grow.

Railroad freight reaching the city averaged 10,000 tons a month and half that weight was sent eastward. By 1876, the Central Pacific was dropping 65,000 passengers a year on the city and hauling away another 47,000.

A DECADE OF DISCONTENT

The Chinese were still arriving, although the long-completed railroad no longer required their services. About 8,000 left for home in 1876, but 10,000 newcomers arrived from Canton in that year alone. This figure spelled trouble for everyone, for the boom of 1876 was about to tumble to the bust of 1877. The economic roller coaster exacerbated class conflict and racism at the same time it encouraged trade unionism. The city's Chinese were the perfect scapegoats for such economic troubles besetting the work force.

As early as 1853, when the Chinese numbered only 4,000, a state exclusion act was passed but judged unconstitutional. Anti-Chinese feeling worsened in the 1870s as the railroad jobs dried up and former gandy dancers or trackmen flooded the city. By 1876 they numbered one-fifth of San Francisco's population. Recession turned jobless whites against the seemingly enigmatic and unintegratable Asians. Their main enemies were those next lowest on the economic totem pole—Irish laborers—who also made up about one-fifth of the population.

The lower middle class began to ally itself with the working class as the Chinese got a handle on San Francisco's upward socioeconomic mobility and started to compete with Caucasian laundries, restaurants, shops and grocery stores. Soon they had almost a monopoly of the cigar-making plants and were doing almost as well in sweatshop clothing manufacture. Some Chinese, like Fong Ching, alias Little Pete—the boss of crime in Chinatown—operated boot and shoe factories thinly disguised as white establishments. Little Pete, for example, called his firm the F.C. (Fong Ching) Peters Company.

In the 1875 city election, anti-Chinese Workingmen's Party candidates practically swept the field. Mayor Andrew Bryant and the Board of Supervisors rammed through a series of restrictive ordinances that upped Chinese establishment license fees, imposed heavy gambling and opium fines, prohibited Chinese peddlers from using the sidewalks, required fireproof buildings of Chinese laundries—even set a 2 a.m. curfew for the Asians. The courts found the most blatantly unfair laws to be unconstitutional and set them aside, but the intent of the majority toward its most conspicuous minority was clear. Trouble obviously lay dead ahead.

Another employment slump in 1877 led to mass meetings in empty lots in which the sandlot orator James d'Arcy denounced the Chinese for causing virtually all of San Francisco's economic ills. He harangued his audience into a mob that set forth to destroy Chinatown like a pack of Hounds. They broke down doors, smashed windows, set fires and cut the arriving firemen's hoses. Mayor Bryant was a loyal union labor man, but he ordered his police to suppress further violence. The press and the pulpit backed him, but the angry—and now numerous—workers were not intimidated.

The employees of food stores on Dupont Gai (Grant Avenue) carefully wound their queues around their heads to keep their hair out of harm's way.

D'Arcy lectured 5,000 men on the evening of July 25, and this time the mob split. Most headed for Chinatown, where they stoned and pummeled Orientals and burned laundries. But another group marched on the Embarcadero and the Pacific Mail Steamship Company docks (the PMSS hired Chinese to crew its steamers). The Sandlotters set fire to a waterfront warehouse containing imported Chinese goods and again slashed firemen's hoses.

For the last time in San Francisco's history, prominent professionals and mercantilists turned vigilantes. They called a hurried emergency meeting and chose Coleman as their chief. He mustered volunteers from his Committee of Safety to patrol the streets and help the badly outnumbered police. He sent 100 of his Pick Handle Brigade to the Embarcadero where a free-for-all ensued. The next day, Mayor Bryant prohibited public assemblies and set a 10 p.m. curfew. This time, the federal government heeded a citizens' committee. Muskets were sent from Benicia Arsenal to arm the vigilante volunteers and the U.S.S. *Lancaster* and *Pensacola* were brought to anchor just off the Embarcadero, with landing parties of sailors and Marines ready to disembark. But Coleman's show of

force was enough to whip the rioters. They dispersed without putting Chinatown to the torch, and the committee shortly voted itself out of existence.

But the class war was not over yet, not by a long shot. Ex-teamster Denis Kearney, whose drayage business had gone under in the depression, had been one of the volunteers brandishing a pickax handle against the Sandlotters, but now he suddenly performed an about face and seized the leadership of the malcontents from d'Arcy. Kearney proved to be a wild, extravagant agitator, dealing in bluster, threats and hatred. Nor did he restrict his attacks to the Chinese—he took on the rich as well, particularly such inviting targets as the mining and railroad barons. Kearney threatened to arm his people and march them to the Capitol where, if the legislators did not pass another exclusion bill, he swore to string them up on Sacramento's lampposts. He also warned Nob Hill mansion dwellers that their flagpoles might become their own gallows.

Apprehension began to spread beyond the middle class to some workers, as the Sandlotters armed themselves and drilled in units, just as the Hounds and Vigilantes had done. Kearney led 3,000 marchers

---

"THE CHINESE MUST GO"

Denis Kearney (1847-1907) was an Irish-born sailor who "swallowed the anchor" (left the sea) in San Francisco in 1872. He married, took out naturalization papers and taught himself to read and write. Kearney bought a drayage firm and became a strong union man, but when he discovered that he had the charismatic presence and persuasive voice of a born demagogue, he used his oratory to lambaste his own working class. He called workers "shiftless and extravagant," loving only liquor and tobacco, both of which he spurned.

When William T. Coleman formed a vigilante-like Committee of Safety to protect Chinatown and the Pacific Mail Steamship Company (which not only transported Chinese but hired them) from a mob of unemployed, anti-Chinese workingmen, Kearney joined the Pick Handle Brigade to defend the Chinese.

Kearney occasionally went too far in his preaching of violence and was jailed—to the delight of Chinatown.

However, Kearney soon made a violent about-face and adopted the line that the "coolies" were taking away white men's jobs with the connivance of capitalists. The Workingmen's Trade and Labor Union was formed with Kearney as its secretary. Overnight he became a radical and a racial bigot. Taking over the (Marxist) Workingmen's Party, he gave it a battle cry—"The Chinese Must Go!"

Kearney fought both extremes, poor Asians and rich nabobs. He promised not only to drive the coolies back to China but to seize government from the rich. He blustered and thundered but, a master of mob psychology, always managed to avoid exhorting his followers to actual violence. His speeches packed vacant lots, so the newspapers dubbed his following the Sandlot Party.

By 1878, Denis Kearney was the most feared man on the Coast. His bombast and bravado knew no bounds. He promised to bring Judge Lynch to town; to replace ballots with bullets. He threatened the state legislature with "hemp" (hanging) and boasted, "If I give an order to hang [Charles] Crocker, it will be done!"

Kearney was arrested several times, to the delight of the much-abused Chinese, but his incarcerations were always brief and only made him a martyr-hero in the eyes of workingmen. In 1879 his power peaked. His Workingmen's Party won Assembly posts and a railroad commissioner's seat, and elected Isaac Kalloch mayor of San Francisco.

Suddenly, a reaction set in. The public repudiated Kearney's bluster and his party crumbled. Kicked out of the presidency and accused of embezzlement, Kearney floundered from party to party—Greenback, Anti-Monopoly, Democratic—but finally retired from politics forever in 1884. He inherited money, and made more in San Joaquin Valley wheat, so that when he died in 1907, he was one of the capitalists he had once threatened to hang.

The agitator Denis Kearney once led a mob to the steps of Charles Crocker's Nob Hill mansion, where he made veiled threats to hang the nabobs.

to storm Nob Hill, protesting not only the vulgar flaunting of wealth, but Charles Crocker's "spite fence." (The railroad man had built a 30-foot-high board fence around the adjacent property to cut off all views and most sunlight when Nicholas Yung refused to sell.)

Now the press, which had generally supported the developing labor movement, did a turnabout of its own, demanding that the city curb the demagogue Kearney. He was arrested for holding unauthorized assemblies but was out of his cell in only two weeks—now a martyr and more popular than ever with his following.

The Workingmen's Party secured control of the 1877 constitutional convention, but Kearney's party now split in two. In the rift between a moderate faction and his own riotous element, Kearney was ousted from the party's presidency. He won it back, but lost it again for good when he was accused of pocketing party funds. He was cleared of the charges, but it was too late. San Francisco was tiring of his strident cry. His career fell overnight, like a spent rocket.

Kearney's crusade sputtered along in the hands of more moderate men who renounced violence but struggled for changes in both the social order and the economic payoff of local commerce and industry. The party's weapons were now ballots. In 1879 its mayoral candidate, Reverend Isaac Kalloch, was elected. It also put its faith in the organization of militant labor unions, and Kearney rival Frank Roney became president of the San Francisco Trades Assembly in 1881.

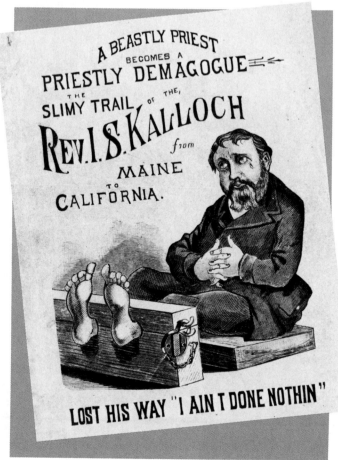

Isaac S. Kalloch, a New England pastor tried but not convicted for adultery, became the Workingmen's Party candidate for mayor.

89

THE CITY BEAUTIFUL

San Francisco began to beautify itself. It replaced street cobblestones with basalt paving blocks and located granite pedestrian crosswalks at intersections. A new and elegant City Hall was begun with ground-breaking ceremonies in 1871. Although the *City Directory* of 1878-79 bragged that it was not only the "largest and most durable structure in the City but [also]...the largest edifice of this description in the United States," it was not yet finished. In fact, it took an astonishing 29 years and $8 million before it was completely finished and occupied in 1900, although it was supposed to take just four years and $1.5 million on a pay-as-you-go basis. It stood, albeit briefly, as a monument to civic corruption and scandal, one of the biggest bureaucratic boondoggles to disgrace American urban history. When the first tremors came in April 1906, it collapsed in a heap, revealing the interior of its proud walls to be filled with rubble, junk and garbage—anything but expensive masonry. The crooked politicos responsible for its Corinthian-French elegance had made "skimming" a science.

A much more successful beautification project and city decoration was Golden Gate Park. Its 1,000-odd

By 1904, the splendid new City Hall was completed (right). By 1906, it looked almost the way it did when Eadweard Muybridge photographed it under construction in November 1873 (above). Poorly built, it literally fell apart with the first tremors of the 1906 earthquake.

Snow, rare in San Francisco, turned Golden Gate Park's Conservatory into a Christmas card scene in 1887 (left). The Conservatory, photographed in 1897 (below left), is almost a dead ringer for its counterpart in London's Kew Gardens. Feisty John McLaren (below right) put his personal stamp on the park during decades of supervision.

The merry-go-round has been a thrill for youngsters in Golden Gate Park for a century.

Al fresco games of checkers and cards became traditions among oldsters visiting the park.

Harry W. Pelt, trainer, posed in Golden Gate Park with his 5½-ton pet Queen Jumbo, who stood 11½ feet tall in her non-stockinged feet.

acres were acquired in an 1871 compromise deal with litigating squatters on the so-called Outside Lands, earlier called the Great Sand Bank. The attempts of the first superintendent of Golden Gate Park, William Hammond Hall (a disciple of Frederick Law Olmsted who designed New York's Central Park), were greeted with hilarity and ridicule by those who predicted that the park would be a white elephant. The *Sonoma Democrat*, for example, described it in 1873 as "a dreary waste of shifting sandhills where a blade of grass cannot be raised without four posts to keep it from blowing away."

Hall stumbled on the solution by accident; he spilled some of his horse's barley. He later found that it had taken root in the dunes. He added soil and leaf mold to barren sand and planted grains and grasses, then followed up with native lupine and finally larger shrubs and trees, the latter in windbreaks. Hall also built a "sea wall"—actually a drift fence of tree limbs and brush—to prevent blowing beach sand from encroaching on the park at its seaward end.

By 1878, Hall's green-thumbed army, led by the park keeper and chief gardener, Patrick Owen, had set out 135,000 trees and shrubs and was raising 32,000 more in the park nursery. Later came tree ferns, azalias and rhododendrons, rose gardens, flower beds, also seven ponds and lakelets, even a Dutch windmill, the largest in the world, and a Mur-

phy windmill that pumped 75,000 gallons of water an hour for irrigation. Hall ran paths and drives through the park to make it a popular place for walks and rides.

The superintendent groomed his assistant, John McLaren, to be his successor in 1887. McLaren, a crusty, opinionated and feisty Scot, held the post for 56 years until he died, aged 96, in 1943. McLaren put his own personal stamp on Golden Gate Park; he called it "My park." He wanted no formal-garden atmosphere, no "Keep Off the Grass" signs and no statues—which he derisively called "stookies."

McLaren's lifelong fight to keep Golden Gate Park simple, untrammeled, natural, ran afoul of Michael De Young's boosterism. The *Chronicle* publisher had been a vice president of the World's Columbian Exposition in Chicago in 1893; now he wanted to show off San Francisco and its year-round benign climate. The result was a Midwinter Fair in 1894-95. It occupied 200 acres of the park. McLaren fumed and frothed as trees crashed down and turf was gouged into roads.

The exposition was an unqualified success, attracting 2.5 million visitors and winning many new friends around the world for San Francisco. McLaren got all of the fair's structures torn down after its closing, except the large Art Museum, a pseudo-Egyptian temple (since replaced by the De Young Museum) and the charming Japanese Tea Garden.

Scrapers, pulled by four-horse teams, were used to level an area of Golden Gate Park for the Midwinter Fair in 1894.

A highlight of the
Midwinter Fair was the
Japanese Tea Garden.
Today, the garden is one of
the most delightful spots in
Golden Gate Park.

A star of the Midwinter
Fair was Achille Philion,
an "equilibrist" who rode a
rotating globe down his
Spiral Tower.

Dock loafers were the 19th-century equivalents of the sidewalk supervisors of today around construction sites.

LABOR FLEXES ITS MUSCLES

By the 1880s, the political power of the Southern Pacific Railroad was absolute in California. John P. Young, editor of the *Chronicle*, lamented that "the real capital of the state was moved from Sacramento to the Railroad Building at 4th and Townsend Streets" in San Francisco. Tough Adolph Sutro and Peter Donahue, among others, took on the Southern Pacific and were bested. It would take the herculean efforts of two anti-railroad governors—George Stoneman, 1883-87, and later (1911-17) the ex-San Francisco attorney Hiram Johnson —to tame the political "devil fish." The so-called Octopus was finally whipped when Johnson made good on his campaign promise and political platform plank to "Kick the Southern Pacific Out of Politics!" The Big Four's heir, Edward H. Harriman of the Union Pacific, merged his line with the Southern Pacific, but got his comeuppance from the government in 1913.

Discriminatory federal legislation—Washington's 1882 agreement with China to a reduced quota of immigrants—followed by exclusionary acts of 1888, 1892 and 1902, eased racial tension in San Francisco by the turn of the century by halting the influx of Asians. But class strife, now bound up securely in unionism, radicalism and socialism, continued to rock the peninsular city like a recurring earthquake.

In the 1880s, Socialist Burnette Haskell led the half-secret International Workingmen's Association and edited a threatening paper, *Truth*. He tried in 1885 to unite all workers into one great citywide union, but failed. Next, he launched the Federated Trades for the whole state. It became powerful as the bargaining agent of various allied unions.

A series of strikes culminated in 1885 in the walk-out of 1,200 members of the Iron Trades Council. When negotiations dragged, the employers reopened their plants with non-union workers. Naturally, physical clashes occurred between strikers and the strike-breakers, but there was no clear victor in this conflict. Both sides tired of the strife and made concessions to end it by compromise. The fight for trade unionism merely shifted to the Embarcadero, since maritime commerce was the lifeblood of the city.

Andy Furuseth organized the Coast Seamens Union into the Sailors Union of the Pacific and the International Seamans Union. Furuseth, a political moderate, had the strongest maritime union in the world with 4,000 members and $50,000 in its treasury. With the help of the editor of the *Coast Seamens Journal*, Walter MacArthur, he lobbied Congress with a pamphlet, the *Red Record*, documenting the abuses of shanghaiing and buckoism—involuntary servitude and brutality, respectively. American seamen had been without civil rights from Colonial times. From the Embarcadero, with the help of congressmen like Robert Lafollette, Furuseth won a bill of rights for sailors by the time of World War I.

However, while Furuseth was fighting the larger battle so passionately, his lofty ideals were frequently forgotten in street scuffles on the waterfront. A demand by sailors for an increase in their paltry wages ($25 a month) and for better food and forecastle quarters was rejected by shipowners who claimed they could not afford it—they would be unable to compete with ships flying foreign flags or mustering non-union crews. The waterfront walkout of 1891 involved frequent bloody clashes between union and non-union merchant seamen. The police could not control the affrays, and a boarding house and bar were dynamited, with five men killed and a dozen injured. Such violence alienated the general public, but it took two years before the opponents settled for a return to the status quo.

The Spanish-American War, the Philippine Insurrection and the usual wartime prosperity distracted labor, but in 1901 workers re-declared their own war. A new metal trades union demanded the closed shop as well as the eight-hour day and better working conditions. The United Railroad Employees next struck. Since labor was really flexing its muscles, an Employers Alliance was formed to counterattack. When the alliance hit upon a boycott of plants yielding to the strikers, it broke the strike; but when it tried the device again in a restaurant workers strike, the fry cooks and waiters called a boycott of their own—with picketing. The International Association of Machinists went out next, followed by the strong Truckers Union. When employers hired strikebreaking teamsters, the regular drivers beat them up.

Finally, the unions got a strike of the City Front Association—all dock workers—on July 30, 1901. The walkout by 13,000 longshoremen, sailors, warehousemen and shipyard workers paralyzed the port for two months. Some 200 ships swung idly at anchor off the finger wharves of the Embarcadero. Street fights grew into riots and acts of sabotage. Hundreds of men were bloodied and five killed in clashes. The press, except for William Randolph Hearst's *Examiner*, lined up with the employers. The suffering public, as usual, was caught in the middle.

The people appealed to both City Hall and the Capitol. Governor Henry T. Gage gave the belligerents just ten days to come to an agreement before placing the waterfront under martial law. Compromises were made and a shaky peace returned to dockside. Well-meaning, honest and moderate Mayor Phelan, who had tried to remain neutral and fair, lost much popular support since workers and others felt that he had sided with employers. The latter, for their part, thought he had been too soft on the "revolutionaries." Labor really won; from 1901 on, San Francisco would remain one of the strongest "union towns" in the country.

In 1881, H.C. Finckler of the San Francisco Bicycle Club modeled a tricycle which, like the parasol, probably appealed more to the ladies.

THE SINGLE TAX

*E*arly San Francisco had its share of thinkers, like Henry George and Josiah Royce, as well as its numerous "doers." Henry George (1838-1899) was first a foremast hand on a sailing ship, as were such disparate spirits as Andy Furuseth and Denis Kearney. In San Francisco, George became a printer, newspaperman, writer and, finally, a world-famous philosopher-economist.

Henry George anticipated Furuseth in the cause for civil rights for merchant seamen, publicizing the brutality of mates and masters of American windships, but he also resolved to do battle against speculation, monopoly and the extortionate "unearned increments" (rents) on land. George fought with his own papers, the San Francisco Times and the Post and the Oakland Transcript, with articles in the Overland Monthly as early as 1868, and with pamphlets. He polished his themes of land use, rents and taxation in an 1871 pamphlet, On Land and Land Policy, and, finally, in his best-selling and influential Progress and Poverty (1879). This book made his doctrine of the Single Tax on land a familiar one around the world.

Henry George, sailor-economist.

The Gilded Age in the West was little different from that of Eastern cities. Materialism, corruption and "bossism" were all present. They fed on San Francisco's traditional tolerance, a belief in what philosopher Josiah Royce termed "irreligious freedom"—the consideration of every man's vices, even those aggressive and offensive ones, as being "a private concern between his own soul and Satan."

A shrewd Tammany-trained saloonkeeper, Christopher Buckley, fine-tuned a machine to run San Francisco from his Bush Street bar. The near-sighted Irishman soon was being called the Blind Boss of San Francisco. He got his slate of hand-picked candidates into office in the municipal elections of 1885, giving Blind Chris the green light to sell City Hall and Police Headquarters protection to gamblers, whoremongers and shanghaiers on the Barbary Coast's Murderer's Corner and Deadman's Alley. In Chinatown, Chris's ally was Fong Ching, alias Little Pete.

Buckley clung to power like a limpet, although he was charged with extortion, ballot-box stuffing, contract frauds and the peddling of streetcar line franchises. San Franciscans, like all Californians, were bemused by the larger problem—the dictatorship of the Southern Pacific which, since 1871, had made San Francisco its headquarters. Reformers who tried to get a new city charter as a lever to pry the crooked Buckley out of office were defeated. Three times in a row, the wily Buckley brought them down by tying the charter movement to increased tax rates.

In 1891, Buckley was finally removed as head of the local Democratic Party. He fled the state a few jumps ahead of an indictment. In 1897 Little Pete was shot to death in a barber chair. In 1898 the voters approved a new charter to replace the antique (1856) instrument of governance, but it was ineffective in blocking the rise of an even more skillful political boss than Buckley.

By the opening of the Gay '90s, San Francisco utterly dominated the West Coast, and not only in finance. By 1900, its population was 342,000; it was the eighth- or ninth-largest city in the United States and second only to New York in foreign and domestic trade. Downtown, including the powerful Financial District, was now a mini-Manhattan. Some of its large structures were ornate and traditional, like the Palace Hotel, the Phelan Building and the Ferry Building with its 235-foot Giralda clock tower. But others were modern steel-framed highrises like the Chronicle (later De Young) Building of 1890—the city's first skyscraper—or the Mills and Flood buildings and, tallest of them all at eighteen stories, the Claus Spreckels Building.

Meanwhile, residential San Francisco was reclaiming the sandy wastelands west of Van Ness Avenue, with the Western Addition leading the way for the post-1900 development of the Richmond and Sunset districts out near the ocean.

A closer look at Downtown toward the turn of the century revealed much decay beneath the cloud-scraping buildings. City Hall grafting was translated into inefficiency and neglect. Streets were potholed,

The new Chronicle *building in 1888 was ugly as sin, but it housed one of the West's great newspapers.*

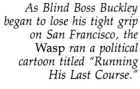

As Blind Boss Buckley began to lose his tight grip on San Francisco, the Wasp *ran a political cartoon titled "Running His Last Course."*

*Proprietors and staff of the Home Market, or
Diamond Meat Market, showed off their wares
in the 1890s.*

The old Ferry Building at the foot of Market Street was perhaps the world's busiest shed (above). Fleets of ferryboats deposited passengers by the thousands. A. Paige Brown's "new" (1898) Ferry Building (right) survives to this day. Its 235-foot clock tower is a copy of that on the Giralda in Seville.

parks ragged and unkempt, schools run-down and decrepit. Merchants hired men to clean up litter and to make temporary repairs to sidewalks and streets in front of their business establishments.

Dissatisfaction with both City Hall and the Southern Pacific began to well up in the public. A reform mayor, the anti-railroad Populist Adolph Sutro, was elected over the Democratic and Republican mayoral candidates in 1894, but the builder of the Sutro Tunnel was no match for machiavellian "civil servants." Sutro admitted that he was whipped: "I could not manage politicians." He left office after a nervous breakdown. His health broken, he died in 1898. In 1897, a younger (37) and stronger reformer than Sutro took office. James D. Phelan was a true visionary—like Henry George and Andy Furuseth—a realistic dreamer. (Phelan's major blind spot was his unreasoning anti-Chinese bias. He even called a Chinese Exclusion Convention in 1901 to discuss the "threat" of the Asians.)

One of Phelan's first actions was to appoint a committee to beautify the city. The major proposal came from a local architect. J.S. Cahill offered to create a harmonious and unified civic center of public buildings tied together with attractively landscaped grounds. It was too costly a plan to implement, but it was important as the beginning of the City Beautiful movement in the West.

UNDERDOG MAYOR

It would be difficult to come up with a typical San Franciscan like the "Typical Texan" of legend, because the city's prominent citizens have always been so varied in personality and character. But Adolph Sutro (1830-1898) would be a better choice than most. A German Jew from Charlemagne's old capital, Aix-la-Chapelle, he migrated to San Francisco in 1851. He became a tobacconist, but Sutro was also a natural engineer; he conceived his Sutro Tunnel to drain the deep Comstock silver mines that were being choked with too much water for the pumps of that day to remove.

Sutro was an outsider, an immigrant Jew with a thick German accent. He had to battle monopolists like Ralston and Sharon and the Silver Kings, Flood and Fair, O'Brien and Mackay, to complete his project. The established mining magnates closed the doors of newspapers, banks and even statehouses to the interloper. But the dogged Sutro, although lampooned as an Assyrian digging a great Coyote Hole in Nevada, won his battle in 1869 with the help of British capital and the miners themselves.

When Sutro returned to the city around 1879 he was the millionaire founder of the Sutro Library, but he still identified with the common people. Not content just to accumulate real estate (at one time he owned one-twelfth of the city), he threw the grounds of his mansion, Sutro Heights, open to the public and built Sutro Baths and a new Cliff House for the pleasure of his fellow citizens. He planted trees and fostered Arbor Day. He gave the University of California land for its medical school. He battled the bullying Southern Pacific "Octopus," once decribing C.P. Huntington as a man who would steal anything except a red-hot stove. A born reformer and friend of the underdog, Sutro ran for mayor as a loner, on the Populist ticket. He beat both regular candidates, Democratic and Republican, and was mayor from 1894 to 1896. He suffered a mental breakdown in office while trying to fight supervisors and entrenched politicians from the inside, and it was his successor, Mayor James D. Phelan, who was finally able to carry out some of the reforms that Sutro stood for.

Adolph Sutro built the Cliff House at Seal Rocks (top) as a gift to San Franciscans. Rarely did he relax in the city, but in the heat of Nevada he sometimes kicked back in the scant shade of the Comstock (above).

103

A Bulletin newsboy rushed an "extra" to the streets around the turn of the century.

In 1904, the Association for the Improvement and Adornment of San Francisco was organized. It, and Phelan, invited Daniel H. Burnham, the idealistic city planner for the redevelopment of Chicago, Cleveland, even Manila, to survey the city. In 1905, Burnham made his recommendations. He borrowed from Cahill by making City Hall the hub of his renovation plan, with broad tree-lined boulevards extending like spokes of a wheel past auditoriums, museums and schools.

Even more than Cahill's plan, the more ambitious Burnham Plan was the subject of debate. Could San Francisco afford such a grand design? Visionaries and esthetes urged its adoption, but irate taxpayers howled that it was impractical and too clostly. Why, it would mean razing entire blocks of the city for rebuilding! They were still arguing when Mother Nature took care of the razing, gratis, on April 18, 1906.

A last fling for many adventurous young San Franciscans occurred with the 1897-98 Alaska-Yukon Gold Rush. More important, San Francisco, after the first shipment of gold ($500,000) reached the mint, profited by fitting out steamers and sailing ships to carry miners north to Nome. The San Francisco-based Alaska Commercial Company, of the Gerstle and Sloss families and Captain Gustave Niebaum, had held a monopoly on Alaska sealing since 1870. Now it began to dominate the territory's general trade.

In April 1898 the Spanish-American War broke out. It was America's first two-ocean war and the San Francisco-built (Union Iron Works) U.S.S. *Oregon* demonstrated the need for the Panama Canal by its 10,000-mile dash around Cape Horn to join Admiral William Sampson's armada in Cuban waters. For the first time, the city was directly involved in a foreign war as Admiral George Dewey took the Pacific Fleet to the Philippines and victory on Manila Bay. Tent camps of the U.S. Volunteer Army soon overflowed the Presidio to stretches of dunes in the Richmond District.

Both the gold rush and the war stimulated the port, and the acquisition of Hawaii as a territory in 1898 and the Philippines as a protectorate strengthened the city's commitment to Pacific commerce. The future of banking and finance was assured a San Francisco base in 1904 when Amadeo P. Giannini founded the modest Bank of Italy (today's Bank of

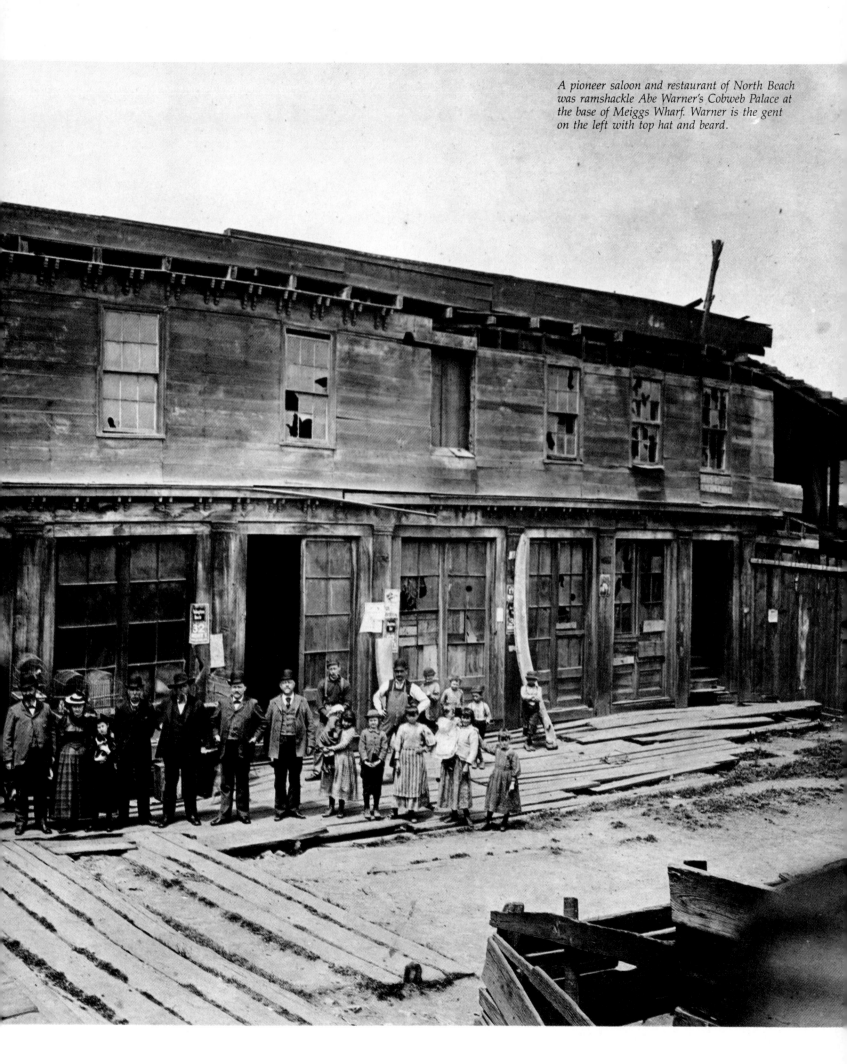

A pioneer saloon and restaurant of North Beach was ramshackle Abe Warner's Cobweb Palace at the base of Meiggs Wharf. Warner is the gent on the left with top hat and beard.

America—the world's largest).

The state's intervention had ended the 1901 waterfront strike, but labor simply went on the offensive again via the ballot box. Working people, feeling betrayed by Phelan, supported a revival of Kearney's old Workingmen's Party. The Union Labor Party was ostensibly headed by popular Irish-German Eugene Schmitz, the orchestra leader of the Columbia Theater and president of the Musicians Union. He ran on a single-plank platform—to give workers a larger voice in city affairs. Schmitz, however, was just a figurehead; the power behind the throne was the unscrupulous, although likeable, attorney Abe Ruef.

Ruef built a more efficient political machine than Buckley's. He waited patiently until "Handsome Gene" Schmitz won his third term in 1905, then threw his machinery into high gear. He put out the word that he was the man to see to get a license, a city contract, a variance, a franchise. He began to rake in the money. His North Beach office, and sometimes the pugilists' bistro that he favored—The Pup—became the center of power.

Abe Ruef was clever and discreet. He did not just send out a bagman to collect; rather, he suggested that his services as an attorney might be had for a price. Some of these retainers ranged from $25,000 to $200,000. Prudent as he was, Ruef had to share the loot with city officials. Naturally, there were leaks. Word spread of the huge cost of maintaining the "Forty Thieves" in City Hall. A clamor rose to end Ruef's rule over San Francisco. The *Chronicle* in 1905 intoned, "His baleful influence covers our city like a pall." Phelan, the *Bulletin* muckraker Fremont Older and a strange ally—aristocrat Rudolph Spreckels— began to lead a reform movement to end the organized shakedown of the city by Ruef and his henchmen. As with the Burnham Plan, however, anti-Ruef reforms would have to wait until after Mother Nature made her seismic play in 1906.

Book binders, always important to culture-hungry San Francisco, were necessary for "nuts and bolts" business ledgers as well as literary masterpieces.

A PLETHORA OF CULTURE

By the century's end, culture was as much a part of San Francisco's persona as was venture capital. Painters of national stature emerged, including those of a "Yosemite School" reminiscent of New York's Hudson River School. They included Alfred Bierstadt, Thomas Hill, William Keith and even a student of London's J.M.W. Turner, Thomas Moran. Sierra photographers Carleton Watkins, Eadweard Muybridge and George Fiske might be said to belong, too. Other favorite artists were William Hahn, Samuel Marsden Brookes, Toby Rosenthal, Jules Tavernier, Virgil Williams (who moved his School of Design into a Big Four mansion, where it became the Mark Hopkins Institute), Ernest Peixotto, Thad Welch of Mt. Tamalpais views, Theodore Wores of Chinatown and Hawaiian subjects, California landscape artists Raymond Yelland and Julian Rix, Charles Rollo Peters, William A. Coulter, G.J. Denny, and the greatest of Southwest desert and Indian painters, Maynard Dixon. Bruce Porter was a muralist who pioneered landsape design and created stained glass windows.

In sculpture were Douglas Tilden, a mute, who was the creator of the Donahue or Mechanics Monument on Market Street, and Arthur Putnam. The latter was famous for bas relief animals, such as the figures on Market Street's ornate lamp standards. Putnam was also the teacher of Ralph Stackpole, who did the figures on the facade of the Stock Exchange. San Francisco's architects were close to sculpture and sometimes skilled in the art; Willis Polk was a bohemian architect who represented Daniel Burnham in the city. He and Bernard Maybeck collaborated with A. Paige Brown, designer of the Ferry Building.

Carleton Watkins and Eadweard Muybridge were splendid landscape photographers and creators of

---

WHEN LUCKY BALDWIN'S LUCK FINALLY RAN OUT

Of all of early San Francisco's speculators, Elias J. (Lucky) Baldwin (1828-1909) had the surest Midas touch. He prospered after his arrival on the Coast in 1853 by dabbling in the hotel and livery, real estate and brick business. But he earned his nickname when he secured such key Comstock Lode holdings as Ophir Mine stock at $2 a share in 1870 and, barely two years later, sold it to Billy Ralston at $1,800 a share. He paid $200,000 for his Santa Anita Ranch in the San Gabriel Valley of Southern California and "lost" a loan of $300,000 to the failing Temple and Workman Bank of Los Angeles. But the property on which he foreclosed was worth much more than that sum, and his ranch became practically a duchy. He later subdivided the towns of Arcadia, Monrovia and Sierra Madre out of it, but there was plenty left for a dairy ranch producing 4,000 pounds of butter a week, a vineyard yielding 400,000 gallons of wine a year, and a stable of thoroughbred racing horses including several Kentucky Derby winners. (Today's Santa Anita Racetrack and the

When the fire was finally conquered, Lucky Baldwin's palatial hotel was a hollow ruin.

Los Angeles County Arboretum occupy the heart of Baldwin's ranch.)

Baldwin's real monument was at San Francisco's busy intersection of Powell and Market streets—the posh Baldwin Hotel, which upstaged the Lick House, James Donahue's Occidental, even Ralston's Palace, because it contained one of the city's major theaters. The Academy of Music (Baldwin Theater) was managed by Tom Maguire till he lost his lease in 1882 during a financial pinch. He opened on March 6, 1876, with Shakespeare's Richard III. *The Baldwin's stock company included Maude Adams; David Belasco, before he became a producer-director; and playright Eugene O'Neill's father, James.*

In 1898, Baldwin's streak of luck broke. The hotel and theater burned in a spectacular blaze. The $3 million loss was completely uninsured and it crippled Baldwin. The career of the aging lady's man now hit the skids, greased by both marital and extra-marital lawsuits.

Before TV, movies and radio, theater was BIG in the West and touring troupes like the costumed family (left) occupied almost as many railroad coach seats as did salesmen. The three runty thespians (below) may have made the try-outs for Snowflake and the Seven Pigmies at Wade's Opera House in 1876.

Three giants of San Francisco letters—Joaquin Miller, George Sterling and Charles Warren Stoddard—posed together before 1909.

Tom Maguire was handsome, dapper, shrewd...and completely illiterate.

ILLITERATE IMPRESSARIO

Tom Maguire was more than a handsome and dapper man-about-town, he was old San Francisco's greatest theatrical entrepreneur and impressario although he could neither read nor write. The ex-New York hack driver and theater bartender became "The Napoleon of the Stage" after starting his first Jenny Lind Theater in the vacant second story of the saloon he ran on Portsmouth Square. San Francisco's fires wiped him out repeatedly, but he finally got a nest egg by selling his (bankrupting) palace of yellow Australian sandstone to the city. The last Jenny Lind became the new City Hall—and Tom got a whopping $200,000.

Now the illiterate Irishman could build his greatest theater, Maguire's Opera House. He hired Junius Brutus Booth Jr. as his manager and he brought the other Booths to the city—Junius Sr. and his two other sons, Edwin and John Wilkes, the latter the future assassin of President Lincoln. It was Maguire who introduced the West to Edwin Forrest, John McCullough, Modjeska, Adah Isaacs Menken, Dion Boucicault, David Belasco and James A. Herne. Tom made—and lost—millions. Charles McClatchy, the newspaperman, claimed that Maguire owed more money to more people than anyone else in the theater.

Maguire was no angel. He was vain; he had a Gaelic temper and he had blind spots galore, thanks to his lack of education. When someone described the plot of Hamlet to him, he called it "the most infernal, confounded rot I've ever heard of. They wouldn't play it in a melodeon!" He could stoop to skullduggery, too, against rivals. (He was practically accused of setting the Metropolitan Theater afire and of drugging one of its leading men.)

But the untutored ex-cabbie and barkeep brought not only legitimate drama to the Coast, but minstrelsy, burlesque, Japanese acrobats, and jugglers. The strong operatic tradition in San Francisco is due to Maguire's willingness to lose $120,000 over ten years producing the grand opera that eventually became an acquired taste in the city.

Tom Maguire ran Lucky Baldwin's theatre, but the two strong personalities did not get along, and Belasco had to act as go-between. Then, in 1879, Maguire made the mistake of assuming that cultured San Francisco was another Oberammergau, ready for Salmi Morse's passion play. Suddenly a Victorian public was hurling the epithet "Blasphemer!" at the bewildered Maguire. The supervisors forbade its presentation. Christ himself (James O'Neill) was arrested. Morse committed suicide. A ruined and crushed Tom Maguire fled back to New York where he died, destitute, in 1896.

stereoscopic-slide photographs. I.W. Taber was almost the peer of Watkins and Muybridge. Arnold Genthe, supposedly a society portrait photographer, made secret photos of Chinatown street scenes that have become classics.

In 1875, the San Francisco Public Library joined the two excellent private subscription institutions, the Mercantile and the Mechanics Institute libraries. (They merged just before the 1906 quake.) Henry George was a founder of the public library.

There was now a "clubland"—women's clubs like the Laurel Hill and Century clubs, also a Press Club and a Browning Circle, organized by Frank and Charles Norris. The California Writers Club was organized by Ina Coolbrith, Jack London, John Muir, Edwin Markham and George Sterling. The Chit-Chat Club provided member-diners and guests with literary talk and lectures. Josiah Royce was an early member. Much like the leather-armchaired male bastions of London were the Bohemian Club, Olympic Club, Family, University and French clubs, all turning away women.

At St. Ignatius College (now the University of San Francisco) Father Joseph Neri made history by devising electric lights before Edison, employing carbon lamps instead of Edison's incandescent bulbs. In 1874 Neri placed a searchlight in the college tower; in 1876 he celebrated the Fourth of July by stringing electric lights on Market Street.

Journalism flourished. There were four major papers, all interested in reform, and many minor papers of note, like Henry George's *Post*, in which he called the public's attention to the plight of America's merchant seamen long before Furuseth appeared. The big four were the *Call*, the *Bulletin*, and today's two rivals, the *Examiner* and *Chronicle*.

Mining magnate George Hearst gave his son Willy the *Examiner* as a present. To everyone's surpise, William Randolph Hearst took journalism seriously. He was a master of both sentimental and yellow journalism, but he made the paper into the dazzling flagship of the Hearst chain. At the time, young Hearst was a pole apart from his later political stance; he was a liberal reformer, pro-union. He signed up Ambrose (Bitter) Bierce as a columnist, young novelist Jack London as a war correspondent covering the Russo-Japanese conflict (1904), and future novelist Kathleen Norris as society columnist. Willis Polk commented on civic planning and architecture; Maynard Dixon was the paper's art director. Hearst also had militant muckraker Arthur McEwen until he departed to found his own (unsuccessful) *Arthur McEwen's Letter* in 1894.

The *Chronicle* was run by a pair of rash reformers and masters of invective, Charles and Michael De Young. In an 1880 political feud over the Workingmen's Party, Charles shot and wounded the Sandlotters' candidate for mayor, Reverend Isaac Kalloch, whereupon Kalloch's son shot De Young dead. In 1885, Adolph Spreckels could no longer take the *Chronicle's* attacks on his family and its Hawaiian sugar interests. He shot and wounded Mike De Young and was himself wounded by a pistol-packing *Chronicle* bookkeeper. De Young recovered and created the Midwinter Fair and De Young Museum (which, ironically, was joined in 1972 with the Palace of the

Legion of Honor Museum—founded by Spreckels!—to form the Fine Arts Museums of San Francisco).

Replacing such literary papers as the old *Golden Era* was the *Overland Monthly*. First edited by Bret Harte, the *Overland's* contributors included Mark Twain; Ina Coolbrith, later poet laureate of California; Henry George, long before his Single Tax and *Progress and Poverty* (1879) made him famous; Charles Warren Stoddard, who popularized Hawaii and the South Seas in American literature; J. Ross Browne, the humorous travel writer who anticipated Twain; John Muir, the West's greatest nature writer; and Prentice Mulford.

John Muir, of course, was not just a writer, any more than was sociologist-economist Henry George. The father of the conservation movement in America, Muir secured the creation of Yosemite National Park in 1890 and founded the Sierra Club in San Francisco in 1892.

In the field of history, John S. and Theodore H. Hittell would have been prominent were it not for the phenomenon of Hubert H. Bancroft. He was the Henry Ford of historical publishing, using assembly-line mass production techniques in his "history factory." He slapped his name on the covers of 30-odd thick volumes of Western history actually compiled by a cadre of hack researchers and writers. But it was Theodore Hittell's "intimate circle" that was affectionately recalled by Mary Austin as the predecessor of Gertrude Atherton's post-quake literary salon, not the prodigious H.H. Bancroft's enterprise.

A tradition of fine printing was established by Edward Bosqui and Charles Murdock; Taylor and Taylor continued it in 1896, and John Henry Nash dominated it not long after joining bookseller Paul Elder in 1901 to form the Tomoye Press.

Writers abounded in 'Frisco. Philosopher Josiah

Poet Herman Scheffauer, left was a protege of the more gifted Ambrose Bierce, at right.

William Randolph Hearst, standing left, was on the portly side as a Harvard student.

His Imperial Majesty, Norton I, decked out in full regalia.

SAN FRANCISCO'S MAD EMPEROR

*E*mperor *Norton (1819-1880) was actually a greedy speculator from South Africa, Joshua A. Norton, who lost his reason after he was bankrupted in a failed attempt to corner the rice market in 1853.*

When Norton surfaced again, it was with a completely different persona. He was mad as a hatter, sincerely believing that he was Norton I, Emperor of the United States and Protector of Mexico. San Franciscans would not argue the point. He wore plug huts decorated with cockades and plumes and affected the brass buttons and epaulettes of the military. Norton was a harmless and dignified fellow, never a nuisance, so he became a sort of civic mascot. He never had to pay for drinks, meals or lodging, though he left signed chits and even formal, imperial promissory notes. He was not only tolerated but humored and flattered as the city grew fond of him.

Norton died suddenly of apoplexy. He was given a funeral at the city morgue, and 10,000 citizens turned out to pay him their last respects. When his loyal followers—the mutts Bummer and Lazarus—died, they were given mock funerals and obituaries (one by Mark Twain) before being stuffed by taxidermists.

Royce was schooled there and poet Robert Frost born and raised there. Bret Harte, Henry George and others headed for greater opportunity in New York. Those who left were more than compensated for by the brief stay of the charming Robert Louis Stevenson in 1879. Jack London began a meteoric career as a novelist, but a better writer, Frank Norris, died young (32) in 1902 after only three powerful novels.

Lighter fare in the Gay '90s came from waggish bohemians like Gelett Burgess ("The Purple Cow"), Willis Polk, Bruce Porter and Porter Garnett who put their social criticism into the short-lived journal, *The Lark.* Agnes Tobin, of the Hibernia Bank clan, was a poet and translator who became an expatriate in London. Journalist-essayists Will and Wallace Irwin were important local writers who also decamped to the East.

Music and theater, shifting to the Bush Street area, continued to charm the city in the last decades of the century. Touring performers ranged from Sarah Bernhardt to dancer-comedienne Marie Dressler and escape artist Harry Houdini. David Belasco—actor, dramatist and producer—served his apprenticeship with Tom Maguire at his Academy of Music before going on to New York to join another San Francisco actor, David Warfield, in greater fame.

Opera went into a slump, as did serious drama, although to a lesser extent. Walter Morosco, who became manager of the Grand Opera House in 1899, had to switch from the serious plays of Ellen Terry and Henry Irving to melodrama. San Francisco now seemed more interested in escapist light fare, like Buffalo Bill Cody's Wild West show of the '80s, Gilbert and Sullivan at the Tivoli Opera House, Victor Herbert's operettas or the Orpheum's vaudeville.

Concertgoers, however, could hear Adelina Patti and Emma Nevada, or catch Madame Schumann-Heink or Enrico Caruso at the Mission Opera House. The star of stars was Luisa Tetrazzini. Her very first San Francisco performance in 1905 began a triumphant career as a concert singer. Old-timers like Lotta Crabtree reappeared, also Eugene O'Neill's father, James, and the Polish patriot Helene Modjeska, Anna Held, Maurice Barrymore, John Drew, Otis Skinner, Lillie Langtry and dialect comedians Weber and Fields and Kolb and Dill.

New names began to appear on marquees as a new century got up steam—Al Jolson, Sophie Tucker, Eddie Cantor, DeWolf Hopper and Lillian Russell. Even Gentleman Jim Corbett of the Olympic Club and Wells, Fargo Bank performed before the footlights, and with the man whom he had beaten in 1892 for the world's heavyweight boxing championship, John L. Sullivan. Briefly, boxing was big in 'Frisco, but Gentleman Jim lost to Bob Fitzsimmons in 1897 and again to Jim Jeffries in 1903, and the town faded as a boxing center.

For all this plethora of culture, the City by the Golden Gate did not become smug. It refused to adhere to the constraints of stodginess. As rustic humorist Opie Read put it, "If'n a feller can't have fun in 'Frisco, he's in hell, sure enough." Despite chauvinism and narcissism, the lively and enterprising city did not take itself too seriously. It was much less interested in power, or even prestige, than in the pursuit of happiness.

In the 1890s, sculptor John McQuarrie posed with students in a jungle setting of the Hopkins Art Institute (left). Michael H. De Young (above) was publisher of the Chronicle and instigator of the 1894 Midwinter Fair and subsequent De Young Museum in Golden Gate Park.

GENTLEMAN JIM

Gentleman Jim Corbett in 1892.

*H*e was not called Gentleman Jim just because he wore clean linen and did not speak out of the corner of his mouth. With his handsome, unmarked face, James J. Corbett (1866-1933) looked like a gent, not a pug. An ex-Wells, Fargo bank clerk and a member of the elite Olympic Club, he popularized the gentlemanly art of boxing as opposed to the roughhouse slugging that passed for prizefighting in the late nineteenth century.

Jim Corbett became heavyweight boxing champion of the world when he defeated the great John L. Sullivan in 1892. He was beaten by Bob Fitzsimmons in 1897 and later fought champion Jim Jeffries twice, but lost both times.

Corbett's most interesting ring battle was one of his three encounters with another local favorite, Joe Choynski. He won all three of the bouts, but the so-called Barge Fight of 1889 in Benicia was a close call. The ring was on a grain barge anchored in Southampton Bay to confuse the police. (Fights to a finish, considered brutal, were illegal at the time.) Jim fought with a broken right thumb and, in the fight, broke his left hand! In desperation, because he could not stand the pain of straight-forward punches to Choynski's head, Corbett "invented" the left hook to spare his broken knuckles. He won the fight with slashing, indirect blows to the Pole's head—and made ring history.

Bank of Italy's Main branch on Montgomery Street, circa 1911 (top). The Market Street branch on a Saturday morning in 1918 (above).

A.P. GIANNINI

*I*n the spring of 1904, 34-year-old A.P. Giannini walked out of the board meeting at Columbus Savings and Loan Society in San Francisco declaring, "I'll start a bank of my own and I'll run it my own way. Banking then was conducted in marble temples and morning coats for clients who were already wealthy. But Giannini changed that when he opened the Bank of Italy in a renovated saloon to serve small customers. He transformed it over the years into Bank of America, the world's largest bank.

Giannini was both friendly and combative. He thrived on business and loved a challenge, but he was always available to even the smallest depositor. Although Giannini exemplified the traditional American success story of humble beginnings and the attainment of power, he never accumulated great personal wealth. Toward the end of his life, he noticed that he was worth almost a million dollars. He gave away half of it.

The Washington Lager Brewery was located at Lombard and Taylor streets in the Gay '90s.

A special attraction of Ocean Beach in the old days was a bird charmer.

The Bird Charmer
at Ocean Beach

Frederick Marriott (above) was California's aviation pioneer. His dirigible Avitor (right), alias Hermes Jr., *actually flew in July 1869, the first such craft to fly in America. It was destroyed by the carelessness of a cigar smoker.*

Dr. August Greth's ugly slug of an airship, California Eagle, *flew October 18, 1903, but crashed into the Bay.*

CHAPTER 6

MODERN TIMES

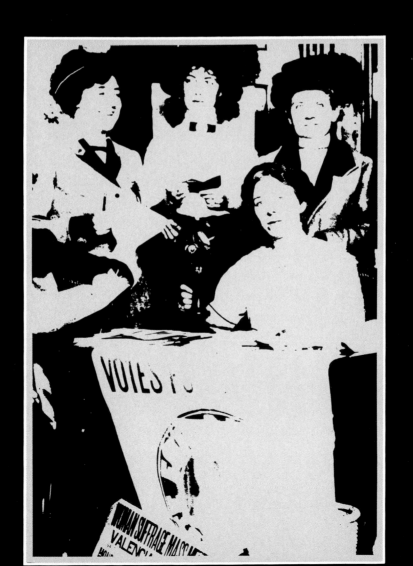

There was little panic during the 1906 earthquake and fire, although crowds gathered downtown to watch the few skyscrapers, like the Call Building, burn.

SAN FRANCISCO

San Francisco has always been a bit shaky on its pins. The Smithsonian Institution logged 465 local earthquakes between 1850 and 1906. Most were minor shakes, but the tremors of 1865 and 1868 shook the town the way the *Alta's* terrier used to handle Embarcadero wharf rats.

DEVASTATION

On April 18, 1906, the San Andreas Fault, running just offshore and parallel with the San Francisco peninsula, threw a lollapalooza of a seismic fit. It registered about 8.3 on the as yet-uninvented Richter scale. There were separate tremors that day, starting at 5:12 a.m. The biggest rattler came at 5:16, when the Ferry Building's clock was brought to a halt.

But old-timers refer rightly to "the Fire" of ought-six. The tremors themselves caused less than twenty percent of the ultimate damage suffered by the city. Although a few structures spat bricks into the street, most—especially those of frame construction—just swayed, twisted and groaned, safely weathering the geological storm. Larger stone and brick buildings, including the city's few skyscrapers, suffered little damage if they sat on solid ground, as opposed to fill. Only a few people were killed by collapsing roofs or falling chimneys. Unfortunately, one of these victims was a key figure in the defense of the city against catastrophe, Fire Chief Dennis T. Sullivan.

The fire that hurried on the heels of the earthquake was lit by tumbled woodstoves and sparking electrical wiring. It fed on ruptured gas lines and was kindled by a cityful of wooden houses. Its temperature soon roared to 2,000 degrees Farenheit. The holocaust was responsible for thousands of injuries and for deaths estimated to number from 450 to 700, including many people initially listed as missing. Fire was responsible for 80 percent of property damage, which was enormous. Some 28,000 buildings in 514 blocks (3,400 acres) of the city's heart—its four-mile-square northeast quadrant, including Downtown and the Financial District—were destroyed. The fire took three days and two nights to burn itself out as professional and volunteer fire fighters watched helplessly. The central fire alarm system on Brenham Place was wrecked by the shake that killed Chief Sullivan. Much worse, almost all water mains were ruptured; virtually every fire hydrant was without water pressure.

Half a hundred small fires sprang up to merge into three major blazes, forming one great tidal wave of fire sweeping over the city as far as the outer Mission and the Western Addition. A few strong structures, like the Appraisers Building, the Mint and the Montgomery Block, survived in good shape. Others, like the Call Building and the Fairmont Hotel, remained standing, but only as gutted shells. Valiant citizens managed to save isolated homes and other buildings by fighting the flames with water- (or wine-) soaked blankets and gunnysacks. The Post Office, as if mindful of its stirring motto, was proudly able to report that not one piece of mail was lost in the disaster.

Mayor Eugene Schmitz took firm action. He huddled with General Frederick Funston of the Presidio to enforce a seeming (but not actual) martial law with 500 Regulars, plus National Guardsmen. It was done pretty much on Funston's own hook, but he was speedily backed up by his superiors. Funston maintained a curfew and had his soldiers patrol the streets against looters, with orders to shoot to kill. At least six thieves were shot dead and a Red Cross worker was killed by mistake. Funston also asked the Army for tents to house 100,000 refugees.

Some San Franciscans claimed the Army did more harm than good by keeping citizens away from buildings where they could have rescued important papers and other property. Some locals were also critical of the Army's dynamiting buildings on the west side of Van Ness Avenue to widen it into a great firebreak. The fire jumped the broad avenue, possibly because the Army blasted brands and embers across it with the explosions, but almost all of the Western Addition beyond Van Ness was spared. In the nick of time, the wind shifted from the east back to its normal westerly direction, and the flames, blown back over burnt-out areas, died.

On the first day, Schmitz figuratively buried the hatchet in the hot ashes of his city. He appointed his political enemy, ex-Mayor Phelan, to head a Committee of Fifty to plan relief and recovery. Mayor and committee were chased all over town by the fire—from the Hall of Justice to Portsmouth Square to the Fairmont Hotel to safety, finally, in Franklin Hall and later the Whitcomb Hotel on upper Market Street. Schmitz ordered looters shot; announced the turning off of all gas and electricity; and requested citizens to stay "at home" from darkness to daylight until order could be restored. He warned hoarders that they were subject to arrest. He also closed all saloons for three months. Although thousands of people fled the city on the Southern Pacific trains to San Jose—some all the way to Los Angeles—and on ferryboats to Marin and the East Bay, most San Franciscans stuck it out.

Many people—perhaps 70,000 of the 200,000 homeless—camped in a dozen tent cities erected in Golden Gate and other parks, in the Presidio, Portsmouth and other squares, and Ingleside Racetrack. As a whole, San Franciscans were not only orderly in their crisis, but remarkably cheerful in adversity. Soup kitchens and breadlines fed at first 250,000 people, most of whom were good-humored. The food came from Army posts and neighboring cities, along with tents, clothing and medicines. Some of the relief kitchens took the names of fallen—and lamented—restaurants, like New Delmonico's, the Hoffman Grill, Techau Tavern and a new Old Poodle Dog. The *Call*, the *Chronicle* and the *Examiner* were all burned out, but combined to issue a joint "extra" on the 19th, run on the *Oakland Tribune's* presses, and were soon back in

PROCLAMATION BY THE MAYOR

The Federal Troops, the members of the Regular Police Force and all Special Police Officers have been authorized by me to KILL any and all persons found engaged in Looting or in the Commission of Any Other Crime.

I have directed all the Gas and Electric Lighting Co.'s not to turn on Gas or Electricity until I order them to do so. You may therefore expect the city to remain in darkness for an indefinite time.

I request all citizens to remain at home from darkness until daylight every night until order is restored.

I WARN all Citizens of the danger of fire from Damaged or Destroyed Chimneys, Broken or Leaking Gas Pipes or Fixtures, or any like cause.

E. E. SCHMITZ, Mayor
Dated, April 18, 1906.

Martial law was not proclaimed in April 1906, but Mayor Schmitz came to within an inch of it with his Army-reinforced emergency proclamations.

*The head of Ms. Liberty, once atop the showy
but shabbily built New City Hall, was salvaged
from the rubble.*

Many frame buildings, especially those on filled land, were destroyed by the 1906 earthquake, but the real devastation came with the subsequent fire.

When the fire finally died out, Grant Street, looking north from O'Farrell, looked like Berlin after World War II (facing page). Many families stayed in their neighborhoods, although their houses were wiped out by fire. They simply relocated to the nearest street (above). The Hoffman Cafe, a San Francisco favorite, survived the fire of 1906 (left).

123

The speedy rebuilding of San Francisco after the 1906 fire marked the city's finest hour.

A.P. Giannini in 1904 founded the Bank of Italy, later the Bank of America, and now the largest bank in the world.

dogged competition, using the presses of three different Oakland papers.

The whole world responded to much-loved San Francisco's plight. Congress quickly voted $2 million for immediate relief, and the donations of states and foreign countries brought the total to about $9 million, plus great quantities of food and other supplies.

San Franciscans shrugged off their misfortune with splendid nonchalance and rolled up their sleeves to get to work rebuilding their city while the wreckage of the old one was still hot and smoking. By July 1906, 25,000 construction workers were laboring at 5,000 temporary (and 70 permanent) buildings. San Franciscans took everything in stride—a six-week taboo on indoor fires, slow-paying insurance companies, even padlocked saloons. Legend to the contrary, most insurers did not renege on their policies, did not repudiate their debts. Some were slow to pay up, of course, and some small outfits could only cough up six bits on the dollar. The delays led Mayor Schmitz to write, prematurely, "The attempts of the insurance companies to avoid paying their losses have become a national scandal....Those that acknowledged their liabilities and paid in full could be counted on one's fingers." Eventually all but $8 million of the $175 million in claims was paid.

"Business as usual" was the motto of the Downtowners. Typical was Amadeo P. Giannini, the young banker who hauled the money of his Bank of Italy away in a wagon to hide it in his hearth in San Mateo. He quickly returned to makeshift banking quarters in the city. Mayor Schmitz bragged that just 80 days after the fire, "banks had so much cash on hand that they could now ship millions to the Eastern states." Most prominent firms—Levi Strauss, Gumps, W. and J. Sloan, Shreve, the White House, Nathan-Dohrmann and the City of Paris—were back in business pronto. Many temporarily took over the grand homes of Van Ness Avenue for stores. Others, like Livingston's department store, made a main drag of far-out Fillmore Street, also outer Mission Street, as the town rushed to rebuild. By July, the mayor reported seven theaters so busy that they were "coining money."

Rubble was dumped in the bay as steam shovels and cranes loaded hundreds of horse-drawn wagons. Twisted car tracks were replaced. Bricks were stacked into neat cubes for reuse. The number of construction workers jumped from 20,000 before the fire to 60,000. Night and day, seven days a week, pile drivers and steam riveters thumped and drummed in a cacophonous accompaniment to the rebuilding activity.

Most natives consider April 1906 and immediately thereafter to be San Francisco's finest hour. In a letter to President Theodore Roosevelt thanking him for federal aid, Mayor Schmitz noted that "the people of San Francisco have shown a remarkable courage in the hours of this great calamity." He then promised T.R. that "within the next five years, we will return to the nation her greatest seaport on her Western shores."

Schmitz was hardly a great mayor, but he was a remarkable prophet. It took barely five years for the City by the Golden Gate to rebound from disaster to prosperity, in absolutely spectacular fashion. Thanks to aid and insurance, 19,000 new wooden buildings, superior in design and workmanship to those de-

Abe Ruef, far left, was driven to the Graft Trials with Detective William Burns at his side and Police Chief William J. Biggy next to the driver (far left).

"Handsome Gene" Schmitz is shown addressing a 1904 G.A.R. Independence Day celebration (left).

stroyed, were soon up. Meanwhile, the 27 pre-fire Class-A buildings were restored and new ones built of steel-reinforced concrete. Building codes were revised upward and the fire department reorganized to prevent the recurrence of such a disaster.

Unfortunately, in the community's understandable rush to get back to normalcy, San Francisco ignored the once-in-a-lifetime opportunity to build Daniel Burnham's dream city, even though Schmitz wrote, "We build not for today, but for all the generations to come....The plan of Mr. D.H. Burnham should be the ideal for which we strive." Interest in the plan revived, but the community was distracted between 1907 and 1909 by a second bubonic plague outbreak in Chinatown. (The first one, in 1900, had foolishly been hushed up by Mayor Schmitz as "bad for business.") It led to vermin-proofed buildings and a massive rat hunt in which 150,000 of the rodents were captured, tested for plague and exterminated.

Once the immediate quake, fire and plague crisis was over, the city returned to the unfinished business of rooting human vermin out of the palaces of government. Arrogant Abe Ruef "asked for it" by pressing the Board of Supervisors to replace cable car lines with trolleys powered by overhead electric wires.

United Railroads had given him a modest "legal fee" of $200,000 to pull it off. Fremont Older obtained from President Roosevelt a federal prosecutor, Francis J. Heney, and an investigator, private detective William Burns. Schmitz fled to Europe, but Ruef persuaded the acting mayor to fire the reforming District Attorney William Langdon and replace him with... Ruef. The courts quashed this ploy, however, and the district attorney hired Heney and Burns and asked the grand jury to indict Schmitz and Ruef on bribery charges. They were convicted of accepting payoffs from French restaurants that were fronts for prostitution, but Ruef's conviction was overturned in 1908 on a legal technicality. Schmitz's conviction was reversed by the Court of Appeals, which found the charges against him unproved. Schmitz was not tried again, perhaps because of his exemplary record in the 1906 crisis, when the secretary of Commerce and Labor told President Roosevelt, "This man, Schmitz, has turned out [to be] 'pure gold' in this emergency."

Ruef was tried again and convicted of accepting street railway bribes, although the trial was interrupted when an ex-con shot Heney in the head for refusing him a place on the jury. Hiram Johnson, later governor and senator, took over the case for the

"Les Girls" of a Barbary Coast bagnio posed for an adventuring cameraman during the wide-open "teens" (far left). Two key reformers of post-Ruef 'Frisco were Mayor (and poet) Edward Robeson Taylor, at left, and ex-Mayor James E. Phelan (left).

The chefs, sous chefs and sauciers of the Old Poodle Dog made it a base for San Francisco's epicureans.

For many years after this 1910 feed Shorty Roberts' Sea Breeze resort at Ocean Beach was a popular hangout. But bear barbecues never caught on in the city.

FAMILY RESORT

Big city or not, San Francisco always has welcomed melon season, as in the 1921 Watermelon Day celebrated at the Free Market at Eighth and Market streets.

"Sunny Jim" Rolph (right), of the omnipresent boutonnierre. Michael M. Shaughnessy (below) harnessed the Sierra waters at Hetch Hetchy Reservoir and led them to the city in 1934.

After 1911 and Dr. Sun Yat Sen's revolution in China, San Francisco's Chinese began to adopt American ways, like this man's cloth cap. Chinatown was the most exotic quarter in town. During festivals, little raised bandstands appeared in the alleyways (facing page).

day in the pen. Upon his release in 1915, Ruef returned to his North Beach haunts, renting an office in the Columbus Tower with a sign on the door reading, "A. Ruef, Ideas, Investments, and Real Estate." He was never again a factor in politics. The able but corrupt attorney died bankrupt in 1936, a victim of Depression reverses.

Schmitz was seen as a naive fellow who was "used" by his sharp friends. Schmitz's character was sufficiently restored (whitewashed, say his critics) by 1917 for him to be elected to the Board of Supervisors. He died in 1928 after having served eight years in office. A "second coat" of lime has been applied in recent years by forgiving 'Friscans ("Cast not the first stone...") to Schmitz as well as to Ruef and even Blind Boss Chris Buckley.

REINCARNATION

From devastation to prosperity took less than five years. The *fait accompli* was formally recognized by the election of Sunny Jim Rolph for the first of his five terms in 1911. This was also the year Chinatown joined the city. The Chinese Revolution and Dr. Sun Yat Sen's republic had a tremendous effect on San Francisco's Chinese, many of whom knew Sun when he was a refugee there. So powerful was the influence of New China that the Asians of *Dupont Gai* and environs abruptly cut off their queues, adopted Western dress, picked up English and decided to join not only the mainstream but also the twentieth century. The bloody tong wars of the *boo how doi*, a sort of Cantonese Mafia, did not cease, however, until the 1920s, despite the attentions of Sergeant Jack Manion and his Chinatown Squad.

Rolph, the "Perennial Mayor," was a master politician of the Tammany stamp. A white mustachioed gent and a dapper dresser, he wore a fresh boutonnierre every day as a kind of reassuring trademark. Hale and hearty Jim personified the city's traditional *laissez faire* philosophy. Although well-to-do from shipping interests, he had the common touch and got along well with workingmen, since he was neither uppity nor intellectual. Rolph ran an open but orderly town, and successfully handled a world war and the city's greatest depression.

In 1912, the Municipal Railway began operations. It was the nation's first publicly owned transit system, thanks to the 1900 city charter promising ultimate municipal ownership of all public utilities. The 1917 boring of the Twin Peaks Tunnel for streetcars opened up the development of southwestern San Francisco.

The Riker Act was signed in 1913 by President Woodrow Wilson and work begun on City Engineer M.M. O'Shaughnessy's brilliant Hetch Hetchy water project, involving a dam on the north fork of the Tuolumne River near Yosemite (which broke John Muir's heart and hastened his death in 1914) and a 156-mile-long aqueduct.

Sponsors of a Civic Center Plaza called it "a monument to the city's cultural traditions," but it was really a token gesture of appreciation for the grandiose plans of Cahill and Burnham. An exposition auditorium (now the Civic Auditorium) and the im-

prosecution. Appeals stalled matters until 1911, by which time the public was weary of the costly graft trials. Ruef was finally convicted and sentenced to a fourteen-year term because he would not squeal on his confederates.

As the trials dragged on into 1912, the public's early enthusiasm weakened, waned and finally shifted from boredom to sympathy for the accused, probably seen as underdogs. Naurally, businessmen involved in paying off Ruef's Forty Thieves only wanted the investigation to go away. The trials were giving Everybody's Favorite City a black eye and were hurting business. An honest mayor who came to office in 1907, Edward Robeson Taylor, had the very devil of a time, like District Attorney Langdon, getting re-elected in 1908.

By 1909, Ruef's once-discredited Union Labor Party roared back into power with P.H. McCarthy. "P.H." promised a return to the style of the years when Frisky 'Frisco was still "The Paris of America." He sensed that the people were tired of the dour do-gooding of the reform crowd, and promised the restoration of good times and the old carefree spirit. But the voters grew leery of P.H. and, fearing a return to bossism, gave the laborite the old heave-ho in 1911 and elected James P. Rolph, who came in on a pledge to clean up Tenderloin and Barbary Coast crime. If he did not opt for a wide-open town, he certainly left the door ajar. His formula worked well; Rolph served five terms as mayor and left City Hall only because he was elected governor in 1930.

"Boodling Boss" Ruef served his time in San Quentin as a model prisoner and was paroled after a stretch of four years and seven months. No one campaigned harder for his release on parole than his old nemesis, Fremont Older. The latter was angry that Abe had been made a scapegoat, the only one of the piratical gang of bribe-givers and takers to serve a

By the time of World War I, Chinatown's children were dressing and playing (above) just like youngsters in North Beach or other parts of town. An important factor in the Americanization of the city's Chinese was Chinatown's press, especially the daily Chung Sai Yat Po (below).

CHUNG SAI YAT PO
THE FIRST & LARGEST CHINESE DAILY
OUTSIDE REPUBLIC OF CHINA
中西日報

On the dawn of the horseless-carriage era in 1909, Mission Street's farriers were nevertheless proud of their trade (left). Congressman Julius Kahn, striking a William Jennings Bryan pose (below), was instrumental in securing a world's fair for San Francisco in 1915.

pressive new City Hall of architects Arthur Brown Jr. and John Bakewell Jr. came first, in 1915. City Hall gave the town a very handsome building with an enormous dome rearing 308 feet above the pavement. It was taller than the Capitol in Washington by some sixteen feet, as Mayor Rolph never tired of mentioning. Best of all, it was solidly built, unlike its notoriously flimsy predecessor, and "came in" well within the $3.5 million budget.

City Hall was followed in 1917 by the impressive but space-wasting million-dollar Public Library, designed by George Kelham, on the site of the old City Hall. A less-impressive California State Building joined the group in 1926. The Veterans Memorial Building (now housing the San Francisco Museum of Modern Art) and the War Memorial Opera House were finished in 1932 to become the first architectural coups of that remarkable Depression era. The last edifice of the complex, the Federal Building, was completed in 1936. (The Opera House is redolent of recent history. It was the birthplace of the United Nations in 1945 and the site of the signing of the Japanese Peace Treaty in 1951.)

Even before "the Fire," the city had petitioned Congress in 1904 at the behest of merchant R.B. Hale, and with the support of local Congressman Julius Kahn, to be chosen the site of a world's fair celebrating the completion of the Panama Canal. By guaranteeing ample financing, reborn San Francisco won out over such rivals as New Orleans. Citizens bought $5 million of exposition bonds and extracted a commitment from the state to back the city with a special tax.

The PPIE, Panama Pacific International Exposition (February 20-December 4, 1915), boasted a large model of the canal. But the locks and Culebra Cut took a back seat to the revival of 'Frisco. Poet David Taylor called the fair "a monument to enterprise," but it was really a tribal celebration of reincarnation. However, the city did look ahead, and for the first time a world's fair included a flying field. Daring Art Smith was the exposition's star pilot.

The fair occupied 635 acres of Harbor Cove, the tidelands between Fort Mason and Fort Point (today's Marina). The exuberant exposition was a smashing success, both financially and artistically. The world seemed to catch San Francisco's own enthusiasm; some 43 states and 27 countries participated, although World War I was on. The fair won many new friends for the come-back city.

The PPIE had no Burnham, but it did not lack for men of talent, even genius. Bernard Maybeck designed the lovely Palace of Fine Arts, the only structure to survive on site after the exposition buildings were pulled down. It was a rival of the sequin-encrusted Tower of Jewels as the most beautiful sight in what poet George Sterling called "the Evanescent City."

Poets like George Sterling and Edwin Markham paid tribute to the exposition. The former described the fairgrounds as "these courts of Beauty's pure universe;" the latter described opening night as "the greatest revelation of beauty that was ever seen on earth." The prestigious Book Club of California was formed by bibliophiles who planned a great exhibit. It never came off, but the fair motivated them to a program that made San Francisco the national capital of

The PPIE was particularly beautiful at night when the Tower of Jewels was ablaze with light (above). The exposition was right on the Bay, so boat races between crews from U.S. Navy vessels were very much in order (right).

On one of his last visits to San Francisco, an aged Buffalo Bill Cody chatted with the PPIE's daring aviator, Art Smith, at the controls of his airplane.

A Maxwell racing car rested before the PPIE's theme building, the Tower of Jewels, still under construction.

*The Panama Pacific
International Exposition
was a phenomenal success;
visitors crowded the
grounds from start to
finish (above). Its only
surviving structure is
Bernard Maybeck's Palace
of Fine Arts (left).*

A great Preparedness Day parade on Market Street on July 22, 1916 was marred by a bombing blamed on socialist workers.

The socialists of the IWW, the Wobblies, won listeners when they held Market Street rallies for free speech or unions, although their advocacy of sabotage and violence fell on largely deaf ears.

fine printing during the "reign" of such presses as that of the brothers Grabhorn. Two great photographers, Ansel Adams and Edward Weston, were turned toward their careers by exposure to art at the PPIE.

SABOTAGE

Labor unrest returned as the tar and feathers finally sloughed off the Union Labor Party. And this time, there was no Father Yorke to make peace. Reverend Peter Yorke, editor of the Catholic *Monitor*, had become the city's labor priest—and its "Consecrated Thunderbolt"—in the 1901 strike. He had been tempered and toughened by years of fighting the Know Nothings of the American Protective Association, whose stated objective was to "save" the U.S.A. for white, native-born and Protestant Americans. Father Yorke backed Mike Casey's Teamsters in 1901, pointing out the rights of labor and the duties of management.

In 1916 a series of strikes by culinary workers and others was opposed by a Law and Order Committee of businessmen protecting the open shop. Strife flashed into violence after the Board of Supervisors adopted an anti-picketing ordinance. Word got out that radical union men were going to protest the July 22 Preparedness Day parade with "a little direct action." An exploding pipe bomb near the Ferry Building killed ten people and injured more than 40.

Two suspects—militant Socialists Tom Mooney and

Warren Billings—were arrested, tried and convicted, more because of their reputations as saboteurs than because of evidence of guilt in the 1916 terrorism. As representatives of trade unionism, they were automatic martyrs to many laboring people. To radicals, they were symbolic heroes. To conservatives, they were murdering subversives.

The fairness of the trial, per se, soon came into question. Prosecution testimony was found to be perjured. The fact-finding Wickersham Committee described "a wierd procession [of witnesses] consisting of a prostitute, two syphilitics, a psychopathic liar and a woman suffering from spiritual hallucinations." Fremont Older, now heading the American Civil Liberties Union, defended the pair, who continued to protest their innocence.

In 1918, President Wilson had the governor reduce Mooney's death sentence to life imprisonment—the same as Billings'—not because he necessarily believed them innocent, but because the case had assumed international importance and was embarrassing Uncle Sam. Mooney was pardoned in 1939 by Governor Culbert Olson. Billings' sentence was commuted at the same time, and he received a pardon in 1961.

The Wickersham Committee of 1929 stated that the investigation was bungled by being turned over to a private detective while the police hunted only for evidence to convict the already-arrested pair. It was an apparent miscarriage of justice; the guilt of the accused was certainly not proved. As usual, the forgotten men and women of the case were those killed and wounded in the bombing.

Labor's momentum was slowed by the port's World

San Francisco's women joined others across the country to secure the 19th Amendment which granted women's suffrage (above). Labor and feminism merged in 1919 when the "Hello Girls," telephone operators, went out on strike (left).

"Can the Rags!" was the battle cry during Clean-Up Week in April 1922 (below). A city tradition is a brisk dip in the Bay on New Year's morning, just as it was in 1916 when these Olympic Clubbers took the plunge (left).

MOTOR
Depen
DE BERR
AUTHORIZED SA
228 DRUMM ST.
UNION GASOL
E
R
A
G
S

During World War I, Victory Gardens sprouted all over town, including the Sutro School on Thirteenth Avenue (above). In 1918, smokers were arrested for failing to wear their flu masks (right).

War I boom and the prosperity that followed the Armistice. The city's population rose to 500,000 in 1920. Shipyards, foundries and mills fattened on defense contracts. Cultural life went on; for example, the Sutro Library opened to the public in 1917. The only scare of the war came not from Germans but from the Spanish—the flu epidemic of 1918, when cotton masks were *de rigeuer*. The war brought legislated virtue, too. A statewide red-light abatement law revoked the licenses of Barbary Coast dance halls and "ended" prostitution. San Franciscans tried mightily to ignore all this, along with the stupefying nightmare of the Eighteenth Amendment which made Prohibition, the Noble Experiment, the law of the land.

During the Roaring '20s, fueled by Prohibition, Mayor Rolph presided over another boom time, with homes spreading like mushrooms over the saharan wastes of the Richmond and Sunset districts, and with skyscrapers, restaurants and ornate movie palaces erupting everywhere like toadstools. Bootleggers made millions from San Francisco's thirst before FDR's Repeal of 1933. Rum runners landed Canadian whiskey on lonely beaches on moonless nights. Barkeeps like Izzy Gomez and Shanty Malone became local folk heroes.

The city was saddened in 1926 when President

140

A kite balloon rose above Civic Center during a World War I recruiting drive.

Warren G. Harding died, suddenly, at the Palace Hotel, the same place in which Hawaiian King David Kalakaua had died in 1891.

In 1927, the first seeds of "SFO" were scattered in the marshes of San Mateo County, just south of the city-county line, as little Mills Field was begun, the direct ancestor of San Francisco International Airport.

PITS AND PEAKS

The stock market crash of 1929 jolted the West Coast's capital out of its complacency. The city was not immune to the Depression, but it wasn't going to take it lying down. Mayor Rolph was elected governor in 1930 and blemished his reputation by defending the 1933 Vigilante-like actions of a mob that stormed a San Jose jail to lynch two murder suspects. Rolph was succeeded as mayor by florist Angelo Rossi.

In the early '30s, there was no evidence of the Depression at the port. The roof line of every finger pier on the waterfront was topped by masts, funnels and cargo booms of freighters, with here and there the white superstructures of passenger liners. The Embarcadero was noisy with steam winches and throttling trucks. Some 150 vessels were employed in the intercoastal trade with an equal number in the coasting trade, including the last of the rugged steam lumber schooners. September 1, 1930 must have set a record; 55 vessels were logged passing in or out of the Golden Gate that day.

United Fruit boats docked in Mission "Crick" near the Third Street drawbridge until a union complaint in San Pedro drove the line and its bananas from the Pacific to Gulf ports. Grace Line's ships tied up at the south end of the Embarcadero, near China Basin. Other prosperous old-timers were Matson, Dollar and Luckenbach Lines, and the frugal American-Hawaiian, its "A-H" said by sailors to stand for "Always Hungry." Matson's sleek *Malolo* pioneered the romantic and lucrative Hawaii tourist trade and was succeeded by the unforgettable *Lurline*.

A half-dozen ferry companies—the Southern Pacific, Southern Pacific-Golden Gate Limited, Northwestern Pacific, Santa Fe, Key System and Monticello Steamship Company—kept 45 ferryboats scuttling forth from the Ferry Building or the Hyde Street Pier to Sausalito, Oakland, Berkeley, Alameda, Richmond and Vallejo. The California Transportation Company's new sister-steamboats, the *Delta King* and *Delta Queen*, plied the Sacramento River to the state capital, offer-

Street musicians remain as constant and distinctive a feature of Downtown as corner flower stands.

141

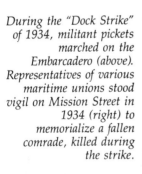

During the "Dock Strike" of 1934, militant pickets marched on the Embarcadero (above). Representatives of various maritime unions stood vigil on Mission Street in 1934 (right) to memorialize a fallen comrade, killed during the strike.

ing handsome furnishings and appetizing cuisine en route, although the Stockton passenger run of the *Fort Sutter* and other paddlewheelers was already being phased out.

Eventually, the Depression caught up with the port. Vessels were laid up, sold or—ironically—scrapped for Japan's war industry, to be returned in the shape of shells, bombs and torpedoes on December 7, 1941 and thereafter.

As shipping stagnated from 1934-36, trouble reappeared on the Embarcadero. In 1934, Harry Bridges' International Longshoremen's Association (ILA) struck the coast's ports, demanding a six-hour day and 30-hour week; a dollar an hour and $1.50 overtime; union control of hiring halls; and a closed shop. Maritime unions supported the longshoremen, as did the Teamsters. Mayor Rossi wanted the harbor open, of course, and promised the Chamber of Commerce and Industrial Association (the latter being the union's opponent) police protection and the clearing away of pickets.

To crush the strike, the Industrial Association formed an Atlas Trucking Company of non-union men and reminded the citizenry that "the waterfront is public property. All citizens are entitled to use it without interference." When the drivers tried to break through the picket lines, a melee erupted. In the fighting of July 3 and 5, 1934, culminating on Bloody Thursday, some 100 men were hurt and two longshoremen killed. Soon 500 National Guardsmen were sent in by the governor, but only to protect state property with bayoneted rifles and machine guns at the ready. Mayor Rossi refused to call in troops and would not declare martial law.

The public, badly split in sentiment, began to favor the unions after the Bloody Thursday deaths and the subsequent funeral parade of 10,000 men up Market Street. But the ILA was not content just to close the port. It now called for a general strike on July 16 to replace the maritime strike; to close down the city. Many theaters, restaurants, liquor stores and other places of business did shutter their doors. "Vigilantes" raided the meeting places of some "radicals." Now the

The waterfront suffered little damage in the Fire of '06 and was soon thriving, with fruit vendors serving Embarcadero workers (left). As the number of lateen-rigged crafts grew, Fisherman's Wharf began to attract tourists, who found it quaint (above).

public turned on the longshoremen's union for its arrogance, and Bridges called off the strike. All outstanding issues were submitted to arbitration.

Labor won, hands down, in 1934. Government attempts to deport Bridges as an alleged Communist failed. But the port began to sink into a slough of despond from which it has not yet emerged. It was

COIT TOWER'S LADY

*L*illie Coit (1842-1929), a Southern belle with a mouthful of a name, Eliza Wyche Hitchcock Coit, was brought to San Francisco by her mother in 1851. Like her mama, she was a Rebel, through and through, and spent part of the Civil War years in Europe and the Confederacy.

As a child, Lillie was a tomboy. She trapped wharf rats under wooden sidewalks and chased fire engines. She became such a fire buff that Knickerbocker Engine Company No. 5 made her its mascot, giving her an honorary membership in the company. She adopted the "5" of the fire brigade as her lucky number. She always wore a gold pin in the shape of the numeral, day and night. (She was buried with the pin.) Lillie signed her name "Lillie Hitchcock 5" until she married Benjamin Howard Coit, then

changed her signature to "Lillie Hitchcock Coit 5".

Lillie's later years were tragic. An insane acquaintance shot one of her callers to death, before her eyes, in her Palace Hotel sitting room. The murderer was jailed, but Mrs. Coit was so shocked and so fearful of him that she fled to Europe and refused to return to her adopted city until the man died in 1924. She came home for her last few years and left one-third of her estate to beautify the city. Coit Tower, the mural-decorated observation point on Telegraph Hill, being a memorial to the city's fire "bhoys" as well as to its donor, is often taken for a great fire hose nozzle in concrete. But the resemblance is only an accident of modern (1934) art.

Fire buff Lillie Coit.

143

raised only temporarily by the extraordinary circumstances of World War II. Oakland passed the one-time imperial city in shipping tonnage in 1969 and has continued to lengthen her lead, while "The City That Knows How" has quarreled over who or what was responsible for the harbor's plight. Poor management, state versus local control, a labor stranglehold, slowness to adopt new cargo handling techniques like containerization—all have been blamed.

Bloody Thursday symbolized the dark, violent side of the '30s, but there was a surprisingly bright side to San Francisco life in the Depression that unemployment, labor strife and even poverty could not dim. During the Rossi years of 1931-44, the city remained a lively place for art and writing, music and theater. John Steinbeck and William Saroyan were often in town. The "WPA School" of art patronage put to work painters who slapped murals on the unsuspecting walls of schools, Coit Tower and Golden Gate Park's Beach Chalet.

Most astonishingly, the depths of the Depression saw a renaissance in world-class engineering and architectural creativity in San Francisco. Some would say that the pits of the Great Depression, rather than 1906, marked the city's finest hour. The splendid War Memorial Opera House was finished in 1932; Telegraph Hill's Coit Tower, a memorial to fire buff Lillie H. Coit, in 1933. That year, construction started on the Golden Gate and San Francisco-Oakland Bay bridges, the two greatest spans in the world.

The Golden Gate Bridge, 4,200 feet long between towers, is still viewed as the world's greatest bridge, and certainly the most beautiful. The two red towers rear up 746 feet, often above the fog banks. It is not

only a masterpiece of engineering, but an immense Art Deco sculpture that does the impossible—actually enhances its setting.

Only Joseph B. Strauss, of all American engineers, was confident that he could throw a structure successfully across the deep, often foggy, windy, tide-ripped Golden Gate. The key was his ingenious South Tower, well out in the stream but built "in the dry" within an oval fender the size of the San Francisco 49ers' playing field.

The Bay Bridge, technically the James J. Rolph Bridge, has been relatively neglected because of its more beautiful mate, but it is a remarkable structure —the longest (8.5 miles) and most expensive ($77 million, to the Golden Gate's $35 million) span in the world when built. It is actually three, even four, bridges in one. A simple truss bridge lifts traffic up from the East Bay approaches over mudflats and duck blinds to meet a cantilevered span over the deepest piers on earth. This leads to the world's largest vehicular tunnel, a two-decker bore (76 feet high by 58 feet wide) through Yerba Buena Island.

From the isle to the Embarcadero are two double-decker suspension spans clearing the old ferry routes by 216 feet and held aloft by four 518-foot towers topping huge piers. The twin suspension spans are joined at Pier W-4, an artificial "high island" of concrete 400 feet tall, half of it under water. The pier itself is an engineering wonder. Having swallowed more concrete than the Empire State Building, it became a larger structure than the biggest pyramid of Gizeh. Briefly—and rightly—it was considered San Francisco's newest isle, like man-made Treasure Island. It was nicknamed Moran's Island for its

Deck or no deck, the Golden Gate Bridge was a graceful sight, an architectural and engineering marvel.

Nonchalant "high iron" men of the San Francisco-Oakland Bay Bridge worked high above the finger piers of the Embarcadero in November 1935.

Even unfinished, the Bay Bridge was a beautiful sight by night as the catwalks and cables were illuminated.

designer but the name, alas, did not stick.

The Bay Bridge, built by the state with considerable federal help since it was a pet project of (Californian) President Herbert Hoover, opened in 1936. The Golden Gate Bridge, a "private" affair paid for by bonds voted in 1930 by San Francisco and the North Bay counties it serves, opened in 1937. About two dozen lives were lost in the construction of the East Bay span. Divers died of the bends and workers fell to their deaths. There was no safety net.

Golden Gate builder Strauss was obsessed with safety. He pioneered hard hats, safety belts, protective goggles, even diets for dizziness-prone "high iron" men on the bridge. He strung a very expensive safety net under the entire deck. Strauss' safety record was almost perfect until just before opening day, when a falling scaffold tore through the tough mesh of manila hemp and carried a dozen men into the waters of the Gate, 220 feet below the deck. Only two survived the fall, and one of them died, shortly after, of his injuries.

In 1939, the Golden Gate International Exposition, a civic celebration to salute the two bridges, opened on Treasure Island. The latter was hand-made by filling 400 acres of Yerba Buena Shoals with mud, sand, dirt and rock from the bay and from the Yerba Buena Tunnel spoil. It held both the world's fair and a Pan American air base for its flying boats to the Orient, the fabled China Clippers of Captain Edward Musick and other pilots.

The fair's theme was "A Pageant of the Pacific," and its architecture was an interesting melange of Southeast Asian, Mayan and pure Buck Rogers. A huge statue of a pouting Island girl—*Pacifica*, by Ralph Stackpole—symbolized this theme. The name of the isle was itself a nice tribute to the Scots author adopted by California bibliophiles—Robert Louis Stevenson. Treasure Island was, indeed, a romantic place, a refuge from the cares and worries of World War II. Although not as successful as its PPIE predecessor (it was a loser, financially), it welcomed seventeen million visitors and is a treasured memory of Bay Area people who knew it.

SIDETRACKED

December 7, 1941, the Japanese raid on Pearl Harbor, marked a watershed in San Francisco history even more than did April 18, 1906. It is the dividing line between Old San Francisco and the city of today. The Japanese did not attack the poorly-defended Coast, as feared; the ack-ack guns and anti-submarine nets turned out to be unnecessary precautions. But the city made itself into a great military and naval base. Hunter's Point Naval Shipyard hummed, as did new yards for merchantmen in Sausalito and Richmond. Workers flocked in, creating a housing crunch. They displaced many "old San Franciscans" who began to move to sunnier climes in the suburbs. Many defense workers—often Southern blacks and Dust Bowl "Okies"—decided to stay put after the war, just as servicemen passing through made mental notes to settle down in 'Frisco when peace should be won.

After World War II, the usual postwar euphoria led

The GGIE was loaded with art and culture, but also with entertainment and female pulchritude on the Gay Way.

THE CHINA CLIPPER

Herb Caen, the Pepys of San Francisco, remembers how the city (when he was new to it in 1935) found a new hero in Captain Edward Musick. He was the pilot who first tied the city to Hawaii and the Orient by air. Musick was at the controls when Pan American's first China Clipper lifted from the water at Alameda and headed westward. (Later, the flying boats' base would be Treasure Island). The four-engine flying boat was the ancestor of all of the "Dumbos" of World War II sea reconnaissance and rescue work.

As the clipper sailed past the twin towers of the unfinished Golden Gate Bridge—en route to Manila in 59 hours and 48 minutes with several refueling stops on Pacific islands—just about everybody in San Francisco seemed to have climbed hills or lined the Marina to wave godspeed to Musick. One of the spectators was a young Italian ballplayer, Joe DiMaggio, watching from Fisherman's Wharf. A few years later, Pan Am launched a companion link between New York and Lisbon, called the Yankee Clipper. The centerfielder for the Seals was now a star slugger for the New York Yankees. He was soon given the nickname "The Yankee Clipper."

The China Clipper opened a new aviation frontier.

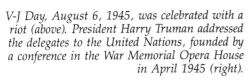

V-J Day, August 6, 1945, was celebrated with a riot (above). President Harry Truman addressed the delegates to the United Nations, founded by a conference in the War Memorial Opera House in April 1945 (right).

Downtown interests to begin an almost maniacal high-rise building program, with the blessings of City Hall. Mayor Roger Lapham actually looked forward to San Francisco becoming the New York of the Pacific Coast. For years, skyscraper building was seen as a cure-all for the city's socioeconomic ills. The old town became lopsided with out-of-scale skyscrapers blocking views and even the sun. Bustling by day, the heart of San Francisco was abandoned by dark, as office workers fled by crowded freeways to safer suburbs. Valuable old historic buildings, like the superb Montgomery Block, were torn down for parking lots or slab-like skyscrapers with neither architectural nor esthetic significance. With insufficient garages, increased traffic brought transportation snarls and even smog alerts to the naturally air-conditioned city.

To many locals, San Francisco seemed to lose its sense of direction—and some of its perennial optimism—in the postwar decades. It suffered from the same Atomic Age malaise that afflicted all American cities. Streets and parks were no longer friendly places, as the makeup of the population changed. It was no longer a small-town city of diverse ethnic groups—Italian, Chinese, Irish—who somehow managed to pull together for San Francisco, perhaps because all in leadership roles had seemed to know one another. The city now became a battleground for rival groups with special interests, all vying for the attention and largesse of City Hall.

Skin-deep rebellious faddism now became "far-out" 'Frisco's trademark. The press, especially television, showed the old town as a nonstop carnival in which actors and audience were one. There was a grain of truth to the indictment, to be sure, but the media became part of the problem as it fed on it, and vice versa, in a sick symbiosis.

Old-style bohemians, often artists and poets, were drowned out by the Beatniks of North Beach cafes, poetry readings and street happenings. Their overrated Shakespeare and Milton were Jack Kerouac and Alan Ginsberg. Instant-poets adopted as their guru the one diehard bohemian, Kenneth Rexroth, who went along with the charade for a while, then pulled out.

The Beats were followed in a downward spiral by the Hippies of the Haight Ashbury district, more interested in drugs and sex, rock music, psychedelic posters, light shows, be-ins and drug-induced "acting out" in general than in writing, spouting poetry or browsing the shelves of Lawrence Ferlinghetti's City Lights bookshop. Pseudo-Buddhism, Hindu philosophy and incense were inadequate protection for the pathetic Flower Children of the Love Generation, often dropouts and runaways. They were abused and brutalized by more violent street people attracted by the garish anarchy of the "Hashbury." The district became a squalid, dangerous ghetto of counterculture freaks. Their show-biz descendants are the handful of Punks, bizarrely painted and coiffed reminders of the wasteful rebellion of youth that became entangled with the civil rights and antiwar marches of the 1960s and '70s.

Sadly, the first police riots occurred in 1960. The cops used fire hoses and billy clubs inside the beautiful City Hall against young people protesting the

Controversial General Douglas MacArthur was given a tremendous popular welcome in April 1951 in Civic Center when he was recalled from Korea by President Truman.

House Un-American Activities Committee hearings in 1960. There would be another—perhaps more understandable if not forgivable—overreaction after the disgraceful White Night Riot of 1978, and an inexcusable orgy of mass clubbing of crowds gathered to celebrate the 49ers finally winning an NFL championship.

Meanwhile, harmless street characters like Emperor Norton or Tiny Armstrong of the bird whistles, were being replaced by so-called freaks and crazies practicing deliberately irrational behavior to attract attention. The streets of San Francisco became dangerous places. Wierd cults were bad enough, but the random, racist Zebra killings, the bloody Symbionese Liberation Army, and the local underpinnings of Reverend Jim Jones' ghastly Guyana murders and mass suicides were truly horrifying.

However, the postwar years were not all bad. There were signs of solid growth, from the Ferry Building's 1956 World Trade Center to the recent, if dragged-out, redevelopment of the old produce area for Embarcadero Center towers I through IV, and the blitzed South of Market sector between St. Patrick's and the *Chronicle*, where the Moscone Center has finally appeared, leaky roof and all. BART, Bay Area Rapid Transit, was once seen as a greater white elephant than even the accidental windtunnel that is Candlestick Park baseball stadium. It has belatedly metamorphosed, like an aging butterfly, into a spectacular success. BART ties the city, via elevated and subway, fast and light rail vehicles, with San Mateo County and, via a transbay tube, with the East Bay.

None of the mayors who followed the lax and

benign Rossi—Roger Lapham, Elmer Robinson, George Christopher and John Shelley—were catastrophes, but neither were they world-beaters. The most dynamic of the lot was controversial Joseph Alioto, who was succeeded by another Italian with a lower profile, George Moscone.

San Francisco's Grand Guignol of civic horrors culminated in 1978 with the aberrant one-man Vigilantism of Dan White. A conservative, middle-class supervisor, he had resigned his seat on the Board of Supervisors, then reconsidered. When Mayor Moscone appeared to renege on a promise to reappoint him, White shot him to death, then—almost as an afterthought—took out his resentment of the growing political power of the homosexual community by killing Supervisor Harvey Milk, the city's first avowed gay supervisor.

White was convicted, but San Francisco was sent reeling again by the verdict and sentence—not homicide but voluntary manslaughter, with a maximum sentence of only seven years. The junk food (or Twinkies) defense and plea of "diminished capacity" seemed to make a travesty of law and justice to a public already disgusted by lawyers' and psychiatrists' misuse of temporary insanity pleas.

The leniency of the sentence enraged homosexuals and their partisans, who rioted, burned police cars and vandalized City Hall in the White Night Riot, as police were leashed by orders from superiors. Shortly after this destruction of a million dollars worth of property, the officers reacted against the mob by having a little riot of their own in Castro Street bars.

The year 1978, with the assassination of Mayor Moscone, marked the bottoming-out of a city finally given its comeuppance by the gods for its excessive hubris. The agony seemed endless, but it took just five years of guilt feelings and soul searching before the city that Bret Harte described as "serene, indifferent to fate" recovered from the trauma of Mayor Moscone's murder. By 1983, the briefly unsure city was finally healing from its multiple wounds, just as a "Strategic Plan" for its future was issued, jointly, by city government and the Chamber of Commerce. But the city's spunky spirits revived only after a time of careful nursing by a remarkably cool, but compassionate conciliator, Mayor Dianne Feinstein.

A heroic statue of Cristoforo Colombo watches from Telegraph Hill over North Beach, San Francisco's historical Italian colony.

CHAPTER 7.

TODAY AND TOMORROW

Luckily, San Francisco had never been deeply mired in violence or, for that matter, racism and urban decay as was the case with many older cities. It had never tolerated a Love Canal or a Times Beach. It even ended an occasional year in the black with a budget surplus! The first of the triple keys to urban health (housing, jobs, transportation) was being addressed not only through the normal avenues of redevelopment or urban renewal, but also in attempts at rent control and limitation of condominium conversions. Along with joblessness, the shortage of affordable housing remained a major problem.

Housing problems in San Francisco were exacerbated by the lunatic prices for real estate, an inflated $130,000 median (some said $225,000) cost of a home in comparison to the national average of $65,000. Costs of labor were high; the costs of climate and scenery even higher. Zoning, lower density requirements for controlled growth, higher permit fees, all added to the tab. Costs of business property, already the highest in the nation, when added to the high-priced homes of the necessary labor force, drove offices out of town in a punishing deterrent to civic growth. Young middle-class parents with children suffered most. They were virtually priced out of the most expensive city in the United States and fled to the suburbs. Steeply rising costs were accompanied by a shrinking total of residents capable of paying the city's bills.

Increasingly, San Francisco in 1983 was in danger of becoming a polarized city of many poor and a few rich, as well as one of singles or loners (as was the case back in 1849) with all of the attendant dangers of isolation—loneliness and homesickness, depression, alcoholism and cirrhosis, drug abuse and suicide. The 1980 census showed 53 percent of the city's 678,974 residents living in non-family households. (The 1970 figure was 44 percent.) This reversion to the days of 1849 was a recent phenomenon that probably could be corrected, for as late as 1953 San Francisco was still "a family town." To return to this healthier social situation, rents and home prices must drop and second units (mother-in-law apartments) must be encouraged in residential areas.

Unemployment remained another terrible problem, but transportation continued to improve as BART belatedly matured and was joined by Muni-Metro LRVs as well as Peninsular SamTrans coaches, the East Bay's AC Transit buses and Marin's Golden Gate Bridge District buses and splendid ferries. The entire cable car system was undergoing a reconstruction project due to be completed in time for the Democratic Convention of 1984.

The quality of life remained excellent in the Golden Gate City which was, after all, national headquarters for the Sierra Club, Friends of the Earth, Save the Redwoods League and Greenpeace—all deeply rooted in John Muir's pioneering—and San Francisco Planning and Urban Research Association; the Save San Francisco Bay Association; People For Open Space; and the important pair—BCDC, the Bay Conservation and Development Commission, and the California Coastal Commission.

With jobs scarce, the number of homeless (swollen by the recession's New Poor) were dumped from the middle class smack into the free-meal lines outside St. Anthony's Dining Room. Mayor Dianne Feinstein attempted to find them places to sleep in small hotels, church shelters and Salvation Army and St. Vincent de Paul Society buildings, even (briefly and unsuccessfully) in strategically parked out-of-service buses.

Crime statistics by 1983 were lowering as the general population, after a continuing slump, apparently began to recover.

The greatest successes in redevelopment brought into being the Embarcadero Center of David Rockefeller and architect John Portman and, later, the Moscone Center. These increased auditorium, office and shop space but, alas, did no more to remedy the housing crunch than did Louise Davies' Symphony Hall or the lovely new shopping center, the Galleria, which followed the earlier innovative triumphs of Ghirardelli Square and the Cannery. There was even hope for the decayed Embarcadero, as Tom Crowley and the Friends of the Port set to work. But the city's real needs were for moderate income rentals, not ad-

The sky over Ghirardelli Square explodes in bursts of brilliance (facing page). No less splendid, and more enduring, the War Memorial Opera House shares the lens with the new Davies Performing Arts Center.

San Francisco's ocean fogs of summer are always in motion, crisp and fresh, torn to tatters by the wind.

ditional meeting rooms, offices or boutiques.

Public education's sad standards sagged further, with students' language and work skills lamentably low. Newcomers, especially those speaking English as a second language, failed even to participate in the city's mainstream, much less enhance it. But a trend to "immersion" of ethnics into English-language life (not necessarily at the expense of their mother tongue) promised to do better for them than politicized bilingualism.

Traditions, history and culture remained in good hands—the Society of California Pioneers, the California Historical Society, the Public Library and the Sutro Library, the Book Club of California. Neighborhood groups and organizations like the Landmarks Preservation Board, Heritage, Victorian Alliance and the Citizens Committee to Save the City of Paris all worked toward the recycling of old buildings of historic and esthetic worth.

The splendid Louise A. Davies Symphony Hall joined the Opera House, and the San Francisco Ballet's new home was under construction in 1983. Sutro Library moved from the University of San Francisco to new quarters on San Francisco State University's Stonestown campus. For efficiency, De Young Museum and the Palace of the Legion of Honor combined their administrations into the Fine Arts Museums of San Francisco, while both the San Francisco Museum of Modern Art and the Academy of Sciences strengthened their public programs.

San Francisco's grandest new asset, the GGNRA (Golden Gate National Recreation Area) was a kind of going-away gift from Congressman Phil Burton, who died unexpectedly in 1983. He was damned as a gerrymandering machine politico by his critics, but lauded by his much more numerous supporters as a superb if hard-nosed politician who was a champion of civil rights and health and welfare services for the underprivileged, with a genuine dedication to the preservation of the outdoors, open space and green belts for urban folk.

Dripping with scrollsaw embellishments and busty with bay windows, San Francisco's Victorian architecture has been copied all over the West (facing page). A city built on seven hills wends its way down to the San Francisco Marina and Yacht Club (below).

Within a month of the 1906 earthquake, Bank of Italy had reestablished quarters on Montgomery Street (above). Fewer than four-score years later, the Bank of America World Headquarters towers 52 stories above the Financial District.

All the world's a stage. . .but San Francisco's cast of players seems more vivid than most cities'. "The Puppet Man" struts his hour with a miniature version of himself (far left). Bufano mosaic "Children Shall Lead Us" makes its statement at the Yerba Buena West Building (left).

An elderly grandfather peruses the theater offerings in Chinatown (far left). A one-man combo, "Uncle Ray Solo" entertains on Fisherman's Wharf (left).

The GGNRA is now a national model for urban and extra-urban parks of the future, bringing clean air, openness, trees, grass and flowers to those who need them most—inner-city dwellers. The Recreation Area protects Ocean Beach, Land's End, Alcatraz and the Marin Headlands. At the same time, it serves Clio, the muse of history, by hosting Karl Kortum's San Francisco National Maritime Museum at Aquatic Park and his fleet of historic ships at Hyde Street Pier. The Fort Mason headquarters of the GGNRA has become a beehive of cultural activity carried out by a cluster of art, history, theater, ecology and other institutions given a home there. The great Army piers are the scene of major art and crafts shows.

LEADERSHIP

The cure for the city's ills could not come entirely from the mayor's office, of course, but leadership could, and did. At first, Dianne Feinstein's friends saw her as essentially a placator of contending constituencies. The latter grew more demanding after the adoption of the supposed reform of district elections in 1976. More and more, a fractured community, seemingly willing to be manipulated by politicians, pulled apart. The pre-World War II small-town atmosphere of Irish, Italians and

Historic reconstruction of a Fort Point officer's quarters captures the light and the austere nostalgia of an earlier time (right). The City by the Bay glows with a charged intensity at sunset (facing page).

San Francisco is a city of human scale—even its "noble harbor" has a friendly ambience.

Chinese seemed one with feudal times. In its place was a city that social scientists, with their love of lumping, would describe as such-and-such percent "non-white", or so-many percent "Spanish surnamed" people. Certainly it was disunified, without consensus. Bilingualism and multilingual ballots became controversial, as possibly converting ethnic pride into functional illiteracy.

Ironically, a series of tough decisions, each requiring courage, changed the role of the incumbent mayor from a sort of passive and healing caretaker to that of a dynamic leader. First, Mayor Feinstein vetoed a divisive "domestic partners" or ("live-in lovers") benefits ordinance and thereby enraged the homosexual community. Next, she secured a ban on handguns (later thrown out as unconstitutional) in a brave attempt to lessen crime and violence. Finally, she fought like a tigress to restrict condo conversions.

Meanwhile, positive things occurred. The mayor handled the visit of Queen Elizabeth II beautifully, then won the 1984 Democratic Convention away from Chicago.

Very likely a turning point in the city's, as well as the mayor's, fortunes was the April 1982 recall elections. The *Examiner's* editorial called it "a frivolous ...wildly irresponsible mis-use of the recall process," and its columnist Guy Wright termed it "a rebellion without a cause... [just] petty gripes and yard-bird bitching." The recall vote was brought about by a handful of far-out Marxists who styled themselves White Panthers. Angered by Mayor Feinstein's anti-gun stance, they won an uneasy alliance of gays, gun lobbyists and disgruntled unemployed looking for a scapegoat.

The recall backfired badly, with its 81.2 percent vote for the mayor fitting her out with a brand-new confidence. With the sudden death of Phil Burton, Mayor Feinstein appeared to come out of her shell to fill the vacuum that many political observers thought

The fortress-like entrance to the Cannery (facing page) supports its own earth-bound star. The smooth, cool curves of a Bufano sculpture at Lake Merced (top left) invite stroking. The sunlit arch of the Crocker Galleria softens the vertical outlines of the Bank of America Building just beyond (bottom left). The classic symmetry of the Conservatory and spring gardens at Golden Gate Park are spiced with riotous color (below).

Alcatraz Island and the angular machinery of a merchant vessel dissolve in the golden glow of an early morning mist.

would be occupied by State Assembly Speaker Willie Brown and became, overnight, a political power broker. She seemed to be gently educating the electorate to the necessity for the long view—broad perspectives, equity, needful compromises and consensus —in order to end social fragmentation and to rebuild the city as a true community of interestingly diversified neighborhoods.

Already, a warm sense of neighborliness, of belonging, was abroad in 1983, certainly in such gentrification projects as the sprucing up of Hayes Valley. Hopes were high that the good times were returning, the times when all of San Francisco was each and every resident's "neighborhood;" when its citizens were completely at home in all parts of town.

Recovery from the city's infections, contusions and fractures must come ultimately from its citizenry, by natural healing. Mayors, supervisors and big wheels cannot do the trick. Like cellular replacement of civic tissue, the losses in recent years of strong, caring, San Franciscans must be replaced. These were citizens like curmudgeon-columnist Charles McCabe; celebrity-capitalists Ben Swig and Louis Lurie; philanthropists Dan Koshland and Joseph Koret; bibliophile David Magee; conductor Pierre Monteaux; Beaux Arts landscape architect Thomas Church; photographer Imogen Cunningham; writer George R. Stewart; painter Glen Wessells; gardener Grace Marchant (beautifier of Will Irwin's "Telegraft Hill"); environmentalist Dorothy Erskine; artists Mallette Dean and Valenti Angelo.

Such staggering losses can only be made up by the efforts of new leaders with a strong sense of community. Fortunately, San Francisco has them a-plenty. Herb Caen remains the city's conscience as well as its Pepys. Cyril Magnin is the city's official greeter. Joe DiMaggio is "Mr. San Francisco." Robert Royston and Lawrence Halprin are talented disciples of Tommy Church. Bibliophiles remain in Albert Sperisen, Franklin Gilliam, Warren Howell and Reverend William Monihan, of the University of San Francisco's symposia. Ansel Adams has removed himself physically to Carmel, but San Franciscans like to think that the photographer is still in San Francisco in spirit. Museum curators include Van Deren Coke; art historians, Dr. Joseph Baird. Writers are legion, led by the city's dean of authors, Oscar Lewis. Poets Vincent McHugh, Kenneth Rexroth and Kenneth Patchen are gone, but Brother Antoninus (William Everson) remains, though migrated to the Santa Cruz coast. Ernest Born is the city's architect emeritus; Allen Temko, a sort of watchdog over architecture and city planning. Ruth Asawa sculpts and Jade Snow Wong pots, and critic Thomas Albright nags painters and other artists to do their best. Harold Gilliam is a latter-day Muir, joined by environmentalists Dorothy Whitnah and Margo Patterson Doss. Of the making of music, like books, there is no end, with Dave Brubeck, Turk Murphy, George Shearing. Hal Lipset is probably a better private eye than Dashiell Hammett ever dreamed of becoming. Adrian Wilson, Andrew Hoyem, et al, continue the tradition of fine printing handed down by John Henry Nash, Taylor and Taylor, the brothers Grabhorn and Lawton Kennedy.

San Francisco's mystique is scented with nostalgia; the long ago seems always at hand, lending the city a

A figurehead on a ship's bow (facing page) and an ancient Spanish hero (left) are apt symbols for a city of adventurers and visionaries.

serenity and dignity beyond its years. To preserve its rich traditions, the city needs turn only to Roger Jobson of the Society of California Pioneers and Al Shumate and Jim Holliday of the California Historical Society, Thomas Chinn of the Chinese American Historical Society, Karl Kortum of the National Maritime Museum, City Archivist Gladys Hanson and Robert Schwendinger of the Maritime Humanities Center.

Alfred and Hanna Fromm have made educational history with their Fromm Institute classes for "seniors" at the University of San Francisco. Julia Porter plants trees, Shirley Sarvis concocts recipes, Friedel Klussmann saves cable cars, Mrs. Henry Potter Russell builds up the Museum of Modern Art, Louise Davies houses the Symphony. Duncan Nicol and Professor Jerry Thomas of the Occidental Hotel are long gone, but North Beach has its *Irlandese* host, Ed the Moose. The city even has a saint, of sorts, in Father Alfred Boeddeker of St. Anthony's Dining Room.

The physical as well as the intellectual assets of the city guarantee a secure future, too. A mere sampler would include Chinese New Years; Mission Street's last jitneys; Larry Halprin's landscaped and fountained Levi's Plaza; the Bay to Breakers run; the Japanese Cultural Center; "Butterball," the jolly manatee at Steinhart Aquarium; the refurbished last Victory ship, *Jeremiah O'Brien*; Judge Harry Low's Court of Historical Review; the Culinary Academy; the enhancement of Strybing Arboretum's Garden of Fragrance, a hands-on botanical experience for the blind; Dusan Mills' restoratian of the handsome and historical (1889) Audifredd Building on the Embarcadero; the International Film Festival; the Police Department's mounted patrol; the Mission District's Latin murals; the St. Mary's Girls Marching Band; the Wattis Hall of Man at the Academy of Sciences; the new Neiman-Marcus store; Fort Mason's American Crafts Council shows; the Wine Museum; Bay cruises; Turk Murphy's Dixieland jazz; the Museo

Italo Americano; free open-air concerts in Stern Grove; enough fine restaurants to feed a city five times 'Frisco's size; a surviving supper club in the Fairmont Hotel's Venetian Room, complete with a big band; French bread—sourdough, of course; Dungeness Crab Louie; abalone.

It is still hard to find another American city with the strong and vibrant personality of San Francisco. In 1983 its Convention and Visitors Bureau polled tourists and found that 82 percent of the visitors were "very satisfied" with the place. Once the town bragged of being "The City That Knows How," as well as the elegant "Paris of America." Gellett Burgess called it "San Francisco the Impossible, the City of Miracles." It still knows how to take its pleasures seriously and its work and problems lightly. So it is bound to re-gain its only slightly dimmed luster, for it remains a city built on a human scale, a place of beauty and even more beautiful vistas and views that make the heart expand. It remains nonconformist, unique, *sui generis*, an unmistakably tolerant and innovative city of the unexpected. Emerging from its brief funk, it is both adaptable and optimistic again, and remarkably unafraid of change.

All of this is so because San Francisco is inhabited by diverse visionaries and adventurers of the same general stamp as the 49ers who always felt that they were "a people unto themselves." Hospitable, cultured and energetic more than idiosyncratic, San Francisco is a magic place, an enchanted city with the verve and style, the freshness and vitality, to dream great dreams of the future, and then to carry them out.

San Francisco's sea fogs can render even Nob Hill an area of magic and mystery.

PARTNERS
IN PROGRESS

*California Brewing Company won first prize in
the Workhorse Parade, September 9, 1909.*

CORPORATE SPONSORS

The Society of California Pioneers

As early as 1850, the very year California became a state, a group of San Francisco's first citizens gathered together to ensure that the history of pioneer days would be preserved. They chose as the name of their association The Society of California Pioneers, and they wrote into its constitution their intention "to collect and preserve information connected with the early settlement and conquest of the country, and to perpetuate the memory of those whose sagacity, enterprise, and love of independence induced them to settle in the wilderness and become the germ of a new state."

Most of the founding group had arrived, as an orator noted on the first day of the following year, when "there were but some twenty houses in the pueblo" that was to become San Francisco. "Now look around you," he added; "we are a mighty city."

That mighty city of 1851, which had sprung into being as the metropolis of one of the world's great migrations, the California Gold Rush, grew from a population of some 20,000 at the time of the Society's founding, to three-quarters of a million in the next century, changing from decade to decade but never losing the unique character bestowed upon it by its pioneers. Throughout the century and a third since its beginning, The Society of California Pioneers has preserved memories, records and mementos of both the city and the state.

Today at Pioneer Hall in the San Francisco Civic Center the Society maintains a museum and a library housing books and a unique collection of manuscripts and photographs. On its walls hang paintings by many of California's most famous nineteenth-century artists. These and objects that vividly recreate the state's early days draw school children, Californians old and new, and visitors from afar.

Here on display are all the flags that have flown over California since Spanish dominion; a crucifix carried by Father Junípero Serra, founder of the mission chain; an iron chest that stored the gold that set off the gold rush; an ore cart used in one of the state's early shaft mines; a stagecoach of the kind that first carried passengers across the nation, then after the transcontinental railroad was completed transported them on local routes throughout the state; and a charred carriage clock found in the ruins after the San Francisco earthquake and fire of 1906.

Among the manuscripts in the library are biographies of members of the Society, invaluable and irreplaceable records of such men as Peter Burnett, first governor of California; John A. Sutter, owner of the iron chest and of the millrace in which the first gold was found; James Lick, whose fortune built the state's first great astronomical observatory; and many others who have played significant roles in the progress of California. In the library are also handwritten reminiscences of men who participated in and observed important events, a collection now being carried forward with the addition of tape-recorded reminiscences of men and women significant in twentieth-century California that the Society has commissioned the Regional Oral History Office of The Bancroft Library to prepare.

Carrying its activities beyond Pioneer Hall, the Society for twenty years maintained custody of the birthplace of Father Serra on the island of Mallorca. It regularly participates in observances of the anniversary of San Francisco's founding, and in placing plaques at

Carriages and horseless carriages share the Boulevard below Sutro Heights.

historical sites. Active in both the state's bicentennial celebration and that of the nation, the Society lent a number of its most cherished objects, among them Mariano Vallejo's chest of traveling silver and the famed Bigler diary page recording the discovery of gold, to the American Freedom Train that carried them to communities throughout the United States.

Today The Society of California Pioneers is planning expansion of

Pioneer Hall to better house its library. This and all its other historical activities carry out its founders' mandate, transmitting the traditions of the state's earliest settlers to present and future generations.

—*J. Roger Jobson*

The ABM story

Give me a lever and a place to stand, and I will move the Earth. *Archimedes.*

Making his weary way along San Francisco's Fillmore Street in 1909, Morris Rosenberg was a man without a lever or an idea any grander than finding a job. The entire country was momentarily paralyzed by a financial panic, and the once-successful son of immigrant parents was unemployed and almost broke. Down to his last $9, Rosenberg was fast becoming acquainted with the trials and tribulations of failure, a state of mind he had never known.

Footsore from two weeks of futile job hunting and lost in his unhappy thoughts, Rosenberg suddenly stopped on the Fillmore Street sidewalk and glanced from one shop window to another. Dirty glass and grimy storefronts greeted him at every turn. A smile came, slowly displacing the grim look he had worn for several weeks, and the man who would eventually build a giant among building maintenance companies looked down the road along which he would follow his destiny.

Without consulting his wife, Rosenberg invested half of his money in a bucket, mop, broom, brush and sponge. The following morning he returned to the hardware store where he had made his purchases, collected his goods and informed the store manager that he, Morris Rosenberg, was now in the business of washing windows. Somewhat surprised, the man gave Rosenberg his first cleaning job.

In that brief moment on Fillmore Street, Rosenberg had glimpsed his destiny. He saw a city filled with dirty windows and began a company capable of providing janitorial services to every need. Washing windows was only the beginning. What he had in mind was nothing less than revolutionary in 1909—contract cleaning for entire buildings, from bathrooms to boardrooms.

Starting with small merchants, Rosenberg worked hard and gave good service. In less than five years he had moved up from the local Fillmore Street merchants to the famed St. Francis Hotel. Prestigious clients like the Bank of America and Stanford University followed, and in the early 1920s he opened a branch office in Los Angeles. Soon after, he bought the Easterday Supply Co., and followed that by organizing the Alta Electric Co. and the American Painting and Decorating Co. The window washer of 1909 then successfully bid on the installation of electrical wiring and decorating the fabulous Fox Theater in San Francisco.

An ABM window cleaner in 1929. The only thing between him and pavement is a thin cowhide strap.

Not long after the Fox opened, the country's economy collapsed and the Great Depression hit San Francisco. Rosenberg succeeded in holding his business together and preserved the jobs of almost all his employees.

Shortly before his death in 1935, Rosenberg was awarded the electrical installation contract for the huge Bay Bridge that would link the city to Oakland. Morris Rosenberg didn't live to see the job finished, but his son Theodore took over and supervised the completion of that job, as well as the same type of work for the world-renowned Golden Gate Bridge.

Joined by his brother Sydney in the late 1930s, the sons of Morris Rosenberg steered American Building Maintenance through the war years and the postwar years, always holding close to their father's creed: "Give the customer more than the contract calls for . . ." The wisdom of that approach can be seen in the success of ABM's record. Today, ABM employs over 22,000 persons to serve more than 11,000 clients in cities and towns across the United States and Canada. The range of services provided includes janitorial services, air conditioning, building engineering, elevator maintenance, lighting, parking, plant rental, pest control, security—all of which began with a mop, a broom and a brush and Morris Rosenberg's vision.

ABM's steam cleaning truck attracted crowds of onlookers when it was first used in San Francisco in the early 1930s.

Innovative responses to client needs fueled growth of Bay Area's largest accounting/consulting firm

Although it was the last Big Eight accounting firm to establish a practice in the Bay Area, Arthur Andersen & Co. has earned a significant and impressive position in the northern California market over the last half-century.

Operating from a base in San Francisco's One Market Plaza, the firm provides auditing, tax, special accounting, information systems and financial consulting services to several thousand Bay Area clients. An Oakland office serves East Bay clients, and a high-tech-oriented office in San Jose serves a mushrooming roster of clients along the booming Silicon Valley area. Altogether, the accounting and consulting firm has approximately 750 personnel to serve the vigorous, diversified northern California market. The firm serves more publicly held companies in California and the United States than any other accounting firm.

The explosive growth of Arthur Andersen & Co. was triggered in large measure by the sustained economic boom that swept the Bay Area following World War II. Although Arthur Andersen had been a part of the San Francisco business community for two decades, it ranked tenth in size in the local market in the late 1940s. By the early 1960s, however, Arthur Andersen had become the area's largest accounting/consulting firm.

One key to the rapid growth over the last three-plus decades has been the conjunction of the market's need for highly sophisticated financial and management information systems and Arthur Andersen's ability to work with Bay Area companies to design and implement those systems. Apart from the firm's extensive work with financial, industrial, regulated utility and health care organizations, Arthur Andersen & Co. has completed a large number of highly significant engagements in the public sector.

One of the first such engagements involved the design and installation of the improved management reporting and control system for the National Aeronautics and Space

Arthur Andersen personnel examine a sophisticated display panel in the control room of Pacific Gas & Electric Co.

Administration's Ames Research Center. More recently, Arthur Andersen undertook the pioneering task of determining the real economic impact of downtown business development. That study has drawn wide scrutiny by the nation's municipalities, and similar studies are now planned for several U.S. cities.

In early 1983, the firm completed another first-ever project—helping a blue-ribbon management committee develop an innovative strategic plan for the city of San Francisco. A broadly experienced Arthur Andersen consulting team adapted its expertise in strategic business planning to the unique needs of the public sector, performed much of the necessary analytical work and provided both leadership and staff support throughout the eighteen-month project.

Among the factors that have enabled Arthur Andersen & Co. to establish and maintain leadership in the northern California market, is the decision made years ago that always striving to be the best in its profession was not enough. The firm also had to be the best in planning the development of its resources and skills. Consequently, the firm devised

a strategy of identifying new factors that would have a significant impact on the local business community. From that point on, its strategy has been to anticipate the impact of changing economic conditions and to help its clients respond to change before anyone else.

Another reason for the firm's success has been its ability to sustain a highly productive recruiting program at area universities, resulting in the hiring of many of the schools' top graduates.

Arthur Andersen & Co. is proud of its record of providing timely and innovative responses to a broad range of client needs. The firm's special ability to understand business problems and devise creative and practical solutions has been the most influential factor in its growth from also-ran status to leadership in the accounting and consulting field in the dynamic Bay Area business environment.

The firm is solidly entrenched in the social as well as business fabric of the community. Arthur Andersen personnel invest substantial time and creative effort in Bay Area civic, cultural and charitable organizations. The firm is deeply committed to using its special skills to help strengthen the communities that sustain it, believing that is an obligation that goes with leadership.

A worldwide financial institution with San Francisco roots

The story of Bank of America NT&SA begins on the morning of October 17, 1904, when a small neighborhood bank opened for business in a remodeled tavern at Washington Street and Columbus Avenue in the North Beach area of San Francisco.

The prime mover behind the bank was a man with a big idea. The man—Amadeo Peter Giannini, the California-born son of immigrant parents. The idea—a revolutionary-for-the-times philosophy to offer wage earners and small businessmen the banking services traditionally reserved for wealthy individuals and large businesses.

Giannini had worked since his early teens for L. Scatena and Company, his stepfather's wholesale produce business in San Francisco. So successful was A.P. in the produce business that Scatena made him a partner at age 21, with a half-interest in the company.

At 31, Giannini retired and shortly thereafter assumed his father-in-law's position on the board of the Columbus Savings and Loan Society. It was a small, conservative bank, with a policy of making loans only to wealthy customers. But A.P. had visions of a more aggressive bank— one that would actively seek the business of the thousands of immigrants coming to San Francisco each year. Most were laborers, but to Giannini the vigor and enterprise of the newcomers presaged their future success. The directors of the Columbus had no wish to change, so Giannini decided to start his own bank.

Twenty-eight new accounts and $8,780 in deposits were received that first day by the Bank of Italy (the name of the organization until 1930). Through hard work, long hours, and door-to-door solicitations, Giannini was able to attract the deposits of people who had never used banking services before and was willing to back them with small loans to start businesses or build homes for their families. By the end of 1904, the little bank showed deposits of $703,024 and resources in excess of $1 million.

Dedication ceremonies at Bank of Italy's One Powell Street headquarters, June 1921. A.P. Giannini is in the center of the front row.

Disaster struck in April 1906, when San Francisco was torn apart and gutted by the worst earthquake and fire in the city's history. As the flames swept toward the bank, Giannini loaded $80,000 cash into wagons and moved it to his San Mateo home for safekeeping. While others were despondent, Giannini saw that immediate action was needed to start rebuilding the city. Within days, he was dispensing loans from a plank-and-barrel counter near the waterfront with only character as collateral, seasoning each advance with his personal dedication to create a better city.

As the new San Francisco rose from the rubble, the young bank grew and prospered. Sound management, sparked by Giannini's imagination and optimism, steered it safely through the banking panic of 1907. In that year the bank's first branch was opened in the Mission District of San Francisco, and in 1909, the first out-of-town branch was opened in San Jose, 50 miles to the south.

Giannini felt strongly that the primary mission of his bank was to bring the benefits of constructive banking services to all segments of the community, and consistent with this was his advocacy of branch

banking. He believed in the virtues of a branch system—the ability to accumulate small deposits from many branches into an immense capital base and then to put these resources to work wherever needed throughout the system. He saw California, with its latent economic potential and great diversity, as a setting that would benefit enormously from the application of this concept.

Despite considerable opposition, Bank of Italy grew rapidly throughout California during the teens and twenties, both by opening new branches and by acquiring other banking institutions. The young bank took a leadership role in lending to the fledgling movie industry, backing such luminaries as Charlie Chaplin, Cecil B. DeMille and Walt Disney. Giannini also put his expertise in the produce business to work in devising new approaches for agricultural credit, and by the mid-1920s, Bank of Italy was the largest lender to agriculture statewide.

In San Francisco, the bank absorbed a number of smaller banks, many of which, like Bank of Italy,

Young depositors at Bank of Italy's Park Presidio branch, San Francisco, 1922.

had begun by serving one or another of San Francisco's ethnic communities. In 1930, Bank of Italy (by then known as Bank of America) acquired the French-American Bank, whose own history in San Francisco dated to 1860, when it was opened as the French Mutual Provident Savings and Loan Society. The French-American Bank had opened its "Oriental" branch in Chinatown in 1923; this is now known as Bank of America's Chinatown branch.

Giannini had a strong sense of civic responsibility, which showed itself time and again in his actions and the bank's. For example, Bank of Italy and Giannini played a key role in the financing of San Francisco's water system in the late 1920s. When the construction of the Hetch Hetchy aqueduct and water system was well underway, it stalled when two critical bond issues needed to continue the project could not be sold in late 1929 due to a weak bond market. In December of that year, the bank stepped forward to purchase $4 million in bonds which provided the

city funds needed to continue work on the Hetch Hetchy aqueduct. At about the same time, it agreed to lead a syndicate to purchase $41 million in bonds issued for the purchase of the Spring Valley Water Company and its key Peninsula reservoirs.

A.P. Giannini and Bank of America also played a critical role in the construction of San Francisco's most enduring landmark—the Golden Gate Bridge. In the decade preceding construction of the bridge in 1933, progress on the project was slow. Despite popular support, opposition from ferry owners and other interests had to be overcome and a legislative structure had to be put in place. In 1930 the key bond election to finance construction of the bridge passed handily, and the district was authorized to issue $35 million of bonds to finance construction.

Continued legal challenges arose, however, which delayed the issue into 1932. With the Depression deepening and the bond market weak, the project appeared to be stalled. Joseph Strauss, chief

engineer, appealed directly to A.P. Giannini; his response was, "California needs that bridge. We'll buy the bonds." As a result, the district was able to continue to meet its immediate operating expenses, and in January 1933, construction of the bridge began. Strauss was later to say that without the bank's support, the bridge would not have been built.

Under Giannini's leadership, Bank of America continued to grow and in 1945 overtook New York's Chase National Bank as the world's largest bank in both deposits and resources. After World War II the bank not only continued to build its California base but expanded strongly overseas as the world economy grew during the 1950s and 1960s. Today, in addition to Bank of America NT&SA, still the world's largest commercial bank, BankAmerica Corporation subsidiaries are active in discount brokerage, mortgage banking, computer leasing, travelers cheques and consumer finance.

While Bank of America has a commanding presence around the world with operations in more than 90 countries, its roots remain firmly in San Francisco. Bank of America World Headquarters—a 52-story facility opened in 1969 which dominates the Financial District skyline—is the administrative center of the bank. More than 16,000 employees work here, in other downtown office buildings, in the bank's northern California data center and in 60 branches scattered throughout the city's neighborhoods. And just as the bank's physical presence is still centered in San Francisco, the commitment to service and to innovative leadership in meeting people's needs which characterized A.P. Giannini's approach to banking is still very much at the core of the bank's philosophy today.

From daring experiment to major medical center

When Children's Hospital began in 1875 as the Pacific Dispensary for Women and Children in $30-a-month "suitable rooms" at 520 Taylor Street, the undertaking was a daring experiment. At the time, women fortunate enough to be admitted to medical schools were not always as fortunate in securing internships. Doctors Charlotte Blake Brown and Martha Bucknell, along with ten San Francisco women, bettered this situation by founding an institution to further the advancement of women in the practice of medicine, to educate nurses and to provide medical and surgical care for women and children.

An all-woman board of directors was formed, and articles of incorporation were drawn up. After numerous moves, a two-story frame structure was built "way out in the sand dunes" on California near Maple. Gradually the entire block around the main building was acquired, and the hospital expanded to include a maternity cottage, a nurses' home and two circular brick buildings on Sacramento Street—the "Little Jim" building for crippled children and the "Eye and Ear" building.

The history and growth of Children's Hospital are interwoven with the history and growth of San Francisco. A male board of trustees of prominent businessmen was chosen to serve in an advisory capacity on financial matters. One of the first trustees was Andrew S. Hallidie, inventor of the cable car. William B. Ralston, builder of the Palace Hotel, and Charles Crocker of the Big Four were made life members of the corporation. The names of Stanford, Flood, Bothin, Sutro, Ghirardelli, Haas, Fuller, Sloss and many others are written in the records of both the hospital and the city.

During the earthquake and fire of 1906, the main hospital was severely damaged. In less than half an hour all patients were removed to the round brick building in the rear. Debris was cleared from the first floor

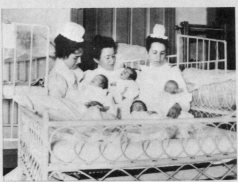

Nurses in the Alexander Maternity Cottage, opened in 1892, proudly show off the first newborns to occupy the famous white wicker cribs. The Cottage had 24 beds and was the gift of Mrs. Charles B. Alexander, the former Harriet Crocker of San Francisco.

From left to right: Eye and Ear, Little Jim, Main Hospital and Alexander Maternity Cottage in 1897. Fund-raising for both round brick buildings on the left was spearheaded by the San Francisco Examiner, with great success.

of the main building to receive emergency patients from downtown.

The damaged frame building was torn down, and in 1911 a new main hospital was dedicated. William Randolph Hearst donated a Contagious Disease Pavilion in 1912, in honor of his mother. Erected at the corner of California and Cherry streets, it was the only facility of its kind in San Francisco.

Children's was the first hospital in the West to install an iron lung. During the '30s and '40s, the hospital was the major center west of the Rockies for the treatment of polio. In 1955 the board decided to admit adult male patients, paving the way to become an acute care general hospital serving the San Francisco community.

From its beginning, Children's trained young physicians, believing that medical education in a hospital setting improved patient care. In 1969 the hospital became a major affiliate of the University of California School of Medicine, the only private, non-sectarian, acute care general hospital

on the West Coast to hold such status.

The transformation of Children's Hospital into a major, 382-bed university-affiliated medical center is a story of overwhelming community support, steady growth and continuous response to changing community needs. Children's today serves a wide range of health care needs of adults and children, yet still retains its special mission to women and children.

Primary medical care, along with numerous medical and surgical specialties and sub-specialties, is provided. Comprehensive cancer services as well as cancer research, education, information and referral, and patient support groups round out the program.

Children's reputation in the area of normal and high-risk maternity and nursery services is well-known and highly regarded. The State of California in 1981 designated Children's a Level 3 (the highest) Perinatal Center for the care of high-risk mothers and infants. Family-centered childbirth is emphasized.

Pediatric services for the critically ill serve Bay Area youngsters as well as children from throughout Northern California who need careful monitoring and intensive care. Patients with neuromuscular diseases come to Children's Hospital from all over the country.

The board established the first private hospital prepaid health plan in 1975. Subscribers numbering 10,000 receive primary health care in the areas of adult medicine, obstetrics and pediatrics, as well as specialty services and hospitalization where needed.

Times change, but Children's Hospital, more than a century after its founding, continues to conquer new frontiers with the courage and daring characteristic of its early founders.

A diversified international food company

"It was gold in the hills that first drew the settlers to California, but they soon discovered the more lasting wealth of its rich soil and wonderful climate. Long before the transcontinental railway was built. . . the founders of the DEL MONTE business were already in California, canning and preserving the golden harvests of its most fertile valleys. They were the first in the field. . ."
—Del Monte advertisement
Pictorial Review, March 1919

One of the first California canners was a young Bostonian named Francis Cutting. Around 1860 he rented space on Sacramento Street in San Francisco and began packing pickles, cider, vinegar and other preserved foods. The business grew and prospered, eventually being absorbed into one of four canning companies that merged in 1916 to form the California Packing Corporation, Del Monte's corporate name until 1967.

Through Cutting and other pioneer packers who had become a part of the four merging companies, the roots of Del Monte's business can be traced to the very beginnings of canning on the Pacific Coast.

The merged organization, with headquarters in San Francisco and a string of 71 canneries and fruit-packing plants, was the largest factor in the California canning industry, which in turn dominated U.S. marketing of canned fruits.

Within a year of its incorporation, the new company began expanding, acquiring canneries in Utah and a pineapple business in Hawaii. Further growth followed in the 1920s as the company added vegetable canneries in the Midwest and started up its first foreign production with a pineapple operation in the Philippines.

Marketing also was a major focus of the newly founded company. In fact, within a decade of its incorporation, the company made one of its most significant contributions—the national marketing

The Cannery, a shopping and entertainment complex on Fisherman's Wharf, in 1920 when it was a Del Monte peach cannery, once the world's largest.

of canned foods under a single, premium label that consumers could trust for consistent quality. The innovative marketing strategy was launched with a full-page ad in *The Saturday Evening Post* of April 21, 1917—the first national ad by a canner. It promoted "California's finest fruits and vegetables," marketed exclusively under the DEL MONTE label.

To ensure that promised quality was delivered, the company initiated quality controls, production standards and agricultural and scientific research programs that came to serve as models for the canning industry.

Following World War II, Del Monte entered can manufacturing to supply its own containers, assumed a controlling interest in Canadian Canners Limited and established a broker network serving 60 foreign nations.

A full-page color ad in a 1917 issue of The Saturday Evening Post *launched the first national marketing program by a canner.*

Foreign operations were accelerated in the 1960s as Del Monte purchased or built facilities in six countries. At the same time, the company was diversifying into such non-canning businesses as fresh fruit and frozen prepared foods.

A major milestone was passed in 1979 when the company became a wholly owned subsidiary of R.J. Reynolds Industries, Inc. of Winston-Salem, North Carolina, whose foods business included such popular brands as Hawaiian Punch, Chun King and Patio. Del Monte blended its food businesses with those of its new parent and, in 1981, added Morton Frozen Foods.

Acquiring Heublein in 1982, RJR established a Food and Beverage Group consisting of Del Monte, Heublein Spirits & Wine Company and Kentucky Fried Chicken Corporation. Added to Del Monte's lines were such established Heublein products as A.1. Steak Sauce, Grey Poupon Mustard and Ortega Mexican Foods.

Del Monte long has been a leader in providing information to consumers. In 1936 it pioneered a labeling format that gave a detailed description of what consumers would find in a can of fruit. And in 1972 it became the first U.S. canner voluntarily to adopt nutrient labeling. The company took a leadership role again in 1982 by voluntarily listing sodium content of canned foods on the nutrient panel and introducing a line of vegetables with no salt added.

Today's Del Monte, employing more than 1,000 persons in its San Francisco headquarters, is one of the world's largest marketers of foods and beverages, with 1982 sales and revenues of $2.3 billion. Directly or through subsidiaries and affiliates, the company markets products in over 60 nations from production facilities and sources it maintains in fifteen countries. The worldwide business is conducted from One Market Plaza, only a few blocks from where it all began more than a century ago.

A retail tradition

More than 100 years ago, when San Francisco was a thriving boom town and the cultural center of the West Coast, a retail enterprise opened its doors for the first time, beginning what would become "California's Largest, America's Grandest, Department Store." The business that was founded in 1872 did not yet bear the name, "The Emporium." In fact, the predecessor of The Emporium was not even a department store—rather, it was a dry goods establishment called the Golden Rule Bazaar and was not even located on the current Market Street site.

In 1872, Emporium-Capwell's current site was the campus of St. Ignatius College. The college moved in the 1880s because the downtown area was getting too crowded and noisy for study, and the way was open for the construction of "The Grandest Mercantile Building in the World." The building that opened May 25, 1896 was a seven-story skyscraper. With its bandstand and restaurant under the Grand Dome, "The Emporium and Golden Rule Bazaar" became an important downtown social center, as well as the paramount California department store. The Emporium was the first West Coast store to send buyers back to the New York markets.

Early in the morning of April 18, 1906, a devastating earthquake struck

The temporary home of The Emporium, in the home of one of the firm's stockholders, was ready almost immediately following the 1906 disaster.

the San Francisco Bay Area, leveling many buildings and rupturing water and gas mains. Many fires began, and with no water available to extinguish them, quickly spread throughout the city. The Emporium, which had withstood the earthquake fairly well, fell victim to the Great Fire. All that remained standing was the seven-story front facade. No merchandise and very few of the firm's records were salvaged. However, the Emporium opened again for business almost immediately, taking over the entire Van Ness Avenue home of one of the firm's stockholders. Because the store had buyers in New York, it took only two weeks for new stocks of merchandise to arrive at the makeshift store.

Rebuilding of the Market Street store began almost immediately after the ashes cooled. It was decided to keep the standing facade wall and construct a newer, more magnificent version of the same seven-story structure behind it. The reconstruction was complete in every detail,

The wonderful bandstand and restaurant under the Great Dome of The Emporium, 1905. The Dome soared seven stories.

including a magnificent mahogany bandstand and restaurant in the center of an even grander glass dome. On October 1, 1908, the new building was opened and the public was invited to "come through the portals of the past into the store of the present."

With the '20s and '30s came tremendous growth in the East Bay Area and massive steel bridges spanned the Bay. The Emporium expanded by purchasing the H.C. Capwell Company in Oakland. Capwell's had always been the leader in the Oakland community, and with this expansion, the two largest and most prestigious department stores in the Bay Area combined to offer the best quality merchandise and service for their customers.

Throughout the next several decades, The Emporium and Capwell's mounted aggressive expansion programs to keep abreast of the rapid growth in the San Francisco Bay Area. BART (the Bay Area Rapid Transit system) became an integral part of the downtown San Francisco and Oakland stores with station stops of the subway in the lower levels of each store. To more effectively and efficiently serve the ever-expanding Greater Bay Area, The Emporium and Capwell's consolidated in May 1980, reflecting that change in the new name, Emporium-Capwell. The aggressive expansion program has continued with the addition of the 21st Emporium-Capwell store at Solano Mall in Fairfield, California, in February 1983.

A pacesetter in merchandising, Emporium-Capwell has been a good neighbor to the community as well. From the vigorous War Bond drives of World War II to the enthusiastic support of major museum exhibitions, the company has provided financial support and expertise to many cultural and civic organizations.

With a rich heritage molded in San Francisco's history and a dominant presence in today's community, Emporium-Capwell is eagerly looking forward to an exciting future as the Greater San Francisco Bay Area's "good neighbor."

The Grand Old Lady of Nob Hill

The Fairmont Hotel, San Francisco, circa 1907.

The Fairmont Hotel was conceived by Hermann Oelrichs, son-in-law of Senator James D. "Bonanza Jim" Fair of the Comstock, one of San Francisco's first mining barons. Oelrichs, who was married to the former Theresa Fair, selected the Nob Hill site despite the critics who said it was much too far from the center of the city. Construction began in 1902.

The architects of record were the Reid Brothers, and the Fairmont Hotel—with stately columns inside and out and a lovely promenade area facing Powell Street—was scheduled to be opened in 1906.

However, this plan was not to be, for San Francisco was dealt the double blow of fire and earthquake the morning of April 18, 1906.

The Fairmont frame withstood the quake, but the fire swept through the foyer—which was then a massive hall—eating up crates of furnishings in its path. The interior was so badly gutted that work had to begin all over again.

One year later, Mrs. Oelrichs was present at the civic banquet held in the Gold Ballroom which formally opened the Fairmont Hotel as an example of the rebirth of San Francisco. Only 300 of the 500 rooms were ready for occupancy.

The life of the hotel was centered in the spacious foyer approached through the massive stone and marble carriage entrance on Mason Street. Inside the lobby rooms, and completely encircling the inner Laurel Court, was a continuous promenade hall, nearly three blocks long.

The Oelrichs family relinquished title to the hotel in 1924 when it was purchased by hotelman D.M. Linnard. After a brief succession of owners, it was purchased in 1945 by Benjamin H. Swig and his partner J.D. Weiler of New York.

The Fairmont Hotel has been operated by the Swigs since then. The concept of the new 22-story Tower addition had been stored in Ben Swig's mind for almost ten years, when the advent of the jet age—plus the healthy population and industrial growth of the San Francisco Bay area—triggered him into action. The November 1961 completion of the multimillion dollar project provided an additional 252 air-conditioned rooms for a total of 700. Atop the Tower was built the spectacular Fairmont Crown, reached by an outside, glass-enclosed Skylift, with its unsurpassed panoramic view of the Bay.

In 1947, Richard L. Swig joined his father Benjamin in the family-owned Fairmont Hotel in San Francisco. He quickly learned every aspect of the hotel's operations and was promoted to president and managing director in 1953. Since that time, he has spearheaded an active acquisition plan; in addition to San Francisco, there are now Fairmont Hotels in Dallas, Denver and New Orleans.

In July 1982, the Swig Investment Company purchased all outstanding stock of the Fairmont Hotel Company, making it the sole owner of the luxury hotel group. Prior to this transaction, the Swig Investment Company held 50 percent of stock in the hotel company, while the remaining 50 percent was held by a New York investment company. This transaction assured the Swig family the ability to provide the finest luxury services and accommodations—a tradition with the Fairmont Hotels—as well as the opportunity to engage in an expansion program.

Lobby of the Fairmont Hotel, circa 1910.

Twelve decades of taking risks

San Francisco burned down five times between 1849 and 1851, the victim of casual architecture, prevailing winds and high spirits.

To Eastern insurance companies of the day, the town was looked upon as a jerry-built Gold Rush backwater with a transient and irresponsible populace. To some of the more venturesome foreign underwriters, it was a primitive outpost where cautious commitment could turn a modest profit.

Even by 1863, protection for serious construction was hard to come by, and community-minded citizens were frustrated in their efforts to attract new capital and build an enduring city on the shores of the Bay.

Firefighting, after all, was left to volunteer organizations—men's clubs, if you will—whose members banded together for reasons of political conviction or place of origin. Fierce rivalries between those groups often worked to the advantage of the blaze, one company waylaying another in a light-hearted effort to be first at the fire.

It was an enterprising sea captain who conceived the idea of founding a home-grown fire insurance company. He proposed that ten percent of the profits of such a company go each year to the benefit fund of the volunteer firemen, thus increasing their diligence in quenching flames erupting from company-insured buildings.

The flinty merchants and businessmen who heard the captain's proposal saw in it the dual appeal of a solution to their needs for insurance protection and the possibility of making a profit in the bargain. They eagerly pledged their support.

The firm was incorporated as the Fireman's Fund Insurance Company. It opened its doors May 6, 1863 with two employees behind its counter, the redoubtable captain at the helm and on its board of directors, some of the most prestigious names in California, as well as an impressive

Early Fireman's Fund building at California and Sansome streets.

number of volunteer firemen.

From the outset, the fledgling enterprise was a resounding success. Loyal San Franciscans flocked to place insurance and to display the distinctive firemark which was used to flag company-insured structures for the benefit of the volunteers.

For many good and sound reasons the arrangement with the firemen was soon terminated by a lump-sum payment of $5,000 in gold coin, and the captain moved on to other pursuits. Yet throughout the changes of those early days and all the changes since, the colorful name has endured, a respected part of San Francisco's history.

In 1867 it became legal for fire insurance companies to engage in the sale of ocean marine insurance. The Fireman's Fund, with less than four years of underwriting experience under its belt, was cocky enough to plunge right into that line of business.

Sitting at the edge of one of the world's busiest and fastest-growing natural harbors, the company soon gained its sea legs and was writing a healthy amount of insurance on ships and their cargoes from around the world.

The Fireman's Fund showed its adventurous spirit in another way by reversing the expansion trend of the day — it moved from West to East when appointing agencies and representatives. So successful was this effort that the company was a well-established underwriter in Chicago in 1871 when that city fell to one of history's most devastating conflagrations. The young company's losses far exceeded its assets. Its president traveled to the scene and pledged payment. San Francisco shareholders paid an assessment and each claim was honored.

Many older, more established insurers defaulted on their Chicago obligations and closed their doors forever. The fact that the young Fireman's Fund, a Far Western upstart, paid dollar for dollar brought to it a flood of national publicity and a spate of new agents eager to display the sign and sell the policies of a company with such dramatic proof of reliability.

The Chicago fire, in fact, marked a turning point in the fortunes of Fireman's Fund. From then on, the company grew steadily and profitably under the direction of some of the outstanding leaders in Western business. It expanded its agency plant, pioneered new coverages for California's burgeoning agricultural community and fashioned ways to handle the special needs of the Alaskan fishing fleets and the imperiled oil-seeking whalers of New England. It covered the heavy gold shipments from the Yukon and issued policies on the railroads probing westward.

By the early 1900s, the Fireman's Fund was an acknowledged leader and innovator in the industry. It had absorbed many another fledgling Western insurer and was experimenting daringly with transportation policies, seeking to cover motorcars— even if they traveled out of their home states. It was a respected force in its always-bustling home city and a creative underwriter of national note.

A few minutes after 5 a.m. on April 18, 1906, San Francisco was jolted awake by a great wrenching of the earth. Buildings throughout the city tilted or collapsed, and gas and water lines were ruptured. And even as people tumbled from their beds in

Flames march unchecked up California Street in 1906 as firemen stand by helplessly without water. The Fireman's Fund building (right) was the next to be consumed by the blaze.

Market Street viewed from the Ferry Building Tower after the 1906 earthquake and fire.

the first moments after the quake, the smell of smoke wafted through narrow alleys. Fire began to prowl unchecked through the heart of the city. Firemen, powerless without water, could not halt the flames. The fire chief himself had been killed when the walls of his home fell in around him. Fireman's Fund was ruined, literally and figuratively. Its head office at California and Sansome streets was a charred skeleton. All of its records had perished. Its total liability took days to determine, the accounting impeded by the dark knowledge that never in history had an insurance company survived such a calamity in its home city. The more than $11 million in claims, unimaginable in terms of the dollars of that day, exceeded any possibility of payment.

Fireman's Fund survived. It did so because its shareholders, its policyholders, its employees and the general citizenry of San Francisco willed the resurgence of the city and its institutions. Survival meant months of frustrating negotiation and compromise as plans were proposed, then discarded. And it meant faith enough on the part of claimants to accept half their payment in stock of the almost-defunct company. It has been said that the miraculous recovery of the city and its commerce could have happened nowhere else but in a determined, unconventional place like San Francisco.

After 1906, Fireman's Fund was never seriously threatened by another catastrophe. It moved forward within the United States and, to the north, in Canada. It joined with other leading U.S. insurers to form associations that carried American insurance abroad with the country's business and industrial interests. It acquired other carriers to broaden its underwriting scope and strengthen its servicing facilities.

Long before its peers, Fireman's Fund reorganized itself as a holding company to permit entry into fields other than insurance. And in 1968, it became part of the distinguished American Express Company family, a compatible union that positioned the combined enterprise as a leader in the field of financial services, where opportunities still are unfolding rapidly today.

Fireman's Fund is now the nation's tenth largest property-liability insurer and provides life insurance, as well, for the business and personal account. It is on the leading edge of the economies and efficiencies automation is bringing to the industry.

The company is equally at home protecting the highly technical risk, the small business on main street, average and affluent homeowners, educational and cultural institutions, entertainment industry endeavors throughout the world, thousands of workers and millions of vehicles, including some that have ventured into space.

With roots still deep in the Bay Area, Fireman's Fund is a presence in major cities around the country and throughout the world. That kind of scope certainly justifies the faith and vision of the California pioneers who decided to take a chance and gamble with the formation of a little San Francisco-based insurance company more than 120 years ago.

185

An impossible dream come true

Dreams have spurred and captivated America since its inception. Owning a successful business is the "impossible dream" for any immigrant, and only in America have so many been given a chance to turn their dreams into reality. For one German immigrant in San Francisco during the 1870s, the impossible dream came true.

His name was Joseph Forderer and he was a sheet metal artisan. In 1873 he was awarded the contract to manufacture two miles of cornices for the Napa State Hospital. During the completion of this project he became so enamored with the beauty of San Francisco that he decided to stay. In 1875 he opened a shop located south of Market at 68 Natoma Street.

Forderer began producing cornices and other ornamental zinc and bronze stampings that were renowned for their intricate detail and fine workmanship. In 1880, at the Oregon State Fair, a Forderer Cornice Works entry won the gold medal for the best galvanized iron work. Some of the firm's early work includes the copper tower on the San Francisco Chronicle Building and the bronze dome on the city hall. Forderer did not limit his company to cornices alone, and in 1890 he designed and patented a ventilated skylight which was awarded a diploma at the Sacramento State Fair. In 1891 the company was incorporated and has since remained a closely held family corporation for four generations.

In March 1906, the firm relocated to its existing Potrero Avenue location and survived the violent earthquake that shook and burned San Francisco just three weeks later. In the ensuing period, the firm expanded its product line to include fireproof windows and elevator enclosures.

Tragedy struck in 1915 when Joseph Forderer was killed in an automobile accident. The days of derby hats, leather aprons and ornamental cornices were coming to a close. Modern architecture and the Industrial Revolution were changing

Workers sporting derby hats and leather aprons relax on some of the cornices they made in 1890.

Founder Joseph Forderer about to depart on business.

the face of America's cities and Forderer Cornice Works.

Shortly after Joseph's death, his eldest son, George, was elected president by the board of directors. In 1925 he began to switch the firm's emphasis to hollow metal doors and frames. In 1930 the last cornice was manufactured and the Great Depression was starting to squeeze the firm. In 1932 George's sudden death shocked the firm and the family.

A young and determined Arthur Forderer (George's younger brother) took over under unfavorable conditions. With construction almost nonexistent during the Depression, Arthur turned to building refrigerators, concrete wire accessories and rolled steel trim. His courage brought

the firm through the very trying period of the 1930s.

Events turned brighter for the company during World War II and the postwar building boom. During the war, the firm did its part by producing accessories for the Navy. As the troops returned home, the building industry, which had been restrained by the Depression and the war, exploded. The luxury of a strong supplier's market allowed for capital improvements needed to offset increasing union demands. Some of the notable work done during this period includes the hollow metal work for Candlestick Park and windows for the addition to the Standard Oil Building in San Francisco.

In 1963 Arthur died of a heart attack and his son Arthur Jr. has ushered the company into the modern age. A stocking division of standard doors and frames was established to complement the firm's manufacturing division. Forderer's emphasis on metal doors and frames continues, as does the family tradition of meticulous attention to detail and quality that was started by Joseph Forderer over 100 years ago.

Providing health care to San Francisco for more than a century.

The second German Hospital had no near neighbors when it opened in 1878 and for years afterwards. The gentlemen in the black bowler hats and a gaslight on the lamppost at left date this view as belonging to the 1890s.

The rather modest beginnings of today's Ralph K. Davies Medical Center were made in 1852 by a group of public-spirited men who had come to San Francisco from the German-speaking countries of Europe. Known as the German General Benevolent Society, this group organized itself out of concern for fellow Germans in need of help. For while these were the heady days of Gold Rush fever when great fortunes were being made, there were many others who didn't strike it rich in California but found themselves down on their luck thousands of miles from home. When such men fell ill, there was often no one to care for them.

The original aims of the Benevolent Society were "To aid the needy and the immigrant with advice and help. To procure work for those needing employment. To take care of the sick."

In 1854 the Society did just that with the purchase of a small home on Mission Street which it turned into a clinic providing free medical care to poor and ill Gold Rush immigrants. Four years later, the first German Hospital was moved into a small building on Brannan Street. The hospital grew to more than 80 beds before it was destroyed by fire in 1876. Less than two weeks later, the Society membership located a new site on which to build a much larger hospital which was necessary to accommodate the city's growing population. Bounded by Castro, Duboce, Noe and Fourteenth streets, the second German Hospital was opened in February 1878 on the very site where Ralph K. Davies Medical Center now stands.

With more than 200 beds, the new hospital was heralded as the most modern in northern California. However, it wasn't long before the Society began to debate whether it was time to replace the wooden structure with a "modern stone edifice." A decision was made to rebuild, and on October 8, 1905, the cornerstone was laid for the third German Hospital.

The devastating 1906 earthquake and fire, however, postponed further construction. Meanwhile, the second German Hospital—despite heavy damage to its facility—turned all efforts to saving the lives of earthquake victims. Records of the time indicate that 2,034 people were helped with food, clothing and relief supplies—including water drawn from the hospital's own wells. More than 1,000 patients were treated at the hospital for free.

In 1908, a tall brick-faced concrete structure—strengthened against the threat of earthquake damage—was completed.

During World War I, the hospital was renamed Franklin Hospital to commemorate the pioneering work carried out by Benjamin Franklin in the fields of medicine and science.

The next major step in building was not to be for another 50 years when construction began in 1965 on a new acute care hospital and comprehensive medical center. Planning for the new center had begun in the 1950s. The last four chairmen of the board have added significantly to the growth and development of the Medical Center. They include Richard Y. Dakin, chairman of the board of trustees until his death in an airplane accident in 1966, the late Ralph K. Davies, who succeeded him, the late Douglas W. Carver, who served from 1971 to 1982, and the current chairman, Mr. Thomas B. Crowley. The Center's Chief Executive Officer, George D. Monardo, has had the pleasure to see the growth and expansion of the Center since he became administrator in 1955.

The new medical center was to be the first in the Bay Area with an acute care facility integrated with long-term care under the same roof. This meant that chronically ill patients and others needing long-term care could receive it at lower expense while all the facilities of an acute care hospital were immediately available.

In 1968, Franklin Hospital and its diagnostic and treatment center opened, forming the nucleus of the new medical center. A medical offices building followed in 1969, the extended care wing in 1970 and the rehabilitation building in 1971. The completed medical center was dedicated in 1971 in honor of the late Ralph K. Davies. Designed to be a hospital-medical complex of connected buildings, the medical center provides services covering the entire range of care, rehabilitation and supportive therapy needed by patients.

Today, Ralph K. Davies Medical Center is a 341-bed nonprofit health care institution serving northern California. The center includes a hemodialysis unit, a comprehensive rehabilitation center, a skilled nursing facility, an orthognathic head and neck surgery service and an emergency room staffed by emergency physicians 24 hours a day.

The center is known worldwide for its pioneering work in research and the clinical application of microsurgery. In 1983, it became the first hospital in San Francisco to provide its own hospital-based ambulance service.

187

Quality care to the community since 1851

French Hospital in 1895 when it opened at its third and present location.

Gold was discovered in California in 1848 and from the four corners of the globe, immigrants swarmed into the territory. It was this magnet that attracted some 20,000 French settlers to the San Francisco Bay Area between 1849 and 1851.

Among the newly arrived Frenchmen were many who suffered from the hardships of the long journey and were unable to work. Others returned from the Placer mines in a state of physical exhaustion, without funds or friends, and unable to speak English. This distressful situation moved some of the more fortunate French residents of the city to provide assistance to their compatriots. Under the leadership of journalist Etienne Derbec, they organized a relief society, known as La Societé Française de Bienfaisance Mutuelle, to "provide for the needs of the sick, and furnish assistance to Frenchmen as well as citizens of other nationalities without resources."

A small wooden house was rented on the northeast corner of Jackson and Mason streets in San Francisco to serve as the first, twenty-bed French Hospital. Dr. D'Oliveira volunteered his professional services and five other physicians soon joined him, all serving without pay. The first patients were admitted on New Year's Eve, 1851.

In August 1853 the Societé purchased a lot on the corner of Bush and Taylor streets for $2,500. M. Huerne, a distinguished architect and engineer who had worked with de Lesseps on the Panama Canal, drew the plans, without charge, for a hospital to accommodate 60 patients. A fund drive among Societé members brought in $9,000, and the building was completed in December 1853 at a cost of $7,195.

On March 15, 1858, French Hospital moved a second time to a building on Fifth and Simmons. It was fully equipped with the latest facilities, such as "running water, ordinary baths, steam baths, and windmills to pump the water." Construction costs—which came to $33,513—were financed by the sale of bonds to Societé members. In 1868 a second story was added, bringing the bed count to 100. The hospital continued in this location for the next 27 years.

In 1895 a 170-bed facility hailed as "the most modern hospital on the Pacific Coast" was opened on the present site on Geary Boulevard, just north of Golden Gate Park. Its equipment was considered the finest obtainable, and the lush gardens and fountains added to the attractiveness of the impressive brick structure. Leading physicians from throughout the city fought for the honor of becoming staff members.

During the earthquake and fire of 1906, French Hospital played an outstanding role in the care of the injured and homeless. Equipped with its own water supply and power plant and undamaged by the earthquake, it was able to provide treatment and care for hundreds. Charity cases were taken in without payment, and the deep well on the hospital premises furnished precious drinking water to a community in need.

For 68 years the outside appearance of the hospital did not change, but extensive internal modifications were made. In 1926, twenty more beds were added to bring the bed count to 190.

By the early 1950s, however, improvements in medical technology had outstripped the building's capac-

ity to accommodate change. The occasion of the hospital's centennial celebration was used to launch a major fund drive among members of the Societé. Under the leadership of Bernard Capou and Simon Toulouse over $360,000 was raised. Escalating costs, however, forced the board of directors to abandon plans to purchase a new site and erect a new building. Instead, a phased-in building program was undertaken at the present site.

On May 4, 1963, the first building of the new French Hospital Medical Center was opened with a bed capacity of 170. In 1964, the west wing was completed bringing the bed count to 197. By 1971, both the Medical Office Building and long-term care facility were completed, concluding the first phase of the hospital's master plan and increasing the licensed beds to 297.

With over 132 years of continuous service and care, pride abounds for the many accomplishments of French Hospital. The same French Health Plan, which once insured total care for the early settlers of San Francisco, still serves qualified groups and individuals from all cultures and backgrounds in the Bay Area. French Hospital has always met the needs and challenges of medical advances, as well as the needs of a changing community. What began as a small infirmary more than a century ago has grown to be one of San Francisco's leading medical institutions.

Growing with the West

In the middle 1800s, the world was bedazzled by the discovery of gold in California. It was a powerful attraction to many who sought a new life in a young country. Even though it was a grueling trip around the horn in those days, many fortune seekers made their way to San Francisco—a bustling hub of energy, finance and optimism. It was during this mad rush in early 1860 that a young Frenchman stepped off the ship onto the docks of the Barbary Coast.

As did thousands of others, Etiénne Guittard had come to San Francisco to seek his fortune in the gold fields. Among the items he brought with him to trade for supplies was a fine French chocolate, for he had spent his early years developing his skills as a chocolate maker in his uncle's factory in France.

After securing his grub stake, he set out to search for the precious yellow metal in the mines along the foothills of the Sierras. He toiled in vain for three years before returning to San Francisco. Little did Etiénne know on this return that success was indeed close at hand. For the shop keepers with whom he had traded remembered him for his fine quality chocolate and persuaded him to seek his fortune by catering to the sweet tooth of the ever-growing San Francisco population.

Etiénne returned to Paris where he scrimped and saved enough money to buy the equipment needed for his new venture. He then returned to San Francisco, and in 1868 Guittard Chocolate opened its doors for business on Commercial Street.

Etiénne Guittard guided the company for 31 years. Although he started from scratch with only a few bags of cocoa beans, by the time of his death in 1899, Guittard Chocolate was an established enterprise with an integral role in the growth of the business community of San Francisco. After Etiénne's passing, his son, Horace C., assumed leadership and led the company to further growth. He was challenged by the great San Francisco earthquake and

Etiénne Guittard, 1838-1899.

fire. The factory, totally destroyed by the ravages of fire, like the Phoenix, was soon to be reborn. New and larger facilities were occupied and the operation gained renewed vigor. In 1921 and again in 1936, the company began to widen its influence by expanding its output with the acquisition of additional property and new and modern equipment.

Horace A. Guittard, the son of Horace C., was instrumental in bringing Guittard Chocolate Company into the modern era of automated production. In 1955 the company sold its San Francisco waterfront property to the city to make way for a new freeway. The company then built a highly sophisticated factory in nearby Burlingame, located a few minutes from San Francisco International Airport. At the time of its construction, the new factory was the most modern created in the entire country in over a quarter century. This modernization and highly organized production system is based on the continuous flow concept which allows all machinery to run full time, rather than the older, less efficient batch production method. This system enabled Guittard to more than double its production capacity. A new construction in 1965 added larger air conditioned warehousing for finished goods along with separate cocoa bean storage facilities. Guittard Chocolate has also kept pace with the rapid changes in chocolate manufacturing techniques with state-of-the-art auto-

mated equipment, an essential ingredient in today's competitive market. This constant upgrading of production capability while maintaining the utmost in quality has allowed the Guittard Chocolate Company to not only keep up with its customers' growth, but to expand into new areas.

Executive leadership in the company has remained in the Guittard Family for its entire existence. Etiénne's son, Horace C., died in 1950 and his son, Horace A. Guittard, became president that year and remains in that capacity today. Three great-grandsons of Etiénne, Jay Guittard, Terrill Timberlake and Gary Guittard, are now members of the company and, besides representing a fourth generation of continuous family operation, are an integral part of its present growth and success. Thus, from the fortunate discontent of a young Parisian gold seeker, Guittard has grown into a major chocolate producer.

Terrill Timberlake, Henry Spini, Jay Guittard, Horace Guittard, Gary Guittard.

Horace C. Guittard, 1878-1950.

Excellence in education since 1863

In 1863, 20-year-old Edward Payson Heald arrived in San Francisco from his native Maine. He quickly realized the vast growth possibilities of the area. What could he contribute to its growth? He had a fine education, including both normal and commercial school. He could teach business subjects and furnish banks, shops and offices with skilled workers. He began by teaching bookkeeping to three students in rooms at 24 Post Street.

In the following formative years, Heald pioneered commercial and technical education on the Pacific Coast, developing a philosophy of training young people in the shortest practical period, based on having them perform the duties they would be given by an employer. By 1870, Heald had established his reputation as the leading business educator in San Francisco.

A revolution hit the business office in the 1870s with the invention of the telephone, typewriter and adding machine. The introduction of shorthand brought women into business and to Heald College.

In 1875, great interest in mining in the Western states and the advance of agriculture in the Sacramento and San Joaquin valleys created a demand for training in mining and civil engineering. Heald named the new department, "The School of Engineering and Mining."

Heald remained at the Post Street location until it was destroyed by the fires that followed the 1906 earthquake. Heald and two teachers were able to rescue 26 typewriters from the burning building and buried them in what is now Union Square. With this equipment as a nucleus, Heald reopened the college fifteen days later, using his home at 1451 Franklin Street as temporary quarters until he was able to lease a building at 425 McAllister Street. Classes were conducted there until 1913 when the city fathers bought the lease and built the new City Hall. Heald moved the school into a newly constructed two-story building at Van Ness and Post where it remained until August 1983,

Typing students at Heald Business College, 24 Post Street, in 1904.

An engineering class at Heald Engineering College, 1215 Van Ness Avenue, 1914.

when the Heald Technical Division was relocated to an all new facility at Yerba Buena West.

The history of Heald Colleges has been one of continuous excellence and progress. As California grew, Heald kept pace, adding new campuses where needed and continuing to offer courses which prepared students for those fields where the greatest number of jobs were available, including such diverse occupations as gold assaying, surveying and radio broadcasting.

Today, Heald students are learning modern state-of-the-art skills in computer programming, drafting, engineering technology and the paralegal and secretarial fields—all occupations which the U.S. Department of Labor projects to have the greatest growth potential for the 1980s.

Heald has taken a number of bold steps in the past few years to make sure that it remains on the cutting edge of the job training field.

Founded five years before the University of California and 50 years before California's junior college system, Heald Colleges had relied exclusively on student tuition for its total income. After 115 years of

operating as a chain of profit-making proprietary schools, Heald converted to individual campuses of a newly chartered and fully approved nonprofit independent corporation, Heald Colleges of California.

By virtue of the nonprofit status, total tuition income from students is channeled into Heald programs, facilities, research and staff development.

Heald has progressed from a few classes conducted by a lone advocate of business education to the largest independent, nonprofit vocational training institution in California consisting of eight business schools, three technical divisions and a paralegal division.

Students come from all over the world to the technical divisions to avail themselves of advanced electronics and computer-aided drafting courses.

Heald graduates are employed by such giants of industry as Pacific Gas and Electric, Pacific Telephone, Bank of America, Standard Oil, IBM, Hewlett-Packard, General Electric and Bechtel.

In its 120-year history, Heald Colleges has had only five presidents—Edward Payson Heald, 1863-1926; Luke W. Peart, 1926-45; Albert L. Lessman, 1945-54; Clarence A. Phillips, 1954-62; and current president James E. Deitz.

The key to Heald's success is its tradition and unmitigated resolve to focus 100 percent of its educational resources on areas of high employability, a tradition that it has maintained for 120 years.

"A gentleman's library set down on a city street"

In October 1912, John Howell opened his book shop at 107 Grant Avenue. His first announcement stated his intention to "specialize in fine & rare books," and for more than seven decades that has been the objective of John Howell—Books. From medieval illuminated manuscripts to the fine printed books of the twentieth century, individual collectors and institutions have been provided the opportunity to acquire the finest works available.

Within a year of opening his shop, Howell was also publishing books by local literary contemporaries, including works of historical and bibliographical interest. By 1918 the firm had become a leading antiquarian book store on the Pacific Coast and larger quarters were needed. The shop's second location was at 328 Post Street, and here the business continued to prosper. In 1924 John Howell moved his shop for the last time, choosing 434 Post Street for the permanent address of the firm which bears his name. Architect Will C. Hays was influenced by Bernard Maybeck in his design for the shop, intended to reflect "a gentleman's library set down on a city street."

In the 1920s many collectors sought to acquire modern literature and fine bindings. During this period Howell's business continued to grow and his publishing activities increased. The Depression dealt harshly with the antiquarian book trade, and many great collectors were wiped out by their losses. It was at this time that Howell called for the help of his son, Warren R. Howell, then at Stanford University. Warren Howell had wanted to be a part of the book shop since his childhood days when he assisted with odd jobs around the store. Despite the fact that 1932 was a dismal year to begin one's career, Warren Howell came into the business with enthusiasm.

The rare book world remained in a

The bookshop of John Howell—Books.

depression until 1946, although there was fantastic activity in new books during the wartime period, and people continued to buy Californiana.

In 1950 Warren Howell became head of the firm. Under his direction the company achieved international recognition specializing in a number of fields—Western Americana and Californiana; voyages and travels; cartography; English and American literature; science and medicine; natural history; fine printing; Bibles; photography; and fine prints and paintings of the West.

Warren R. Howell, a bookman.

During the 1960s and '70s there was further development of the sales market in Europe and the Orient. Carrying on the legacy of the founder, the publishing program of the firm has continued to flourish, with publications of California interest and the rare book catalogues quickly becoming collector's items, noted for their content and fine typographical design.

An important facet of the operation of John Howell—Books is its association with many libraries, museums and historical societies. Having been a part of San Francisco cultural life for more than 70 years, Warren Howell and John Howell—Books look toward the future with renewed desire to serve book collectors and the community from "a gentleman's library set down on a city street."

From clipper ships to computer chips

The history of Johnson & Higgins is closely intertwined with the history of business insurance in the United States. As the country's oldest insurance brokerage firm, dating from the clipper ship days of the mid-nineteenth century, J&H has helped to guide the scope and character of the entire insurance community for nearly 140 years.

The company was founded in 1845 on Wall Street in New York by two young men, 24-year-olds, who started in business as marine average adjusters and insurance brokers. Because insurance companies in those days generally dealt directly with their clients, the brokerage business developed slowly at first.

But the young partners were exceptional marine adjusters. They decided how losses were to be shared when more than one party was involved in a marine incident—such as a collision, a need to jettison cargo or piracy. As the partners' reputation for arranging equitable settlements spread, shippers began to use their services as brokers to negotiate insurance terms as well.

Even before California was admitted to the Union in 1850, the territory played a substantial role in the firm's early business. Indeed, the partnership was barely three years old when news of the discovery of gold in California in 1848 reached the Eastern Seaboard. During the next few months, nearly 200 vessels sailed for California from Philadelphia, Baltimore, Boston and New York. The Gold Rush was on, and unquestionably the fledgling firm benefited greatly from the resulting marine adjusting and brokerage business.

The golden age of the American merchant marine survived the Civil War, and J&H prospered accordingly. In 1883, the firm sent James B. Dickson to the West Coast to handle transactions involving the *Queen of the Pacific*—a large new passenger steamer that had been stranded near the mouth of the Columbia River. That same year, Dickson opened the first J&H branch office in San Francisco.

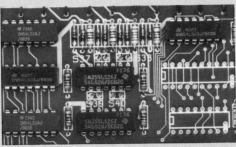

Johnson & Higgins has built a tradition of customer service from the days of the clipper ships to the high-tech business world of today.

By 1899, the Johnson & Higgins organization had been restructured as a corporation and had established a network of offices that reached from the Eastern Seaboard to the Pacific. Moreover, J&H had formed its first international connection—with Willis Faber, the leading English brokerage firm; the arrangement continues to the present day.

Shortly after the turn of the century, J&H moved its office in San Francisco from 315 California Street to number 416. And by 1905, the office had broadened its activities beyond marine insurance to handle fire insurance coverages and claims handling.

That additional capability was taxed to the utmost only a year later by the 1906 earthquake and fire. In San Francisco, property worth about $325 million was destroyed, and total claims against insurance companies exceeded $200 million. J&H employees were among the many thousands of San Franciscans dispossessed by the fire. For a brief time during the six months required to collect and conclude outstanding claims, members of the San Francisco staff operated from a tent located at 120 Battery Street.

Today, some 200 J&H employees in San Francisco occupy three full floors and part of a fourth in the International Building at 601 California Street. In previous years, the office had several other addresses on California Street, including a 39-year span in the Robert Dollar Building at number 311.

Walter H. Clemens, president of Johnson & Higgins of California since Edmond S. Gillette Jr. retired in 1981, is managing director of the San Francisco office, and a director of the parent corporation. J&H of California also has major offices in Los Angeles (second largest in the J&H worldwide system), San Diego, Riverside and Orange County.

The firm's client portfolio in San Francisco reflects the wide range of business activity in the Bay Area and in Northern California. In addition to the services it has traditionally provided for shipping interests, the office has long served companies associated with agriculture and food processing, forest products, banking and finance, and the professions—medical, dental and legal. More recently, high technology businesses have assumed increasing prominence on the J&H list of distinguished clients located in the region.

As the J&H San Francisco office celebrates its 100th anniversary, it takes particular pride in its history as a member of the California business community and in the contributions of its people to the civic, cultural and charitable life of a great American city. From clipper ships to computer chips, Johnson & Higgins values its long tradition of service in San Francisco.

Hard work and high ideals: a recipe for sweet success

Contrary to San Francisco mythology, Just Desserts' cheesecake recipe did not come from God—not directly, anyway—but from the kitchen archives of a friend's grandmother, and was presented to co-founder Elliot Hoffman on his brithday. From the home of Elliot and his wife-to-be, Gail Horvath, the cheesecake went public in a neighborhood cafe. The rest is local legend—the two sold their Volkswagen, borrowed $10,000 and, with the help of Barbara Radcliffe, a friend-turned-partner, worked eighteen-hour shifts building and baking until, in 1974, the first Just Desserts bakery opened on Church Street.

One year later, with annual gross sales exceeding $100,000, the kitchen was moved to roomier quarters on Pacific Avenue, where a second retail store was opened. A fourth partner, Jane Fay, graduate of the Cordon Bleu School in London, joined the team in 1976 to manage the kitchen, broaden the product line and streamline bakery operations. Wholesale business expanded, and in 1978 a third store opened at Three Embarcadero Center, where the downtown clientele mandated high-tech service, the Sweet Account (a business charge account) and the company's morning line— Danish, croissants and coffeecakes. In 1980 the company acquired the Edible Express, a food distributorship delivering Just Desserts' products to more than 700 wholesale clients from Santa Cruz to Sacramento.

"Crack your own eggs? Grate lemons? Peel and core your own apples? You can't run a bakery like that nowadays," scoffed the skeptics. But for imitators all over the Bay Area, Just Desserts' style became the archetype for a new generation of bakers— traditional American pastries baked each day from pure butter and fresh, natural ingredients. No mixes, no preservatives, no freezing.

Along with "the best cheesecake west of the East" and the acclaimed cakes, pies, cookies, Danish and croissants, the *coup de gratification*,

Patrons enjoying pastries and coffee.

Chocolate Velvet, became a landmark dessert. Splendid wedding and party cakes soon followed.

Just Desserts had paid its dues and was now enjoying overwhelming public success and media notice: "Best giant chocolate chip cookie"— the *Bay Guardian;* "Fantastic chocolate cake"—Herb Caen of the *San Francisco Chronicle;* "Best bakery in the City"— *The San Francisco Paper.* For those preferring their dessert with local color, Just Desserts was the place to be. "It's a great place for people watching," wrote Ruthe Stein of the *Chronicle.* "Writer Herb Gold, for instance, can be found there almost every morning, working on his latest novel."

From its inception, the company embraced an ethic of service to the community that had nurtured it. Just Desserts donates thousands of pastries to the city's needy through the St. Anthony Dining Room; it sponsors fund-raising events benefiting local theater groups and the Children's Cancer Research Institute; its walls served as free gallery space for young artists; it sponsors bake-offs for amateur bakers competing for prizes and recognition; it gave senior citizens a twenty percent discount. In 1981 the U.S. Small Business Administration named Just Desserts "Small Business Advocate of the Year," in recognition of "exemplary services to the small business community."

Just Desserts' dedication to quality established it as San Francisco's freshest tradition. Taking note of this, the retiring proprietors of an old San Francisco tradition, the Three Mills Creamery on Irving Street, encour-

aged the bakery to open a fourth store where the Three Mills had operated for over 40 years, and thus, old-fashioned soda fountain fare was added to the Just Desserts repertoire.

With an eye to the future and plans for more growth, the company found a new home in 1982—a whopping 30,000 square feet on Carroll Avenue near Candlestick Park which had been vacated by Armanino Farms. The building houses the bakery, administrative staff, Edible Express, a full-time R&D kitchen and the thousands of desserts that exit the ovens daily.

Asked if they had anticipated their company's rapid growth, the four partners respond in unison, "No!" But personal vigilance over their precocious bakery is apparently a sweet burden, judging by the frequency with which they refuse opportunities to sell out or franchise.

If Just Desserts' future is a piece of cake, it can still evoke awe in the young owners, who insist, "We just wanted to have a nice little store and bake good things."

A tempting array of desserts.

A Nob Hill landmark with a continuing dedication to luxury

The original Mark Hopkins residence, largest and most opulent of Nob Hill's palatial mansions during San Francisco's golden era. (Photo courtesy of California Historical Society, San Francisco.)

Robert Louis Stevenson wrote, "Nob Hill, the Hill of Palaces, must certainly be counted the best part of San Francisco."

It was then—with the homes of Stanford, Crocker, Fair and of Mark Hopkins on its crest—and it still is today. Of the stately mansions of the past, only the Flood Mansion, which now houses the Pacific Union Club, stands as an imposing reminder of the opulent grandeur of early Nob Hill. Now, however, Stevenson's "Hill of Palaces" is a place of elegance and charm in a different manner.

Throughout the world, the name of Mark Hopkins summons not the image of a man, but of a great hotel which has stood for over a half-century on the exact site of the gabled mansion built by the railroad tycoon for his wife. So elaborate and demanding were Hopkins' plans for his home, that his health failed and he died in 1878 before it was completed. Mrs. Hopkins lived in the ornate mansion for only two years before returning to her native Massachusetts. After her death in 1891, the home was donated to the San Francisco Art Association as a cultural center. The Hopkins house, greatest of all the Nob Hill mansions, might have survived the Great Earthquake of 1906, but it was consumed in the terrible fires which followed. Ironically, a secret half-million gallon cistern lay buried beneath which might have saved the home if anyone had known about it. Only the massive foundation remained, built from the same granite Hopkins used to bridge the Sierra canyons for his railroad. Perhaps it was the scale of these magnificent ruins which inspired the next man of vision to acquire the hilltop site.

When George D. Smith, former mining engineer, purchased the property in 1925, he incorporated a portion of the monumental stonework into his own dream. In December 1926, he opened the doors of that dream, and ushered the luxury hotel industry into the twentieth century. Smith designed and executed a startling original structure—an open-winged tower which gave every guest room a panoramic view of the city and the bay. He then furnished his hotel with the most lavish appointments available, and the results proved the wisdom of his decision. The hotel, named to honor Mark Hopkins, became the social center of the Golden Gate City. Newspapers and magazines were filled with accounts of the fashionable wedding receptions and glittering debutante balls held in the opulent Peacock Court, and the great dance bands and supper club entertainers of the era played there. Smith's brand of thoughtful bravado kept The Mark Hopkins always at the head of the pack. His introduction of the glass-walled "Top of The Mark" skyroom in 1939 was such a master stroke. The Top, with its matchless 360 degree view, quickly became the most famous cocktail lounge anywhere, and it remains today a magnet for locals and for tourists from around the globe. With its status as a world

The Mark Hopkins, world-famous hotel which continues a tradition of elegance on Nob Hill.

landmark, the Top was undoubtedly the crowning achievement of Smith's lifelong love affair with the hotel.

Eager for retirement, Smith sold the hotel in 1962 to Louis Lurie. Lurie, in turn, passed the management to a series of well-meaning proprietors, but their piecemeal redecorations lacked the mixture of affection and lucidity which had marked Smith's tenure. It became increasingly clear that if The Mark Hopkins was to remain a world-class hotel, it needed world-class management.

Inter-Continental Hotels Corporation operates over 100 of the world's most luxurious hotels in 50 countries. They agreed with The Mark Hopkins' owners that it belonged in the top ranks, and in 1974 they assumed the management. A major renovation, the most extensive in the hotel's history, was completed in the fall of 1982. The four-year, $12 million project saw complete redecoration and air conditioning of all guest rooms, upgrading of safety systems and expansion of guest services. Inter-Continental Hotels Vice President Sandor J. Stangl states that the objective of the project was, "To ensure that guests at The Mark Hopkins will be provided with the most luxurious and comfortable features and services available in the world."

If that objective was a familar ring, it may be because it hearkens back to the spirit which prompted George Smith to build the hotel in the first place, at the other end of the century.

The oldest large law firm in California

Edward J. McCutchen, 1857-1933.

The McCutchen law firm is celebrating its centennial in 1983. It was founded in 1883 when two San Francisco lawyers, Charles Page and Charles P. Eells, formed a partnership for the practice of law under the name Page & Eells at 316 California Street. The firm has been an ongoing partnership of practicing lawyers ever since. Edward J. McCutchen, whose parents were survivors of the ill-fated Donner Party, joined the partnership in 1896. Its name then became Page, McCutchen & Eells. The present name was adopted in 1958.

From its beginning as a two-man partnership the firm has grown steadily to its 1983 size of 145 lawyers, consisting of 55 partners, 2 full-time and 6 part-time counsel and 82 associates. In addition the firm has 40 legal assistants (paralegals) and a support staff of approximately 180 secretaries, accountants, computer operators, word processors, receptionists, calendar clerks, telephone operators, file keepers, printers, librarians, messengers, mail clerks and administrators. The firm is now housed in the top floors of Three Embarcadero Center.

The firm has had three branch offices. The first—possibly the first branch office of any American law firm—was established in Nome, Alaska, in 1900 to handle legal problems of clients who had invested in gold mining ventures. It was closed a few years later. The second was opened in 1929 in Los Angeles, primarily to serve the firm's admiralty clients having business in the newly created Los Angeles Harbor. This branch grew steadily in size and strength. In 1971, by mutual agreement, it became an independent law firm which is now one of the largest and strongest in Los Angeles' — McCutchen, Black, Verleger & Shea. The third branch was established in 1981 in San Jose, California, to take care of the firm's clients in Silicon Valley.

The firm provides legal services in virtually every field of the law. Its clientele includes many of the nation's leading commercial, industrial, financial, agricultural, public service and educational organizations. Some of the firm's major clients have been with it for decades.

Litigation has always been the major part of the firm's practice. In the early days there was a concentration in maritime litigation, Charles Page having been a nationally recognized expert in admiralty law. As time went on, the litigation extended into every known field. For example, the firm recovered a large judgment, affirmed by the California Supreme Court in 1915, in favor of the owners of a salt mine in Imperial County, California, that was inundated by the man-made flood which created the Salton Sea.

In more recent years the firm has been heavily involved in many newly invented species of litigation, such as product liability cases, charges of violations of the securities laws, suits involving labor relations, charges of discriminatory treatment of employees, antitrust treble-damage actions, malpractice suits, cases arising under the environmental protection laws and dealer termination cases.

In addition to its litigation team the firm has a large corporate law department; a group of experts in estate planning, trust law and probate administration; a tax and employee benefit department; specialists in the law of agricultural cooperatives and in environmental law; and a sizable and growing real estate law department. The firm does much *pro bono* work, both through the organized bar and through individual contacts.

The lawyers in the firm have been active in civic, community and educational circles and in the work of the organized bar. The firm has produced two presidents and one vice-president of the State Bar of California, five presidents of the Bar Association of San Francisco, one member of the Board of Regents of the University of California, two presidents of the Board of Trustees of Stanford University, four members and one chairman of the Mills College Board, one member of the Board of Overseers of Harvard University and two presidents of what is now the United Way of the Bay Area.

The McCutchen firm is one of the largest in California, and is the oldest of all large California firms. Its primary policy is to provide its clients with the highest quality of professional legal services at reasonable cost.

From left to right, Robert Minge Brown, Burnham Enersen, Owen Jameson and Morris M. Doyle.

After 150 years, John McKesson wouldn't know his little company

The date was April 18, 1906. A steady drone pervaded San Francisco's early morning streets as city dwellers prepared for the working day. As the drone developed into a loud rumble, the residents of the city experienced a 48-second disaster which would alter lives and history books throughout the nation. Among those inhabitants was Charles Frederick Michaels, co-owner of Langley & Michaels Co., an importer of wholesale drugs and chemicals. After the earthquake, Michaels rushed to the building on the northeast corner of Front and Pine streets. Discovering the building intact, he and a handful of employees dashed inside, retrieved the inventory records and brought them to their homes. Hours later, the building was consumed by fire.

Langley & Michaels employees gathered in front of the San Francisco building before the 1906 earthquake.

The Langley & Michaels employees worked quickly to set up tents several blocks away and reorder from the inventory sheets they had saved. As a result, the firm was able to replenish stocks and was one of the first in the city to reopen business.

Langley & Michaels became the San Francisco division of the reputable McKesson & Robbins' unique wholesale enterprise in 1928.

It was in 1833 that John McKesson, the fourth-generation scion of a distinguished colonial family, formed a partnership with Charles Olcott to import and wholesale drugs and chemicals in New York. Soon they were joined by a young assistant named Daniel Robbins, and when Olcott died in 1853 the firm was renamed McKesson & Robbins.

McKesson & Robbins' reputation journeyed west with stagecoaches and wagon trains that streamed across the country in the 1840s and 1850s. Among those in the trek was Charles Langley, who secured some of Langley & Michaels' first stock from the company in the form of gold dust.

McKesson & Robbins continued to expand its lines of proprietary products, and also became one of the first wholesale drug houses to install a drug manufacturing laboratory, which earned medals in expositions of the 1870s.

By the turn of the century, however, the company's wholesale business faced growing competition from newer firms in the Midwest, and its import business was hard-hit by high tariffs and domestic competition. By 1926, when a small, bespectacled man named F. Donald Coster purchased the company for $1 million, little remained but the McKesson & Robbins name.

Coster, who claimed a Ph.D. and M.D. from Heidelberg University, quickly earned a reputation as a financial genius for reviving the century-old drug firm. The company introduced a new line of products and had persuaded many of the nation's largest wholesalers to become McKesson & Robbins subsidiaries. The company held on through the stock market crash and the Depression that gripped the country into the next decade.

In 1933, Prohibition was repealed, and the manufacture and sale of alcoholic beverages once again was made legal. An importer of spirits since its earliest days, McKesson & Robbins quickly created the forerunner of today's Wine & Spirits Group.

In 1938, the company suffered another setback when revelations about Coster stunned Wall Street and the nation. It was discovered that several of Coster's drug divisions in Canada were actually ficticious operations designed to inflate the company's profits, and that Coster himself was an ex-convict named Philip Musica. The scandal ended shortly afterward when Musica committed suicide.

Despite the bleak episode, the company survived. In 1945, McKesson & Robbins set up a chemical distributing business to meet manufacturers' increasing needs for chemicals. In the booming postwar economy, the chemical business grew so rapidly that it was formally separated from the drug business, forming McKesson Chemical Company.

Throughout the 1950s and 1960s, the three branches of McKesson & Robbins—drugs, liquors and chemicals—continued to expand. In 1967, the company merged with Foremost Dairies, founded in 1929 by the legendary retailer James Cash Penney. Foremost had grown by acquisition into a prosperous dairy company with operations all across the nation and abroad.

Under the leadership of president and chief executive officer Thomas E. Drohan, the company divested some $225 million of assets and reinvested $650 million in new growth businesses from 1976 to 1982, which led to the selling of Foremost Dairies in 1982. On July 27, 1983, the shareholders approved the company's name change to McKesson Corporation.

Today, the company's three largest businesses—McKesson Drug, McKesson Wine & Spirits and McKesson Chemical—are the leading distributors in their industries.

It's a coincidence that the name change to McKesson Corporation occurred during the same year the company observed its founding 150 years ago by John McKesson. But it does mark the start of a new and exciting future under a name that is both new and 150 years old.

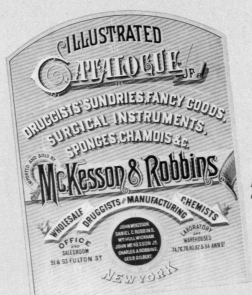

McKesson & Robbins' wholesale drug business was established in 1833.

San Francisco's largest photographic company grew up with the city

Earthquake and fire 1906.

Many have photographed the city of San Francisco throughout its history, but nowhere is there a more complete record of its growth and development over the last 100 years than in the archives of the Moulin Studios. Here are to be found, amongst others, classic photographs of the disastrous 1906 earthquake and fire, the reconstruction of the city, the building of the Golden Gate and Bay bridges and the evolution of the city's towering skyline. These photographs, however, go beyond the mere recording of events and architecture, to capture the true character of the people and landscape and the ever-changing atmosphere of the times as the city grew from a boisterous boom town to a cosmopolitan metropolis.

In 1884, when Gabriel Moulin left school at age 12 to work as a photographic assistant, the art of photography was in its infancy. By the turn of the century he was an accomplished photographer and in 1906 opened his own studio in the aftermath of the San Francisco earthquake and fire.

Both Gabriel's sons showed an early interest in photography, and by 1930 Irving and Raymond Moulin had joined their father in business. In 1933, Irving pioneered the use of photography for retail advertising in San Francisco, and by the end of the year every store in the city that used illustrated advertising was a Moulin client. Raymond, meanwhile, had just designed an aerial camera for Moulin Studios and began taking panoramic photographs of the city.

Moulin Studios was commissioned as the photographers for the construction of both the Golden Gate and the San Francisco-Oakland Bay bridges. One of Raymond's photographs of the Bay Bridge was used on a postage stamp issued in 1938.

By the late 1930s, Moulin Studios was the major force on the West Coast in commercial and portrait photography. During World War II, it worked day and night reproducing and enlarging maps and charts for the Department of Defense. Raymond traveled the United States

taking pictures for Greyhound's yearly calendars. Moulin Studios has photographed every president of the Bank of America, and Irving took the picture of A.P. Giannini that was later reproduced on a 25¢ postage stamp. In the late '30s the Moulins began to create photomurals, then coming into vogue for interior and exterior design, and in 1939 the studio was official photographer for the Golden Gate International Exposition.

Gabriel Moulin died in 1945 after more than 60 years as a photographer; in 1982, four years after his retirement, Raymond Moulin died in Hillsborough. In 1957 Irving relinquished his share of the business, and Raymond's son Thomas, who had worked with the studio since 1949, now takes the business into its third generation of Moulin photographers.

After Gabriel's death, Irving and Raymond closed the original Kearny Street studio and opened larger premises on Second Street. Thomas now runs the business from a site on Green Street.

Today Moulin Studios is still the city's largest photographic company. It is still involved in recording the yearly changes in the city, and the commercial scope of the business is more varied than ever—executive and personal portraiture, advertising, aerial photography, photo murals,

multimedia presentations, family and social functions and, more recently, videotape recordings.

In 1978 the Fine Arts Commission of San Francisco held an exhibition at the De Young Museum documenting the city's growth through the eyes of the Moulin photographers. Moulin Studios later donated part of this exhibition to the city; the photographs are now on display at the San Francisco International Airport.

Three books have been compiled using photographs from the extensive Moulin archives—*San Francisco, Creation of a City; Motor Touring in Early California* and *High Steel*. The contents of the archives are available for public viewing and print purchase, and there are continuous requests for copies of photographs used in the books and from individuals asking whether photographs are available of specific locations at specific periods or of historical events.

Thomas's wife Jean now takes a full-time role helping with the business. Their children Philip and Samantha have both developed a sensitive eye for creative photography, which will likely lead to a fourth generation of Moulin photographers in San Francisco.

A commitment to progressive, compassionate health care

Since November 4, 1882, an area of San Francisco's Pacific Heights has been dedicated to patient care, medical education and research.

That date marked the opening of Cooper Medical College on the northeast corner of Webster and Sacramento streets. It was the new home for a medical school that had been established ten years earlier by several independent-minded, progressive physicians who had broken away from the established Toland Medical School. They named their college in honor of the late Dr. Elias Samuel Cooper, another medical maverick who had founded the West's first medical school in 1854. Cooper Medical College was the predecessor to Stanford University's School of Medicine, the forerunner to today's Pacific Medical Center.

Through the continuous commitment by Pacific Medical Center and its predecessor institutions, generations of San Franciscans and patients referred from throughout the United States have received care. Pacific Medical Center annually records over 11,000 inpatient admissions and 53,000 visits to clinics and laboratories.

The main campus site, located at Clay between Buchanan and Webster streets, includes the 341-bed Presbyterian Hospital and outpatient, research, administrative and library facilities. Other locations include the 129-bed Garden Sullivan Hospital on Geary Boulevard near Masonic Avenue; outpatient and day treatment facilities for psychiatric care; and the Pacific Pyramid Health Center located in the downtown headquarters of Transamerica Corp.

Along with general medical and surgical care, specialized services include the diagnosis and treatment of heart and eye diseases in adults and children; digestive disorders; adult and children's cancer; the application of advanced imaging technology; microsurgical capabilities; progressive rehabilitation programs; organ and tissue transplantation; and psychiatric care.

At the 1882 opening of Cooper Medical College, Dr. Levi Cooper Lane, dedicated the college: "To suffering humanity and the healing art in the hope that the former may here find refuge and relief; the latter exercise of human skill and intelligent sympathy."

The college became Stanford University's School of Medicine in 1908. Nine years later, Stanford Hospital was built near Lane Hospital. In 1921, the Stanford School of Nursing opened.

In 1959, the medical and nursing schools moved to Palo Alto. But because many of the faculty physicians wished to remain in San Francisco, leading citizens representing the Presbytery of San Francisco entered into negotiations with Stan-

Dr. Levi Cooper Lane (white beard) operates in the surgical amphitheater of the new building in 1883.

ford, and on April 30, 1960, the Presbyterian Hospital and Medical Center came into existence as a unique private institution which combines private medical care with academic attention to education and research.

Pacific Medical Center was formed in 1967, providing the organizational basis for future expansion. Also that year, an affiliation was begun with Children's Hospital of San Francisco. Growth began with a merger with Callison Hospital in 1969. A new Presbyterian Hospital was opened in 1973, followed by the remodeling of the "Stanford Building" to house physicians' offices, a kidney dialysis unit, laboratories and administrative offices. The Cooper Medical College and Lane Hospital were torn down in 1974 to make room for a medical office complex featuring progressive clinical and social services.

Garden Sullivan Hospital, which joined Pacific Medical Center in 1978, offers specialized caare for acute and long-term rehabilitation and the treatment of alcoholism and drug addiction.

Other important entities include the Pacific Medical Foundation, which was established in 1980. Also the Northern California Transplant Bank at Pacific Medical Center is now among the nation's most comprehensive multi-tissue and -organ procurement centers.

To enable physician/scientists to continue research, the Medical Research Institute of San Francisco, a private organization of affiliated institutes, was established at the medical center more than 20 years ago.

In 1982 the parent company of Pacific Medical Center, Health Pacific Corporation, was formed to allow increased diversification of services and programs. This innovative structure, is a legacy to the commitments first promised through Cooper Medical College.

The future physicians who attended Cooper Medical College selected courses from this curriculum guide, which featured an illustration of the widely admired new building.

Portrait of a pioneer

Baywood was the name John Parrott chose for his 450-acre San Mateo estate. Amid rolling hills, native oak and bay trees, this wealthy financier and shipping magnate built in 1868 a home for his wife, nine children, a staff of 10, plus gardeners and a dozen or more Chinese laborers.

The vast reaches of Baywood were once included in the great Rancho de la Pulgas, a Spanish grant to that distinguished branch of the Arguello family which gave two governors to California "before the Gringo came."

The house was of modified Queen Anne Victorian design with finials rising from a balustrade that swept along the length of the second floor. The unusually symmetrical architecture and the elegant but restrained interior furnishings made an impression as dignified as was the owner himself.

Although the family also had an impressive residence in the city, it was at Baywood amid landscaped gardens and surrounded by his children that Parrott, then aged 57, lived out the active and well-ordered routine of his life.

This gracious existence was the culmination of 40 years of adventure, work and shrewd investment.

Tennessee born, John Parrott at age 18 joined his brother's mercantile and importing business at Mexico City. His passport at that time describes him as "six feet tall, hazel eyes, large mouth, pugg nose, dark hair, round face and fair of complexion." The business was successful and flourished. He was appointed United States Consul at Mazatlan from 1837 to 1846 and reappointed in 1848 until his resignation and move to San Francisco in 1850.

After leaving Mexico, but before settling permanently in San Francisco, 42-year-old Parrott traveled to Mobile, Alabama. There he met and married 24-hour-old Abby Meaher. Miss Meaher was reluctant to marry at first and so Parrott, reminiscent of his years in Mexico, engaged musicians to serenade her in front of the hotel where she and her family were staying.

It is true that many of the pioneers to California were men of restricted means and education. Some came to seek their fortune, others to make a fresh start, or in some cases to escape capture and punishment by the law of the land. None of this can be said of Parrott, however, who by 1849 with his California interests well-established from previous visits, arrived in San Francisco with a fortune. He had already proven to be a man of learning and astute business acumen.

Within a few years Parrott established a banking exchange to purchase gold dust and bullion that adventurous men were digging from the hills and panning from the Sierra streams. A partner in this venture was non other than W.B. Comstock, the man whose name lives in the annals of the West of the famed Comstock Lode.

The mid-nineteenth century on the Pacific Coast was a period of expanding commerce. California, no longer restricted by Spanish and Mexican jurisdictions, began to attract the shipping attention of the world. A notable characteristic of financier Parrott was his ability to foresee and adapt to the times. Soon sailing vessels owned or chartered by the Parrott Company sailed the trade routes; quicksilver to Hong Kong, wheat to Liverpool, rice and spices from the Orient and coffee from

Baywood, 1868-1927. Photo courtesy of Barbara Donohue Jostes.

Central and South America.

Meanwhile, John and Abby Parrott's nine children grew, attended school—here, in England and in France—traveled abroad, married, participated in the social and cultural life of the city, continued their father's business interests and had children of their own.

Today's descendants of the private and conservative Parrotts continue to be a force in the Bay Area where their lives thread through and contribute richly to the tapestry of the city, giving it continuity, color and durability.

In her definite biography about her illustrious ancestor, Barbara Donohoe Jostes tells of the death in 1884 at age 73 of John Parrott. "His had been an active life, spanning the years of early trade on the West Coast of Mexico and California; the war with Mexico and the Gold Rush. His was the age of sail, the Pony Express, the Overland Mail, the Telegraph, the first steam ships and the building of the Transcontinental Railroad.

"He experienced the devastating fires in the early years in San Francisco, the violent days that brought into being the Vigilantes, and survived the panics in the banking world. Friend of many, exacting of himself and others, John Parrott contributed to the advancement of the state and to the city of his choice."

John Parrott. Photo courtesy of Barbara Donohue Jostes.

The West's most experienced and diversified cargo-handler

Today, the Port of San Francisco is an active center of worldwide trade and the most diversified seaport on the West Coast. With over 1,000 acres of land area, 11 terminals and 40 berths—the largest number in the Bay Area—the Port has the capability of handling every type of ship and cargo. It has the only cruise ship facilities on the Bay.

Well-known as a natural, deep-water port, the Port of San Francisco extends 7.5 miles along the western shore of San Francisco Bay from Hunter's Point on the south to the world-famous Fisherman's Wharf, the number one tourist attraction in San Francisco and home of an important commercial fishing industry.

For over a century, the Port has been the crossroads of world trade and the historical port of entry and exit for Pacific cargos.

It all began in 1775 when the Spanish supply ship *San Carlos,* under the command of Lieutenant Don Manuel de Ayala, sailing up the then unknown coast of California, slipped through a narrow, tide-torn channel and into the magnificent natural harbor beyond. It was the first ship ever to drop anchor in San Francisco Bay. And from that day on, history had a new port of call.

But it wasn't until 1848 and the discovery of gold that San Francisco became a busy, bustling seaport. Nugget-hungry prospectors flooded California by the thousands. Then came the farmers, merchants and mechanics. Soon the harbor was crowded with sailing craft of every description, all in search of berthing space.

The Ferry Building in the early 1920s.

In 1863, California's legislature established the Board of State Harbor Commissioners and gave it full administrative control of the San Francisco waterfront. Control of the Port remained under the state until it was transferred to the City and County of San Francisco in 1969.

The Harbor Board's prime objective was the construction of a seawall to stabilize the city's waterfront line. This seawall, which underlies today's Embarcadero, created more than 800 acres of prime metropolitan land, including what are now San Francisco's downtown financial and commercial districts.

In 1898, San Francisco celebrated the opening of the Ferry Building at the foot of Market Street. It, like the rest of the waterfront, escaped virtually unscathed the 1906 earthquake and fire which destroyed much of the city, and has become one of San Francisco's most famous landmarks.

Before the opening of the Golden Gate and Bay bridges in the mid-'30s, the Ferry Building was the world's second busiest terminal, surpassed only by London's Charing Cross Station. It served over 100,000 commuters per day, averaging 170 daily trans-Bay crossings.

By 1908, 23 piers had been completed along the Port's newly established waterfront. Water commerce continued to flourish, and San Francisco grew rapidly into an international trading center.

During World War II this was interrupted when San Francisco became the principal point of departure for the Pacific offensive.

In the 1960s a new mode of shipping was introduced—containers—that required new configurations of ships and terminals, special cranes and acres of storage space.

The older finger piers on which San Francisco's thriving shipping trade had been built were no longer adequate to meet this new generation of larger ships and containerized cargo that was to dominate the '70s.

Although a new container terminal was built on the southern waterfront in the early 1970s, it was not until later in the decade that the new direction and future of the Port was determined.

The Port's northern waterfront contains some of the most valuable land in California for commercial development, and the southern waterfront has the most available, accessible and appropriate land in the Bay Area for maritime expansion.

The Port's decision in 1978 to capitalize on the commercial potential of the northern waterfront property, and use this economic advantage to support maritime development on the southern waterfront, resulted in the renewed growth and vitality of the Port. In only four years, the net income of the Port increased 25-fold.

Today the Port of San Francisco has embarked on a Capital Improvement and Maritime Expansion program that will add nearly a dozen new container berths along the southern waterfront by the mid-1990s. With cargo volume expected to double by the year 2000, San Francisco will be ready.

The Port with a past has become the Port with a future.

Advancing without a pause through another golden century of service

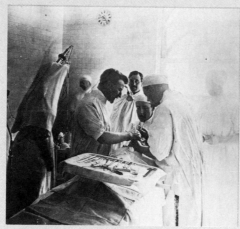

Surgery in the St. Mary's Hospital operating room in 1911.

The histories of San Francisco and of St. Mary's Hospital and Medical Center are woven together by a golden thread extending into a second century.

Thousands of argonauts, the few successful and the vast majority disappointed, had multiplied the population of San Francisco many times over when eight Sisters of Mercy arrived in 1854 from Ireland. The Sisters came to California to be teachers and to perform pastoral work for Archbishop Joseph Alemany.

Within a year they were operating the State Marine Hospital on Stockton Street and working as nurses. They had been pressed into service when a cholera epidemic struck the city, spreading death and panic in its wake. The compassion and efficiency of the nuns in caring for the sick so impressed the County Board of Supervisors that they invited the sisters to assume management of the hospital, which had been abandoned by the state.

Sister M. Baptist Russell, leader of the small band, possessed no formal training as a nurse, but she and her companions were superior to the mostly male and mostly unconcerned nurses who had staffed the hospital. She accepted the invitation.

After two years, during which the county successfully ignored its financial obligations, she terminated the agreement. Instead the sisters, who had purchased the building, removed the county's legend and replaced it with one bearing the name "St. Mary's Hospital." The date was July 27, 1857, and St. Mary's was the first Catholic hospital opened on the Pacific Coast.

Sr. M. Baptist Russell knew immediately that the building would be unacceptable in the long run, and in November 1861 the hospital moved to Rincon Hill on land which now serves as the western approach to the Oakland-San Francisco Bay Bridge. This St. Mary's, four stories tall, became a Bay Area landmark as "The Hospital on the Hill."

A grammar school and home for the elderly also were built on the grounds. Unskilled young women were trained for employment and the destitute could always find shelter there.

The sturdy hospital survived the earthquake of 1906 but was destroyed in the holocaust that followed. Between 1906 and 1911 St. Mary's occupied the former Maudsley's Sanitarium on Sutter Street while a new 150-bed hospital was being constructed adjacent to Golden Gate Park. With typical foresight, the Sisters of Mercy had purchased the property prior to the earthquake. The site remains the location of today's St. Mary's.

Another wing was added to the hospital in 1926, increasing the bed capacity to 374 and providing space for new services.

In 1966, the Sister M. Philippa Memorial Clinic was dedicated. The Clinic centralized the service to the poor and aged that is a vital part of the mission of the Sisters of Mercy.

Construction of new facilities has proceeded through the years without extending beyond the Stanyan, Shrader, Fell and Fulton streets boundary. The most recent addition to the 555-bed hospital is the acute care tower opened in 1975. Almost all of the patient rooms are private.

Throughout its more than 125 years, St. Mary's has prided itself on the quality of its patient care by physicians and highly trained nurses. They are supported by health professionals and other employees using the most modern equipment available. The caring spirit of the Sisters of Mercy is constantly present.

Other milestones in St. Mary's history include the following: established St. Mary's College of Nursing (1900); opened a child care clinic (1922); approved a tumor registry (1948); opened a medical physics department and operated a nuclear medicine department (1953), both "firsts" for San Francisco; appointed a full-time medical education director (1957); dedicated the McAuley Neuropsychiatric Institite (1961); opened a surgical intensive care unit (1962) and medical intensive care unit (1966); adopted the Medical Center concept and broadened the scope of the hospital's responsibility (1967); merged with another Sisters of Mercy Hospital, Notre Dame (1971).

There is no faltering in St. Mary's approach to its mission in San Francisco as both approach new golden ages.

The acute care tower opened in 1975 on land purchased before the 1906 earthquake.

Photo by Lawrence Migdale

201

Fifty years of innovative firsts in American dance

Founded in 1933, the San Francisco Opera Ballet (SFOB) was established to train dancers by the San Francisco Opera Association following the opening of the War Memorial Opera House. The Ballet also presented independent "all-dance" programs, under the direction of ballet master Adolph Bolm.

In 1938, Willam Christensen became the new ballet master, adding a new repertory of works including *Coppelia* in 1939, *Swan Lake* in 1940 (the first complete version ever produced by an American company) and *Nutcracker* in 1944 (the first complete production ever seen in the Western hemisphere). The nationwide tradition of presenting *Nutcracker* during the Christmas holidays began with SFB's production.

In 1942, Willam's brother, Harold Christensen, was appointed director of the SFOB School which became the largest training institution outside of New York and the primary source of dancers for the Company.

In 1952, Willam moved to Salt Lake City and his younger brother, Lew Christensen (America's first premier danseur who had performed with and choreographed for the companies of Lincoln Kirstein and George Balanchine in New York) was named SFB's new director. Lew created several major ballets and established an exchange policy with New York City Ballet whereby Balanchine ballets entered SFB's repertory for the first time.

SFB made its East Coast debut in 1956 at Jacob's Pillow in Massachusetts, bringing the Company its first major national exposure. Subsequently, the U.S. State Department sponsored SFB on three international tours from 1957-59 to the Far East, Central and South America and the Middle East.

After moving into several theatres from 1960-72, the Company eventually occupied the Opera House for a "home" season in 1974, beginning in December with *Nutcracker* followed by a repertory season from January

Company member Evelyn Cisneros in Michael Smuin's Emmy Award-winning The Tempest, broadcast live in 1981 from the War Memorial Opera House on PBS's "Dance in America" series. (Photo by Rudi Legname.)

A rendering of San Francisco Ballet Association's new $11.5-million home, scheduled for occupancy in December 1983 and located in the city's historic Performing Arts Center.

through May. (The School, Company and Administration had had rehearsal and office space since 1956 in a converted parking garage in the Richmond District.)

In 1972, SFB's various components were established under the auspices of a single organization, the San Francisco Ballet Association. Michael Smuin returned from American Ballet Theatre in 1973 to accept a position as SFB's associate artistic director. He began a Company rebirth and an extraordinary grassroots effort which focused national attention on the Company. In 1976, he was appointed co-director.

The reorganization of SFB Association into the institution as it's known today began with the appointment of Dr. Richard E. LeBlond Jr. as president and general manager. The Company also created its own resident orchestra under music director and conductor Denis de Coteau. Harold Christensen, school director since 1942, was succeeded in 1975 by Richard L. Cammack.

SFB became the first West Coast dance company on PBS's "Dance in

America" series when Smuin's *Romeo and Juliet* premiered in 1978, winning an Emmy Award. SFB scored major successes with tours in 1978 and 1980 to New York's Brooklyn Academy of Music and in 1981 at the Edinburgh International Festival in Scotland.

Another milestone for SFB was Michael Smuin's *The Tempest* (1980), considered the first full-length American ballet created with original choreography, music and designs. The work was broadcast live in 1981 on "Dance in America," winning another Emmy Award. In 1982, the 49th repertory season showcased the company's resident choreographers (now numbering seven) and produced an acclaimed group of ballets including Smuin's *Stravinsky Piano Pieces*, a movement which premiered on a national broadcast from The White House, and Assistant Director Robert Gladstein's *Symphony in Three Movements*, broadcast by KQED-TV.

On May 26, 1982, the groundbreaking ceremonies for the Association's new $11.5-million home united all of San Francisco's major performing arts in the Performing Arts Center. This four-level structure is the first new building in the history of American dance ever designed expressly to house a major professional dance institution.

The following year, SFB became the first U.S. dance company to celebrate its 50th anniversary with a Gala on January 29, 1983—conceived, produced and directed by Michael Smuin. The 50th anniversary year also featured SFB's third "Dance in America" broadcast, a tour of Italy, Israel and Greece, and a new history book on SFB's first half-century of innovative achievements.

Upholding world-class standards

The San Francisco Opera, one of the world's leading companies, is second only to New York's Metropolitan in this country for the length of its international seasons and number of annual productions. Founded by Gaetano Merola, San Francisco Opera gave its first performance on September 26, 1923, in the Civic Auditorium. On October 5, 1932, the company gave its first performance in the War Memorial Opera House, which has been its home ever since.

Merola served as general director until his death in 1953, by which time San Francisco Opera had established a reputation as a world-class company and introduced a large number of major artists to this country.

After Merola's death, Kurt Herbert Adler was named artistic director, becoming general director in 1957. Under Adler's leadership, San Francisco Opera expanded its Fall Season from 22 performances in 1953 to 70 in 1981 and, just before Adler's retirement, inaugurated an annual five-week Summer Festival season of international grand opera. Adler also initiated numerous affiliate programs for the company, including the Merola Opera Program, a ten-week summer course for young singers; Western Opera Theater, a touring company that has since played to over one and one-half million people in 29 states; and Brown Bag Opera, which presents short, informal concerts in a wide variety of locations from shopping malls and parks to schools, hospitals and senior citizen centers.

Adler retired at the end of 1981 and was succeeded by Terence A. McEwen, former vice-president of London Records. One of McEwen's first organizational changes was to create the San Francisco Opera Center to unify, streamline and coordinate the network of affiliate programs for the training and encouragement of young singers. The various auditions for these programs were also consolidated into the nationwide San Francisco Opera Center Auditions, held each year in New York, Chicago, San Francisco and other regional centers.

During the 1983 Summer Festival, San Francisco Opera launched a new production of Wagner's monumental four-opera cycle, *The Ring of the Nibelung*, starting with *Das Rheingold* and *Die Walkuere*. *Siegfried* will be added for the 1984 Festival with the complete Ring, including *Goetterdaemmerung*, constituting the 1985 Summer Festival.

In 1979 San Francisco Opera became the first American opera company to offer a live telecast to Europe via satellite with a new production of Ponchielli's *La Gioconda*, also televised nationally in this country. Other telecasts include Saint-Saëns's *Samson et Dalila*, seen on the PBS network in America, and Verdi's *Aida*, again televised live to Europe, with a special closed-circuit relay to the Civic Auditorium, the first such showing in the company's history. Performances from the War Memorial Opera House have also been heard by millions on the San Francisco Opera radio broadcasts, which received the George Foster Peabody Award for excellence in 1980.

Every year San Francisco Opera

Cast of La Traviata on stage in 1932, the first year San Francisco Opera performed in the War Memorial Opera House. Third from left is Gaetano Merola, who founded the company in 1923. To his left is the production's star, Claudia Muzio. (Morton photo)

presents a free Opera in the Park concert in the Music Concourse of Golden Gate Park. The concert, which draws tens of thousands of opera lovers, traditionally features artists from the Fall Season's Opening Night, which has become the principal social event on the West Coast.

San Francisco Opera offers a wig and makeup training program, the first professional training school of its kind in the United States. The company also maintains fully equipped costume and scene shops, in which sets and costumes for San Francisco Opera productions are consructed.

The merchandising division of the company has developed the San Francisco Opera Shop, which has grown from a small space in the Opera House, open before performances and during intermissions, to a full-time store at 199 Grove Street, open year-round to serve those interested in all the performing arts.

Critic Andrew Porter has written that "internationally, the San Francisco Opera has the reputation of being America's first: the big company that most successfully combines excellent casts, enterprise in the choice of repertory, and a serious approach to dramatic presentation." The ever-increasing numbers of San Francisco Opera's audiences would seem to confirm that reputation.

Educating generations of San Franciscans

In 1855 San Francisco citizens, outraged by the "quackery and empiricism" of the city's public school teachers during the gold rush, began to demand that the city insure the quality of education for their children.

City officials responded by starting teacher training classes on Saturday mornings. By doing so, San Francisco became the first city in the West to offer a regular program of teacher training.

It wasn't until 1899, however, that the San Francisco State Normal School was established. That date marks the founding of what has become San Francisco State University.

The normal school was established by a noted educator of the times, Frederic L. Burk, whose goal was to provide the Bay Area with more and better qualified teachers. Classes were held in a small brick building on the crest of Nob Hill, on Powell Street between Clay and Sacramento. The first class of 36 young women graduated in 1901, ready to step into the classroom.

The school and all its records were destroyed, along with most of San Francisco, during the great fire and earthquake of April 18, 1906. After only ten days, Burk was able to continue classes in temporary quarters in Oakland. Never one for delay, he quickly found a new site for the San Francisco State Normal School—on Upper Market Street—and classes resumed in June of that year. San Francisco State was the first public school in the city to reopen after the fire.

The school grew quickly, particularly after World War I. Its name was changed to San Francisco State Teachers' College in 1921. In 1923 the institution was authorized to grant the bachelor of arts degree, and three years later, enrolled men in the school for the first time. By 1930 the teacher training program was extended to four years.

The liberal arts became an integral part of the school's curriculum by the 1930s. Originally taught only as an

In 1911, San Francisco State Normal School—later San Francisco State University—used a geometric motif in graduating its class of young ladies.

adjunct to the teacher instruction program, liberal arts courses came to serve the purpose of rounding out the students' education and providing them with the materials and methods for leading lives as educated citizens. In 1935 the state legislature formally recognized this new educational mission by renaming the school San Francisco State College.

By this time, it was clear that the Upper Market Street facility was no longer adequate for the school's continuing growth and climbing enrollment. A large tract of land was acquired in the southwest corner of San Francisco near the shores of Lake Merced, a Pacific Ocean inlet. Ground was broken for a new campus in 1939.

World War II intervened and delayed construction of the new facility. The first permanent structure, the Physical Education Building, wasn't actually started until 1949. The col-

San Francisco State Normal School was the first public school in the city to rebuild after the 1906 earthquake and fire. Among the new buildings was College Hall, circa 1917.

lege officially dedicated its 100-acre, $12-million campus in October 1954. Enrollment at that time was nearly 12,000 students.

By the 1950s and early 1960s, SF State was offering graduate programs and had earned a reputation as an outstanding institution of higher education, respected for both its educational programs and faculty.

The college, however, was one of the first to experience the wave of campus unrest that swept the country in the late '60s and early '70s; but it survived and emerged with a renewed sense of vitality and purpose.

The school's name was changed once again in 1973, to California State University, San Francisco, but widespread protest brought back the San Francisco State University name a short time later. That name was officially proclaimed in January 1974.

Today San Francisco State is a modern urban university with an enrollment of more than 24,000 and a faculty of about 1,800. Bachelor's degrees are offered in 89 areas; master's in 73. A number of the university's programs are known throughout the country.

For more than twenty years SF State has been an outstanding part of The California State University system, the largest system of public higher education in the world. And for almost a century, it has been the city's leader in educating generations of San Franciscans.

Commitment to musical excellence over 70 years brought prestigious reputation

Described as a "West Coast Success Story" by *Time* Magazine's Michael Walsh, who ranks the orchestra in the nation's top ten, the San Francisco Symphony has garnered a prestigious international reputation built upon nearly 75 years of historic tradition.

The strains of symphonic music in San Francisco arrived close behind the sounds of gold-diggers panning for gold in the mid 1800's as small ensembles gave performances throughout the city over the next 50 years. Late in 1909, 21 citizens organized the Musical Association of San Francisco and after two years of fundraising, the Association presented Henry Hadley and the new San Francisco Symphony Orchestra in its premiere performance on December 8, 1911 at the Cort (now the Curran) Theatre.

For the next four years, Hadley led an ensemble of 65 musicians, most of whom had been recruited from the hotels, theatres and cafes of the city. Alfred Hertz mounted the podium in 1915. Though a flu epidemic caused the cancellation of five weeks of the 1918-1919 season and a lack of funds continually worried the Association, Hertz led the Symphony for the next fifteen years, enlarging the size of the orchestra and hiring the first woman in a major American orchestra. Youth concerts began in 1923, recordings for Victor Records and broadcasts on the Standard Radio Hour in 1926.

The people of San Francisco came to the rescue of their orchestra in 1935 during the Great Depression when they voted a half-cent increase in the tax rate to assure financial assistance for the Symphony. In that year, Pierre Monteux became Music Director of the Symphony, and the man who introduced the world to *Petrushka* and *Rite of Spring* infused the orchestra and its audiences with a sense of excitement and class.

With special dispensation from the Rationing Board, San Francisco Symphony concerts continued throughout World War II. Transport buses and Red Cross wagons delivered wounded members of the armed forces to box seats at the Opera

San Francisco Symphony conductor Pierre Monteux and his wife wait between trains during the orchestra's transcontinental tour to 53 cities in 1947.

House and the orchestra held War Bond admission concerts and performed in Army camps. Fleet Admiral Chester Nimitz, stationed in the Pacific, used the sound connection between his headquarters and neighboring ships in the fleet for San Francisco Symphony broadcasts.

After the war, the San Francisco Symphony undertook a tremendous tour across the United States and Canada in the spring of 1947, performing 56 concerts in 53 cities. President Truman was the honored guest at the concert in Washington's Constitution Hall.

Spanish conductor Enrique Jorda was Music Director for nine years beginning in 1954, and Josef Krips led the Symphony from 1963 to 1970, taking the orchestra on its first overseas tour to Japan in 1968. Seiji Ozawa became the orchestra's next Music Director in 1970; highlights of his tenure included the formation of the 125-member Symphony Chorus, a 30-concert tour through Europe and the Soviet Union in 1973 and a return trip to Japan two years later.

Edo de Waart became the San Francisco Symphony's Music Director in 1977. The Dutch-born conductor began annual Beethoven and Mostly Mozart Festivals, and his programming of contemporary music earned the orchestra three ASCAP awards for adventuresome programming. With the opening of Louise M.

Davies Symphony Hall and the orchestra's first live national telecast in September 1980, the San Francisco Symphony moved into its own home for the first time and expanded to a 52-week season. Season subscriptions broke every previous sales record in the history of the orchestra. Edo de Waart was instrumental in the signing of a new recording contract with Philips Records and helped establish the San Francisco Symphony Youth Orchestra. He embarked with the orchestra on its first East Coast tour in over 30 years and the most extensive transcontinental tour since 1947. In the 1983-84 season, the San Francisco Symphony's new Ruffatti organ, the largest concert hall organ in North America, received its premiere in an Inaugural Gala.

After over 70 years of tremendous growth—both in artistic excellence and audience expansion through extensive touring, recording and presenting the highest quality performances and guest artists—the San Francisco Symphony has earned its place among the top major orchestras in the nation and the world.

A tradition in fine German dining since 1893.

When Henry Schroeder opened the doors of Schroeder's Cafe in 1893, he started a tradition that would span nearly a century in San Francisco. A Prussian gentleman, Schroeder immigrated to San Francisco and opened the restaurant on the south side of Market between First and Second streets.

The devastating earthquake and fire bolted through San Francisco April 18, 1906 and destroyed the cafe. It temporarily relocated at the corner of Sixteenth and Mission streets. Slowly the city began to rebuild, and the determination of Schroeder and others like him helped to restore the now thriving Financial District. In 1911 Mr. Schroeder moved his restaurant to 117 Front Street. Schroeder's was then a "men only" establishment and attracted a varied clientele of

Interior of 111 Front Street during the early '50s.

Schroeder's original bar at 117 Front Street.

businessmen, sea captains and merchants. Five years later the cafe moved next door to 111 Front Street.

Henry Schroeder passed away in 1921 and left the operation to his widow, Mrs. Schroeder. She decided to sell it the same year and advertised for a buyer in a local newspaper. A young man named Max Kniesche was vacationing in Germany at the time and read about the sale. He had lived in San Francisco since 1907 but had never seen Schroeder's interior. On January 10, 1922 he purchased, with gold pieces, Schroeder's Cafe sight unseen. That afternoon Max walked into the restaurant and announced "All right, I'm your new boss." This marked the

beginning of a dining tradition that now spans three generations of family management.

Having purchased Schroeder's during Prohibition, Max had restrictions on alcohol and could serve only 3.2 beer. The restaurant was also badly in need of repairs. Max and his wife Alma worked diligently making necessary repairs while creating an authentic German-style atmosphere. Max ran the business "his way," which meant many changes. Menu revisions and additions transformed the three-entree lunch choice to a full bill of fare complete with German dishes. In time, all who worked with Max and patronized the establishment grew to respect him as an honest, hard working businessman.

Changing with the times was an ingredient for success, so in 1935 Schroeder's began serving dinner and opened its doors to ladies after 1:30 p.m.

The 1939 Exposition on Treasure Island brought thousands of tourists to San Francisco. Schroeder's prospered from increased business and secured a fine reputation for authentic German dishes. Sauerbraten and potato pancakes, wiener schnitzel and frankfurters with sauerkraut are just a few dishes that have become synonymous with the name Schroeder's. Boasts Max Jr., "Our food's not fattening—just strengthening. It doesn't add any curves—just fills out the ones you have."

In 1940 Max and Alma's only heir, Max Jr., joined the team. He was raised around the restaurant and learned the business from the "bottom up." His youth and enthusiasm was a welcomed addition to the management.

Being a German restaurant, Schroeder's faced a temporary setback with the onset of World War II. Fritz Wiedemann, German consul general, had been arrested on suspicion of being a German agent. His photograph, taken in front of the restaurant, was published in *Life* Magazine and created quite a stir around San Francisco. Many friends came to Max's aid and helped convince the patrons that Schroeder's was not in the business of German espionage.

In 1956, after 40 years in the same location, Schroeder's moved to its present locale at 240 Front Street. In an attempt to preserve the same warm, friendly atmosphere so familiar to regular patrons, the famous Herman Richter murals, beer steins and the rosewood bar were carefully moved.

Current exterior of 240 Front Street.

As times changed, Schroeder's was forced to open its doors at lunch to ladies on October 7, 1970. With a great deal of feminist persuasion, the management made the decision, and today women make up 25 percent of the noon-hour trade.

Continuing the family tradition, Max Kniesche III joined Schroeder's in July 1975 and brought in many fresh, progressive ideas. Realizing the challenge of operating a business in the '80s, Max Jr.'s eldest daughter Linda stepped in in April 1982. Max Sr. contends that the secret to Schroeder's longevity is the family-owned tradition. Assuring this continuation are Max IV and Mark Wells Kniesche waiting in the wings.

A San Francisco story, too!

Mary See with her grandson, Laurance, who was to succeed his father as president of See's Candies.

When the San Francisco World's Fair opened in 1939, a relative new-comer—See's candy shop and its tempting displays—quickly became one of the most popular attractions. The Fair proved to be a "seeding" operation that opened San Francisco and all of Central and Northern California to a small company from Los Angeles.

Turn the clock of history ahead 43 years to the Knoxville World's Fair of 1982. By this time, the corporate headquarters of See's Candies had long been firmly established at the company's general offices and pro-duction facilities on El Camino Real in South San Francisco. The small company had grown to more than 200 candy shops spread across a great expanse of geography from Hawaii to the Mississippi River, all shops operated by See's own locally hired and trained employees.

Millions of visitors to the Knoxville World's Fair took the taste and image of See's candies back to their own home towns, and it looked like the San Francisco story was starting all over again. But let's get back to the beginning . . .

Mary See had emigrated with her family from Canada to Los Angeles right after World War I. Her son Charles A. See had been a pharma-cist in a small Ontario mining town. After a fire destroyed his two drug-stores, he had started over as a chocolate salesman and took this knowledge with him to Southern California.

In 1921, when his mother was 71 years old, he opened his first candy shop in her image, using many of her recipes. The company grew steadily, focusing on an image of quality, backed by shrewd marketing.

During the Depression of the early 1930s, Charles See cut his price from 80 cents to 50 cents a pound and told his landlords—lower rent is better than no rent; reduce the rent and we'll survive together. He then took the visionary step of sending Edward G. Peck to San Francisco to establish a Northern California base. Came the World's Fair of 1939, and See's never looked back.

During World War II, the quality image of See's candy was indelibly impressed on all Californians then old enough to be interested in a candy shop. Rather than compromise quality by using inferior ingredients, See's curtailed production, keeping shops open only a few hours and creating long, not-to-be-forgotten lines of waiting customers.

When Charles A. See died in 1949, the Los Angeles *Times* described him as a man who had built a three-man candy company into a chain of "78 establishments employing more than 2,000."

His son Laurance took over leader-ship and made the decision that tied See's to California's shopping center growth. After Laurance See's death in 1969, his brother Charles B. "Harry" See gave the company the forward momentum it had lost during Laur-ance's final illness. He also named Charles N. Huggins, who had come to top management under Edward G. Peck, as the new president of See's.

The crowds were enthusiastic for See's candies at the 1939 World's Fair in San Francisco.

A short time later, Harry See negoti-ated the sale of the family company to Blue Chip Stamps.

Under Charles Huggins' leadership since 1972, See's has enjoyed its greatest period of growth, combining tradition and the skills of the indi-vidual candymaker with all the quality controls, technological advances, management techniques and human and product resources available to a company like See's. And it was President Huggins who took a leaf from the San Francisco story to put See's into the Knoxville 1982 World's Fair.

Huggins stresses a point that has always been basic to See's business philosophy:

"We are grateful for our growth and success, but we still like to think of ourselves as an individual candy shop serving its own community. That is the only way we can continue to give the best quality in product and service."

All See's candies are made today in the kitchens at South San Francisco and Los Angeles and transported in a matter of hours to all shops.

The company doesn't look back, but neither does it forget the lessons of the past. The experience of surviv-ing the Depression of the 1930s keynotes See's marketing approach during the current recession: "Qual-ity at a price no one matches."

Helping to create the future for more than 100 years

There was a time in San Francisco's colorful past when the construction of a 22-story office building was considered an extraordinary architectural achievement.

A writer in a 1925 magazine *Shapes of Clay* praised a "noble structure erected (in 1923) by the Standard Oil Company at California . . . achieving with easy grace the domination of a truly beautiful skyline." While "domination" was short-lived—the Russ Building went 30 stories in 1927—the Standard Oil Building at 225 Bush Street remained the *largest* office building west of Chicago as late as 1950.

Today, of course, the building is dwarfed by other downtown high-rise buildings, including two just a block away that house additional headquarters offices of Standard of California and the Chevron companies.

As a rich, diverse city has changed and grown beyond the vision of those who were its leaders in 1925, so has the company which began in 1879 as the Pacific Coast Oil Company.

In that year a gambling wildcatter named Frederick Taylor gathered a group of investors to form his fledgling company. Taylor had found oil north of Los Angeles, subsequently turning his Pico No. 4 well into the most productive in California.

The new company, Pacific Coast, was set up to market what was then considered an unmanageable quantity of crude oil.

Meanwhile, John D. Rockefeller's Standard Oil Company (Ohio) had merged its western interests and was doing business as Standard Oil Company (Iowa) from a marketing office in San Francisco. By the turn of the century, it had markets from Canada to Mexico. Unfortunately for Standard of Iowa, its oil supplies were back East. Its booming western market couldn't be served unless the company found a source of crude on the West Coast.

To meet the need for crude oil, Rockefeller acquired Pacific Coast Oil Company in 1900 with its established oil fields and track record of aggresive exploration and frequent success.

By 1910, the merged enterprise boasted two major West Coast refineries (one at Richmond, across the Bay from San Francisco, the other at El Segundo near Los Angeles); a promising new oil field in Kern County, California; and a burgeoning new market in road-paving for plenty of the thick California crude being found.

On the horizon, however, a crisis loomed for Rockefeller and his Standard Oil Trust. In 1911, the U.S. Supreme Court ruled that his empire must be broken up into 34 separate, competing companies.

Among the corporate descendents well equipped to carry on was Standard Oil Company (California). It had oil fields, refineries, pipelines, tankers, markets and a fine foundation in exploration.

Today, Socal—Standard Oil Company of California (the name was modified in the 1920s)—is the world's fourth largest oil company based on 1982 net income. Some 13,000 employees working in the San Francisco Bay Area are among nearly 42,000 employees operating in more than 90 nations on six continents.

From its humble beginning, the company has become a diverse natural resources concern engaged in crude oil and natural gas exploration, production, refining and marketing; the production of a wide range of chemicals and fertilizers for industry, farm and home; and development of geothermal and mineral resources throughout the world.

Over the decades, Socal has compiled an assortment of major achievements. They range from those that are technical—the development of the first diesel engine lubricating oil—to those of tremendous historic significance beyond a single corporation.

One of these, the discovery and development of oil resources in Saudi Arabia, propelled this once-regional oil company from San Francisco to its role today as a multinational corporate giant. The same achievement also spawned two major Eastern Hemisphere oil enterprises known today as Caltex Petroleum Companies and the Arabian American Oil Company (ARAMCO); both are affiliates of Socal.

Elsewhere, the company's history is rife with anecdotes, accomplishments and twists of fate.

In 1926, as experts were being quoted widely with predictions that "air travel will someday be common," Socal was aiding pilots by putting beacon lights on the tallest peaks along the West Coast. One of the first was on Mt. Diablo, just east of San Francisco.

Company painters, meanwhile, were atop the roofs of Socal bulk plants from Seattle to San Diego, painting north-facing white arrows

Charles Lindbergh refuels his plane at Rockwell Field, San Diego, prior to his trans-Atlantic flight, 1927.

and town names in huge block letters to help flyers navigate.

The following year, Charles Lindbergh chose Socal's old Red Crown Brand gasoline for his legendary flight across the Atlantic.

Standard of California, in fact, was first in the West to market a special fuel for airplanes. And in 1928, the company bought a Ford Tri-Motor to help promote public acceptance of aviation. The *Standard of California No. 1* flew more than 200,000 miles and carried more than 30,000 civic, government and business leaders on their first flights. Later, the first U.S. jet plane was powered with Socal fuel.

Motorists driving the first cars found filling up a tedious—sometimes dangerous—task, until a Socal employee developed the West's first service station (Seattle, 1907). Later, Standard was first in the West to issue credit cards to its customers.

Standard of California has long been an industry leader in exploration. In addition to its discoveries in the Middle East, the company made the first commercial oil discovery off the Texas coast; was first to drill a commercial well off the California coast; and the first to drill in the Western Arctic and on native-Alaskan lands.

Exploration success has been complemented over the years with strides in drilling technology and pioneering improvements in oil refining around the world. And as the world looks for long-range energy solutions, Socal is a leader in synthetic fuels research and development.

As busy as Socal people are in the energy business, they are also proud of their involvement as corporate citizens. In San Francisco, that involvement dates back to the earliest days. Company vessels were pressed into service to house earthquake refugees in 1906, for example.

Since then, diversity in service has been the key. Today's allocation for community involvement is planned for $19 million, with more than $4 million targeted for the greater San Francisco Bay Area.

The company may have set an

Socal President K.R. Kingsbury lays the cornerstone of the 225 Bush Street home office building in 1922.

American precedent for corporate voluntarism with a $10,000 grant in 1926. In those days, such a sum was considered tremendous—and was not tax deductible. Socal employee Phil Patchin heard that the San Francisco Symphony was in trouble. He came up with the somewhat revolutionary idea that Standard of California could bail it out. Company president K.R. Kingsbury saw the merits of such action and followed through.

In exchange, the symphony granted Standard exclusive radio broadcast rights. In 1928, in another unprecedented move, the company initiated the Standard School Broadcasts, which became the longest running radio series in history. The weekly shows were first heard by students in 72 schools. Today, some 25,000 schools nationwide receive free audio-visual tape/slide presentations designed to enrich the learning process.

The creative human spirit has long been celebrated by Socal, and in 1979 that quality became the company's centennial theme.

Socal developed a 4,000-square-foot museum exhibit, "Creativity—The Human Resource," which opened a national tour at San Francisco's Cal-

The signing of concession agreements in 1933 by Socal's Lloyd Hamilton and Saudi Arabia's finance minister, Abd Allah as-Sulayman. The discovery of oil in Saudi Arabia in 1938 marked a major milestone in the company's history.

ifornia Academy of Sciences. During three years on the road, it was seen by nearly four million Americans in thirteen cities.

The company often extends its generosity in areas other than education and the arts. Socal's domestic subsidiary, Chevron U.S.A., recently gave San Francisco $1 million toward the renovation of the city's beloved cable car system. The gift was the first from a major company and sparked a flood of similar contributions.

Some contributions are not monetary. A Socal employee, for example, was loaned out to serve on a citizens' Energy Policy Advisory Committee in San Francisco, looking for ways to save the city energy and money. Another Socal employee studied the city's non-revenue fleet and made recommendations on how to conserve fuel.

Hundreds of thousands of Bay Area residents have benefited from the company's co-sponsorship of a series of week-long health fairs since 1979. The fairs offer walk-in diagnostic services aimed at the early detection of potential health problems. Chevron U.S.A. contributed $1 million in 1982 for fairs in all 50 states.

As Standard of California continues to develop energy resources in the next century, it will also continue to look for ways to participate in the excitement that has been San Francisco's development. And who is to know today what achievement that development may include in coming decades?

The company that helped win the West

Southern Pacific is a company with its roots in the West—and in San Francisco. It actually helped start the city's tradition as a "headquarters town" in 1873, when the Central Pacific Railroad (SP's predecessor) moved its headquarters from Sacramento to a spacious new building at Fourth and Townsend streets.

Less than five years before—on May 10, 1869—the company had made history by driving a gold spike at Promontory, Utah, to meet the Union Pacific, building from the east, to form the nation's first transcontinental railroad.

The "Big Four" founders of SP—Leland Stanford, Charles Crocker, Collis P. Huntington and Mark Hopkins—were Sacramento merchants who accepted the great railroad-building challenge set up when Abraham Lincoln signed the Pacific Railroad acts. These men were builders and movers, and their names live on in dozens of California cities and landmarks.

Between 1869 and 1920, Southern Pacific truly built the West. SP extended a rail network that linked California to the rest of the nation, advertised and promoted the new land to bring hundreds of thousands of settlers west, formed irrigation districts, sponsored "scientific" farming, helped form the national parks,

Early "colonization" poster of the Central Pacific (now Southern Pacific) helped populate the West.

attracted industry and contributed heavily to making San Francisco the lively international business center it became.

San Francisco's connection to the western terminus of the transcontinental railroad in the East Bay was a fleet of ferryboats. Scores of boats carried passengers, whole trains, livestock, freight and, later on, automobiles. Southern Pacific and its affiliates had the world's largest ferryboat fleet—numbering 43 boats at the 1930 peak and carrying more than 40 million people and six million autos. The ferryboats did their job well. They made it possible for suburban communities to mushroom around the Bay—and made the bridges that supplanted the boats an inevitability.

The 1906 earthquake and fire destroyed SP's first general office building and other facilities. But the railroad immediately pitched in to help the stricken city. Relief supplies of food and medicine—1,600 carloads—were brought in by rail, and 224,000 refugees were moved out free of charge. The company opened its warehouses to the homeless and laid tracks on city streets to remove debris and bring in rebuilding materials.

From a sturdy, no-nonsense new general office at the foot of Market Street, SP kept playing its major role in the development and economy of the West over the next decades.

It was a giant in the World War II war effort. Nearly 300 military and naval establishments were located on SP lines, more than on any other railroad. San Francisco Bay was the focus of moving men and material to the Pacific War, and SP was the major rail artery of supply.

Following the war, Southern Pacific invested billions of dollars in modernizing its rail and highway transportation system and diversifying into other fields—petroleum product and coal slurry pipelines, intermodal traffic, telecommunications, natural resources and real estate development and management, leasing and financial services.

Its nineteenth century rail-building activities made Southern Pacific one of San Francisco's major property

San Francisco's initial Ferry Building in 1886, built by the Central Pacific Railroad, predecessor of today's Southern Pacific. This was the terminal for transcontinental train passengers (arriving by ferryboat from Oakland) until 1896, when the present Ferry Building was built.

owners, and today much of this land is being transformed into important elements of tomorrow's city.

In 1975, One Market Plaza, a full-block office complex, arose around SP's headquarters, featuring two office towers (43 and 28 stories high), a shopping mall and a galleria with a six-story-high glass ceiling.

A block away on Mission Street is the 30-story Pacific Gateway office building, another SP project completed in late 1982.

A few blocks south of the downtown district and surrounding China Basin is Southern Pacific's 195-acre Mission Bay property. Development plans are being worked out with city planners and a group of respected consultants—including architects I.M. Pei & Partners and urban planners Wallace, Roberts & Todd—for a multifaceted new "community" with office, residential and commercial space. It could become one of the largest urban developments ever seen on one parcel of single-ownership property and could revitalize an entire part of the city.

And so through the '80s, San Francisco and Southern Pacific, partners through both troubled and the best of times, continue to grow comfortably together, as old friends do.

Bay Area designers for over half a century

From its beginning in 1924, Stone, Marraccini and Patterson has grown to become one of the largest and oldest continuously practicing architectural firms in San Francisco. Still headquartered in the city, SMP (as it is generally known) now has branch offices in several other major American cities and has achieved an international reputation as a leader and innovator in high-technology architecture.

In the 1920s, Douglas Dacre Stone, AIA, was one of a handful of flamboyant San Francisco entrepreneur-architects who built successful careers based on a combination of design talent, social and political associations, quick-wittedness and business acumen. During those halcyon years Doug Stone produced a spate of apartment buildings, hotels, commercial structures and residences designed in the popular idioms of the day: Spanish Baroque, Norman Chateau, Tudor Gothic and Art Deco. Some of these still exist downtown, in Pacific Heights and in the East Bay—albeit much modified.

The Depression, which saw the demise of many architectural firms, challenged Stone's combative and survival instincts. The paucity of money for new construction diverted him into the field of restoration and remodeling. The repeal of Prohibition brought some commissions for new hotel restaurants and nightclubs. The then-famous and now-lost "Persian Room" of the Sir Francis Drake Hotel was one of Stone's Art Deco glass and chrome designs of this period. A series of projects for modernization of

The Olympic Club before renovation, early 1920s.

Entry detail of a San Francisco apartment building, early 1920s.

various downtown buildings and, particularly, a major interior renovation of San Francisco's exclusive Olympic Club, carried the firm through this unsettled period.

The advent of World War II brought new challenges to the survival of the firm, since there were few if any opportunities available then for private construction. The Lanham Act, which provided federal funding for war-related communities, led to the company's first hospital commission—the 250-bed Vallejo Community Hospital. Thus was initiated the development of a health-care design expertise which has continuously increased to this day.

During the war, Stone formed a partnership with Lou Mulloy, and in 1950 and 1951 expanded it to include Silvio Marraccini and Norman Patterson. This was the beginning of the modern, strongly managed, technologically oriented architecture and planning firm. The next 30 years were a period of vigorous growth including incorporation in 1957, and the addition of more and younger principals.

A series of prestigious commissions followed which included San Francisco General Hospital, Presbyterian Hospital (on the site of the old Stanford Hospital in Pacific Heights), the Sequoias retirement complex on San Francisco's Cathedral Hill, large

The new San Francisco General Hospital, 1973.

bulk-mail facilities in San Francisco and Oakland as well as major teaching and research buildings for the University of California, Stanford and other universities. By 1970, the firm had achieved a national reputation and had been selected to design (in joint venture) the new Walter Reed Army Hospital in Washington, D.C. More recent commissions include research and manufacturing facilities for Rolm Corporation, Chevron Chemical Company, Stauffer Chemical Company as well as office buildings, a new conference center at Asilomar in Pacific Grove and major buildings in Germany, Saudi Arabia and Canada.

By the early 1980s, SMP had made a full commitment to the computer age by acquiring its own computer-assisted design system. This technical augmentation enables its professional staff to respond to client needs even more efficiently and provide a greater range of services. In addition, a group of interior designers and space planners reinforces the firm's architectural capabilities.

Patterson, one of the shapers of the SMP of today, retired in 1982, and is the sole surviving original partner. Were he alive today, Doug Stone would be gratified at what was spawned out of those turbulent early years of trial, bravado and risk—an expanding, innovative, youthful firm dedicated to "architecture as a social and economic art." He probably would not be surprised since, after all, he, Mulloy, Marraccini and Patterson were the dynamic progenitors, exemplars of a tradition of architectural excellence and commitment to San Francisco's spirit of optimism and endless renewal.

Character and values shaped an old partner of the city

Sutro & Co. traces its beginnings to the 1848 discovery of gold in California, for it was this glittering lure which caught the imagination of men who would develop the final land frontier. One such was Adolph Sutro, then a young man in Aachen, Prussia, still in his teens and restless for life. Nearby, his cousins Charles and Gustav, of much the same age and cut, were also feeling the repressions of a German government rife with factions and suffering an economic imbalance of classes. Assessing the situation, they opted for the opportunities that beckoned from the New World. Adolph, assuming the role of leader since his father's death a short time before, guided his mother and siblings to the United States, and by fall 1850 was eking out a living in California. A few months later, he was joined by his cousins in the new and turbulent town of San Francisco.

Of good background and well educated, impatient Adolph became, at one time or another, engineer, commodities broker, tobacconist, hotelier, miner, visionary and mayor of San Francisco. His dedication to the job at hand was unswerving until it was completed or successful, and then he moved on. Brothers Charles and Gustav, with much the same background and schooling, were of steadier natures and, upon their arrival, devoted themselves to the tobacco business that Adolph initiated. They expanded; they advertised; and they were accommodating to their clientele, weighing and exchanging the miners' gold dust as a courtesy during their normal transactions as tobacconists. Their reputation for both good cigars and honesty grew. By the mid-1850s, Adolph was on the move, trying first a gold strike in Victoria, then a silver strike in Nevada. He left the tobacco business in the hands of the brothers, who soon found the tail wagging the dog. They had, in fact, evolved into Gold Dust and Exchange merchants, and began to serve as a Silver Coin and Bullion Exchange, as well. On

Founders Charles and Gustav Sutro, circa 1885, in front of 408 Montgomery Street, which they occupied for twenty years. Sutro & Co. moved off "The Street" to 201 California in February 1980.

Cleaning up after San Francisco's 1906 earthquake and fire. Sutro & Co., located at the time at 412 Montgomery, was spared damage, while buildings on either side were gutted by fire. Only Sutro's wire service was operable and able to inform the rest of the country of what was happening.

November 13, 1858 they opened their new enterprise in earnest, keeping the original tobacco shop located on Montgomery Street.

In 1861, the first liaison between firm and city occurred when Sutro & Co. promoted and financed a new enterprise, the Omnibus Street Railroad. Horsedrawn, it was the first railway transportation in San Francisco, and was to become a part of the Market Street Railway System some years later.

Over the early decades of its growth, Sutro & Co. participated greatly in the development of municipal services for the city. It financed those gas utilities which brought the first flickering light to the growing town's muddy streets; it was influential in financing Spring Valley Water Company, which ultimately would be a substantive part of the city's water system; it participated in promotion and financing of the California Electric Company, as well as of California Electric Light Company, both destined to be in the ancestral lineage of Pacific Gas & Electric Company.

In 1882, Sutro executed the first transaction on the San Francisco Stock and Bond Exchange (eventually the Pacific Stock Exchange). The second transaction that day was made by

H. Berl & Co. Decades later, in 1957, Edwin D. Berl & Sons, successor firm to H. Berl & Co., merged with Sutro to form the roots of the present-day organization. The pioneer firms were both manned by strong personalities and, as the years went on, drew to them other leaders of integrity.

Over its long history in San Francisco, the firm has had but six chief executive officers—Gustav Sutro, serving from 1858-98, Charles Sutro Jr. from 1898-1929, Sidney L. Schwartz from 1930-59, Alaistair C. Hall from 1959-71, Warren H. Berl from 1971-83 and Ross L. Cobb, elected in 1983.

Now in its 125th year, Sutro is headquartered in new offices at 201 California Street and is connected by wire service to its nineteen California branches. Further, this modern investment banking firm unifies its offices with its own, wholly owned computerized information system, giving its 250 brokers fingertip research and account information at their desks. Still, since 1858, Sutro's values have remained based on those which inspired the founders—"Is it right? Is it for the good of the clients?"

From a coffee stand to a San Francisco tradition

In 1849, during the California Gold Rush, three Yugoslavian immigrants began a business which later was to become Tadich Grill. Their coffee stand in a little tent-like structure hovered on the edge of San Francisco's Long Wharf (now Commercial Street), serving merchants and sailors coming off the square-rigged vessels docked in Yerba Buena harbor. In 1852, however, San Francisco's major landfill project forced them to relocate to the New World Market, a popular produce area on Commercial and Leidesdorff streets. They now named their thriving business The New World Coffee Stand. In 1868, the first of San Francisco's great earthquakes devastated the city, forcing another move—this time to 624 Kearny Street (near Commercial Street). It was here that John Tadich, a young immigrant from Yugoslavia, arrived in San Francisco in 1871 and began his restaurant career. In 1879, the steadily growing business moved to a larger coffee saloon at 221 Leidesdorff Street (at Commercial Street).

In 1882, a quite infamous county assessor, Alexander Badlam Jr., ran for re-election. His arrogant election slogan, "It's a cold day when I get left," so infuriated his opposition and the San Francisco voters that he was overwhelmingly defeated. The boisterous Badlam, who frequented the coffee saloon with his cronies, sought refuge there after the election. His triumphant opponents mocked Badlam by dumping a wagon load of ice at his doorstep. This incident, along with the severe November cold of 1882, supplied the newspapers with ample material to lambaste the shady former assessor. Thereafter, the coffee saloon was popularly referred to as "The Cold Day."

In 1887 John Tadich, having worked at the coffee saloon for sixteen years, took proprietorship. But in 1906, the great earthquake demolished his restaurant at 221 Leidesdorff. Tadich, along with another Yugoslavian restaurant owner, John Sutich, temporarily set up business at 417 Pine Street and, a

The beginning of another day.

240 California Street, San Francisco.

year later, moved to 441 Pine Street. In 1912, the partnership broke up and Tadich established himself at 545 Clay Street (at Leidesdorff Street). Sutich, however, retained the moniker The Cold Day Restaurant. Tadich, enraged by this and believing that this rightfully belonged to his restaurant, named his place, Tadich Grill, The *Original* Cold Day Restaurant.

In 1913, Tom Buich, another immigrant from Yugoslavia, came to work for John Tadich. Tom's brothers followed—Louie in 1922 and Mitch in

1924. In 1929, after 58 years with the restaurant, Tadich sold his interest to Mitch Buich and, in 1933, brothers Tom and Louie became partners. They operated Tadich Grill until 1961, at which time Louie and his sons, Steve and Bob, took over the business. In 1967, redevelopment of the area, which was once a bustling wholesale marketplace, forced the restaurant to move to its present location at 240 California Street.

In 1980, Steve and Bob Buich purchased the building at 240 California Street, establishing the first permanent address for Tadich's. Today, they are proud to carry on the family business, a restaurant which has been in continuous operation and Yugoslavian ownership since 1849.

Meeting customer needs through innovation

Transamerica Corporation was founded in 1928 by financial pioneer A.P. Giannini as a holding company for his Bank of Italy (later to become Bank of America) and other interests.

Transamerica today is a far different company—a diversified international corporation with operations in insurance and financial services, travel services and manufacturing (its banking interests were spun off in the 1950s as a result of federal legislation). Although it has changed over the years, Transamerica has continued to flourish by retaining its founder's philosophy of meeting customer needs through innovation.

Transamerica initially expanded into insurance in the 1930s by acquiring Los Angeles-based Occidental Life of California, known today as Transamerica Occidental Life, the largest company in the Transamerica family. The corporation also purchased several property/casualty insurers and a number of manufacturing operations.

With the eruption of World War II, Transamerica began shifting resources to meet the country's new needs. Its banks moved funds into war bonds and urged customers to invest in government securities, while its manufacturing operations repaired some of the ships bombed at Pearl Harbor and produced parts for other military ships and aircraft.

The death of founder Giannini in 1949 closed a chapter in Transamerica's history, and seven years later the law was passed which forced the company to choose between its banking and non-banking activities. To comply with the ruling, the corporation divested itself of all banking operations.

Transamerica lost no time in building upon its strong foundation in insurance and manufacturing. New president John R. Beckett, a former investment banker, launched a "quiet" revolution to guide Transamerica from a classic holding company to a diversified operating concern.

The elaborately turreted building at 701 Montgomery Street served as Transamerica Corporation headquarters for over 30 years.

The 1960s and '70s saw Transamerica expand into title insurance, equipment leasing, entertainment and travel. In 1972 the company built its distinctive corporate headquarters, the Transamerica Pyramid, just a short distance from the site of Giannini's original Bank of Italy. Now a San Francisco landmark, the Pyramid stands as a literal expression of Transamerica's belief in innovation and quality.

The Transamerica Pyramid, a San Francisco landmark since 1972.

Under current chairman James R. Harvey, Transamerica's many acquisitions have been streamlined into three areas of related operations, with each operation a leader in its particular industry.

• Insurance and financial services include life and health insurance, property/casualty insurance, title insurance, insurance brokerage, consumer lending and equipment leasing.

• Travel services include low-cost passenger and cargo airline service and automobile and truck rental operations.

• Transamerica's manufacturing operations specialize in precision-engineered machinery and components.

Transamerica today remains a low-cost producer and marketer of products and services attuned to changing consumer needs. Thanks to the commitment of its employees, agents and licensees, the corporation continues the Giannini tradition of serving customers through innovation.

A tradition of innovation

Like the city, the University of San Francisco (USF) offers a rich history and fresh new challenges. What began as a one-room schoolhouse with an enrollment of about 25 students has grown to a prestigious university with more than 7,500 students.

Founded by the Jesuit fathers in 1855, USF proudly carries on the centuries-old Jesuit tradition of scholarship and dedication to the humanities. In this tradition were a few Italian priests who had fled from the political upheavals in Italy to venture into a raucous, gold rush boomtown which a few years earlier had become incorporated as the City of San Francisco. One such Jesuit, Father Michael Accolti, described the disorder, the open immorality, the reign of crime, which, he said, "triumphed in a soil not yet brought under the sway of human laws." Clearly, the town was overdue for education.

In this setting, San Francisco's first institution of higher learning was created, amidst the sand dunes of Market Street, now the site of one of California's largest department stores. St. Ignatius Academy, as it was then known, opened its doors on October 15, 1855. Father Anthony Maraschi was its first president.

Immediately the Jesuits contributed to this booming city. Scientists at the academy developed methods for assaying the gold that was brought to San Francisco, discoveries which resulted in one of the finest and most complete collections of scientific equipment in the country at that time. Further illuminating the Jesuits' contribution was Professor Joseph Neri, S.J., a pioneer in experiments with electricity. On the nation's centenary on July 4, 1876, Neri gave a dazzling electric light show from the academy's steps on Market Street —quite a display in the days of horse-drawn streetcars and gas streetlamps.

The young institution soon outgrew its facilities on Market

San Francisco's first institution of higher education in 1855—Saint Ignatius Academy, on Market Street (site of present Emporium).

Ignatian Heights, campus of the University of San Francisco from 1927 to the present day.

Street, and in 1880, ambitious plans were made to build a college at Hayes and Van Ness, now the site of San Francisco's grand new Performing Arts Center. There the Jesuits built a magnificent church, library, laboratories, and even a gymnasium with a pool. By the turn of the century, San Francisco boasted a full-fledged college of elegant detail and neoclassical splendor.

On the morning of April 18, 1906, it all came crashing down. Half a century of sacrifice, toil and the dreams of Jesuit fathers and the community for its university lay in ashes as a result of the earthquake and fire. What follows, however, is glowing testament to the resourcefulness of those hardy pioneers. The college was virtually back in operation the following Monday—in an abandoned factory up the street. Those temporary quarters, fondly referred to by alumni and faculty of those days as "the shirt factory," were to serve as home for the university until 1927 when the present campus on Ignatian

Heights was acquired. Three years later, the mayor asked the university to take the name of the city.

The university now consists of more than eighteen buildings (including the basilica-sized Saint Ignatius Church) covering 51 acres on a hilltop in the center of San Francisco—next door to Golden Gate Park, overlooking downtown and the Pacific Ocean.

If founder Father Maraschi were to return to USF today, he would find his college had fulfilled his dreams of becoming a major university. USF now offers undergraduate and graduate programs in six colleges and professional schools—Arts and Sciences, Business, Professional Studies, Education, Nursing and Law. Like the city of San Francisco, students at USF come from all over the country and all over the world, are multiracial, multiethnic and of many religions. Some of San Francisco's finest attorneys, educators, business executives, humanitarians and civic leaders (including two former San Francisco mayors) are USF alumni. Under the direction of President John Lo Schiavo, S.J., and Chancellor Charles Dullea, S.J., USF will continue to fulfill its motto: *Pro urbe et universite*— for city and university.

The oldest bank in the West

In March 1852 Henry Wells and William G. Fargo, two well-known Eastern businessmen, brought together a group of associates at New York's famed Astor House and formally launched the banking and express enterprise that carried their names westward into American frontier history—Wells, Fargo & Co. The new firm opened its first office in July of that year on Montgomery Street in San Francisco.

Through a network of banking and express offices in the 1850s, Wells Fargo purchased gold dust, transferred funds throughout the Pacific coast region and eastward, guarded and shipped bullion, accepted deposits, made loans, conveyed mail and acted as agent in commercial and legal matters. When a financial panic destroyed California's two other leading banks in 1855, Wells Fargo emerged with new prestige.

As the only Western partner in the Overland Mail Company, Wells Fargo hurried letters between San Francisco and St. Louis, via El Paso and Los Angeles, in 1858. On the shorter Central Overland route in 1861, the company ran the western half of the

famed Pony Express during the last six months of its existence.

By 1866 Wells Fargo stagecoaches rolled between the workcamps of the advancing transcontinental railroad in California and Nebraska, and headed northward into Montana and Idaho. In fact, the Concord stagecoach became so identified with Wells Fargo during this period it eventually became the company's official symbol.

The firm kept expanding. Wells, Fargo & Co.'s Bank had branches in Nevada, Utah, Oregon, New York and California, as well as numerous correspondent banks in other states. In 1888 Wells, Fargo & Co.'s Express became the first to offer "Ocean to Ocean" service from San Francisco to New York, and by 1918 had 10,000 offices and agencies throughout the United States and abroad.

Change came with the new century. In 1905, the bank joined with the Nevada National Bank, founded in 1875 on the wealth from the Comstock Lode, to form the Wells Fargo Nevada National Bank. On April 18, 1906, a great earthquake

Today, the Wells Fargo Bank History Room at 420 Montgomery Street, San Francisco, hosts thousands of visitors a year.

Photo courtesy of Sunset Magazine

and fire severely tested the institution. Though much of San Francisco lay in ruins, Wells Fargo's spirit did not waver. The bank immediately telegraphed its correspondents:

"Building destroyed. Vaults Intact. Credit Unaffected." Business quickly resumed in a private home, while bank President Isaias W. Hellman pledged support to San Francisco's future: "I will do all I can to help build the City again, and it will be done."

The Great Depression challenged Wells Fargo in the 1930s, but President Frederick Lipman's conservative banking policies carried the bank through the period unscathed. Under his guidance, Wells Fargo grew in trust and corporate banking.

A major merger in 1960 with the American Trust Company, descendant of California's earliest savings bank, created one of the largest retail banking systems in California and the country.

Today, Wells Fargo Bank, N.A., with $25 billion in assets, nearly 400 offices worldwide and 17,000 employees, is the twelfth largest bank in the nation and a leader in electronic banking. Under the guidance of chief executive officer Carl Reichardt, Wells Fargo offers financial services throughout the United States and around the world, while it remains inseparably a part of San Francisco and the American West.

Daguerreotype of Wells Fargo's first office on Montgomery Street, San Francisco, 1852.

Through earthquake, fire, flu, depression and war, "the Spirit of the West" prevails

West Coast Life was founded in 1906 by a group of men who wanted to provide Westerners with insurance service which until that time was only available from the insurance giants of the East and Midwest. In many ways, these men were a cross section of the kinds of personalities and mix of talents and backgrounds that composed the social and economic backbone of America's "doers" early in the century. They made things happen and in so doing, they determined the style of the times and the direction of the West.

Business commenced April 2, 1906, just sixteen days before the San Francisco earthquake and fire. Although the company's offices and physical assets were reduced to ashes, the officers were determined to maintain their goal. With a fighting spirit, the company began to grow and, in fact, offered the city of San Franciso a loan for reconstruction purposes, the first company to do so. The early formative years included the establishment of a general agency in Honolulu in 1907, which was a first for any American life insurance company. In 1915 the company merged with the San Francisco Life Insurance Company to alleviate costly promotion, expenses and business duplication. As West Coast-San Francisco Life Insurance Company, the firm entered and began doing business in Texas and Montana and became the first American life insurance company to operate in the Philippine Islands.

These successes were quickly interrupted by the worldwide flu epidemic of 1917-19 in which one percent of the world's population died. The abnormally high mortality among policyholders reduced the company's capital and surplus and forced the sale of its industrial (weekly, debit policies) business. This setback was only temporary as the subsequent years were marked by aggressive efforts to expand. Between 1919 and 1930 the company entered Colorado, Wyoming, Alaska, Oklahoma, New Mexico and was the first American life insurance

The West Coast Life Chinatown agency has been serving the public since 1921.

company to do business in China and Hong Kong. It was also during this period that the company reverted to the name West Coast Life.

Although the 1929 "crash" adversely affected the company's domestic investments, it did not have such an immediate effect upon its overseas operations. The company continued to expand in the Far East and did not suffer a financial crisis until the onset of World War II. No other American life insurance company had such a high percentage of its insurance in-force resources, premium income, new insurance sales and agencies affected by the war, nor suffered the premium income loss as a result of World War II as did West Coast Life. As a result, the company discontinued business in the Far East and concentrated all

efforts on developing markets closest to home. This decision led the company toward a greater pursuit of professionalism and contributed to many outstanding accomplishments.

In addition to being the first American life insurance company established in Honolulu, the Philippines, China and Hong Kong, West Coast Life was also the first to issue a group policy west of the Mississippi, first to issue an unemployment compensation disability policy in America (off-the-job disability), the first to underwrite association business, the first to respond to the Tax Act of 1981, the first to introduce a universal life product based on the 1980 CSO Table, the first to bring parenting seminars to the public as a community service and the first to use the Check-O-Matic concept, whose name West Coast Life gave to the rest of the industry at the request of the industry's leading marketing research organization.

Today John U. Metzger, CLU, presides over a company and marketing organization that still represents the international populace of the West Coast and, in particular, California, Texas and Hawaii. The company's agents serve a variety of publics, both individual and business, and that is reflected in the people who not ony work for the company but also represent its sales force. "The Spirit of the West", the company slogan since 1910, prevails. West Coast Life is the oldest, largest and most innovative life insurance company home based in San Francisco.

John U. Metzger, CLU, president of West Coast Life.